Date

One man's diary about the
ultimate dating challenge

Dave Cornthwaite

www.davecornthwaite.com

Sleeve photography by Sean Conway
www.seanconway.com

With permission from and thanks to Kris Hallenga, Maren
Hallenga, Jenny Hao, Melika Harris and Nikki Jarryn Baker.

www.davecornthwaite.com
@DaveCorn

ISBN-13: 978-1492153351   ISBN-10: 1492153354

Other books by Dave Cornthwaite

Available in paperback and for Kindle on Amazon

BoardFree (2008)

Two weeks after Dave Cornthwaite tried riding a long skateboard for the first time, he woke up and made the biggest decision of his life. BoardFree is the story of one man's extraordinary determination to escape a rut.

Within two years Dave taught himself how to skate, quit his job, set up a charitable initiative, then embarked on two incredible skateboard journeys to raise money and awareness for three charities. He pushed the length of Britain and the width of Australia, breaking two world records and inspiring many others to go on and do something similar.

Life in the Slow Lane (2013)

Six years after quitting a job in order to chase his passions, Dave Cornthwaite hit a crossroads: one way, consistency, and the other, adventure.

From the relative solitude of a 3000 mile sailing voyage across the Pacific to a dangerous yet soul-enriching ride through the   American South on a unique four-wheeled Bikecar, Dave's determination, grit and indomitable humour is matched by candid storytelling that shows what can happen if you follow your heart and allow the smallest seed to transform into something so much bigger. Not just once, but time and time again.

"Not all men are idiots.
This book is proof."

Amazon Reviews

"Adventurer Dave Cornthwaite has done it again, a must read for all single men and women out there. Open, honest, charming and funny - this book has it all."

"The author's description of rejection and recovery is one of the most moving I have read in recent memory (and I teach sonnets for a living)."

"A fantastic insight into how men think and interpret women. Not only funny, it's poignant, thought-provoking and inspiring."

"A fascinating window into the world of internet dating and human relationships."

"If you like Danny Wallace and Dave Gorman, then Cornthwaite's latest adventure is definitely up your street."

"Dave manages to make the ordinary very amusing."

"Witty, insightful and, dare I say it, emotionally observant, this is not your typical Adventurer."

"Capable of being brutally honest: a meditation on the nature of relationships."

"Not all men are idiots. This book is proof."

"Written by a genius! Laugh out loud funny, compassionate and incredibly moving."

"What a sensitive, straight from the heart book but with lashings of humour. Dave Cornthwaite manages to capture human behaviour (good and bad) in the written word so easily."

"Dave reminds us that those people who set our hearts on fire, turn our lives upside down, and make the world more beautiful are out there, for all of us."

"If you feel your faith in men needs justification read this book."

"Addictive, witty, entertaining, extremely funny, insightful, reflective and thought-provoking."

"If you're expecting to read a misogynist's account of intense dating, you'll be very disappointed."

"One of the funniest books I've read in quite a while. I sat giggling uncontrollably at my desk."

"My girlfriend couldn't put it down after I had finished reading it."

"Date made me wish my commute was longer…"

"Cornthwaite never loses the sense of gentle, chatty humour that makes this book such an absolute pleasure to read."

"We all make mistakes in our love lives, but we don't all share them with the nation - Dave does, and he does it well."

"A wonderfully witty book."

"Amusing, emotional and very frank indeed."

"Blooming hilarious. Who knew that men thought so much?"

"Refreshingly honest and self-deprecating."

"I was expecting lighthearted, fun, cheeky and entertaining, and I got so much more! An easy read but with hidden depths."

"Date seemed like it might be an amusing story, even if it didn't appear to be the author's usual genre. How wrong was I?!! This is SO his genre!"

"Outrageously honest revealing innermost thoughts and offering reflections on life, love and more. A great page turner."

"I started to master the skill of reading while walking just to read more!"

"A complete change of subject matter compared to his previous book but Date is a clear sign that the author can turn his hand to anything."

Dave Cornthwaite is a Nutella-loving record-breaking adventurer, author and motivational speaker. He was once quite a bad graphic designer, but outside of work hours was a total whizz on any games console you care to mention. Eventually, recognising that he only had so many brain cells left to lose, he decided to pursue a new career doing something he enjoyed, which strangely had been a life path not much encouraged throughout his education.

Dave's Expedition1000 project is recognised as one of the most ambitious adventures around. At the time of publishing he had completed eight from a series of twenty-five journeys, each at least 1000 miles in distance, each using a different form of non-motorised transport.

Dave is also the founder of Say Yes More, an organisation designed to encourage people to love their work and make the most of their time on this lovely planet of ours. The key is quite simple; he just wants you to say yes more. Find out more at www.davecornthwaite.com

For Mum, who pushed me into existence.
For Kate, who pulled the words all the way out.
For Nina, who squeezed them into shape.
For my dates, you were lovely,
I hope you don't recognise yourselves.

And for you, for reading this far…

For such a vast amount of people on this planet,
it seems that we find love too rarely.
Without it, life is bleak and lacking colour.
So this book is dedicated to everyone
who has loved me and brightened my life.
It gives me hope that one day
I'll be free of all this bloody dating.

Foreword

By Kris Hallenga, Founder of CoppaFeel!

At the age of 23 I was very much on the dating scene, living a relatively carefree existence, until the day I was diagnosed with breast cancer. As nuclear bomb–sized curveballs go, this was right up there with the best of 'em. My immediate thought was '*I am 23 and I'm going to die*'. No sooner did that thought pass when I was steamrolled by the next: '*who on earth would fancy a bald-headed, bloated and boobless twenty-something?*' But, above all that came the realisation that I had not checked my boobs for breast cancer and I didn't even know it could happen at my age. Both were factors that could have impacted on my life as I now live with stage 4 breast cancer at the age of 26.

There is no stage 5.

One month after the diagnosis I turned my shock and anger into pure kick–ass, immediately making it my full–time mission to encourage friends, my generation and *young people* everywhere to keep hold of their wonderful, carefree lives by getting to know their boobs. Breast cancer can affect *young people* at any age, and from this message CoppaFeel! was born. We exist to remind every young person in the UK that checking their boobs isn't only fun, it could save their life. Awareness is at the core of our operation - we're like a friendly bop on the head when you least expect it, encouraging a lifelong, proactive habit. We're not here to scare the bejeezus out of people, we aim to educate and empower so we can reduce the number of fatalities from this horrific disease. I refused to let breast cancer wreck my party, and I refuse to let it wreck yours too.

Thank you to Dave for being endlessly supportive of our cause, the most wonderful thing to have come out of having cancer (yes, it's not all bad) is getting to meet so many cool people, and Dave is a big shiny beaming light of a cool person. I'm honoured to be forewording this very insightful and entertaining book, I hope you too will fall in love with Dave's unrivaled humour, compassion and honesty. I doubt he ever fully comprehended what he was letting himself in for and, with hindsight, skateboarding across a continent probably seems like a doddle in comparison, even if the dating involved more laugh-out-loud moments than you can shake a stick at.

You may now be wondering if I am one of the women in these pages, being paid off for his sneaky little plan by being allowed to write a few words about our ill-fated love affair, disguised as a charity dedication. Alas, I'm not and no, he genuinely cares about Britain's boobs. We're really thankful to Dave for dedicating this book to helping us reach more young people with our life saving message. And finally, in case you're wondering, I do have a boyfriend, whom I met when I had NO HAIR and a bloated crusty face, so take it from me, there is hope for us all.

Now, off you go to www.coppafeel.org and check your boobs immediately. And check your partners' too, although that's **not** guaranteed to happen on your first date, I'm hastened to add.

10% of all profits raised by sales of this book will be donated to CoppaFeel.Org

ONE

Dating Cowboy

I stand at the bar, clinical with its swilling, suited clientele and chrome surfaces, and watch: two women in the corner clinking glasses of white wine. One man and a woman a bit further down the bar, shoulder to shoulder, facing the dance floor. Four women who are joined by a fifth, clip-clopping in her heels back from the toilet. And there, over there by the mirror, another lady. Very pretty, short brunette hair, sat on a cubic leather stool, checking her phone, looking around. She's been there for about twenty minutes doing exactly the same thing and, frankly, she looks lonely. So I gulp down my drink and stroll over, nervous as hell because this is the first time in my life that I've ever approached a strange woman in a bar and I have no idea what's about to happen. She looks up as I reach her and I want the shiny black tiles to part and swallow me whole. I shouldn't be here. I shouldn't be doing this, talking in a silent goldfish-type way to this lady who doesn't know me. My arms swing by my side and I don't know what to do with them as they feel kind of … well, limp. I tuck my thumbs into my pockets and then realise I'm standing like a cowboy, but one without a hat, or a pistol, or appearing to be cool, and I wish I hadn't necked that drink, because I could really do with a glass to nurse right now.

'Can I help you?' the lady asks.

'Ah.' I say, looking at her. 'Ah.' She cocks her head slightly and frowns at me, drawing her legs into the stool and leaning back a little bit too far for her to be entirely comfortable. I realise that I'm scaring her and decide to do something about that. 'Hi. My name is … er, Dave.' I breathe deeply, scratch my head quickly and then triumphantly finish my bit, 'and I … I, well, I'm single.'

She straightens up, smiles, pushes herself off the stool into a standing position, and then she moves towards me slow and feline, sexily, gripping my jacket with both of her perfectly manicured hands before pulling my face towards her slightly parted lips, all red like strawberries, her eyes closing behind a hundred thick, curly black lashes. And she kisses me, flicks her tongue against my teeth, snake-like, as though she wants to taste me with all of her senses. She moves her lips across my cheek, towards my earlobe, nudging, squeezing, whispering, '*let's go…*'

Oh bugger, I really cocked that up. She's not kissing me. Of course she bloody isn't. She's still sitting there on her stool, reaching down and gathering up her bag, staring at me one last time before jumping to her feet and spinning towards the door. 'Good for you,' she growls, and she's gone.

I've always had a hunch that I'm not very good at approaching women in bars, and now I've actually tried it my fears have been confirmed. I'm left alone in the middle of a crowd, standing in front of an empty stool with red cheeks and a pounding, painful heart, looking very much like a rubbish cowboy.

TWO

London

I'm new to this city. It's late September now and I arrived in early June, already comfortable with London life after regular trips to the capital in past years, but never having actually *lived* here. The first three months were spent locked in a room halfway up the Victoria line, writing. Basically, I was a hermit, but I had a job to do and shut myself off from the outside world until the last word of the book had been typed out.

Then, suddenly, I was on a social rebound; rushing around, catching up with friends, moving to a new home in South London, putting my energies into new projects and generally carving myself a new life. Yet despite the flurry of refreshed human interaction I can't help feeling lonely. Maybe it's something about being in a big city; the rush of feet, heads down, everybody is going somewhere and usually somewhere fast. You don't talk to strangers unless they're behind a counter, and because you're in the middle of the throng no one talks to you, and in turn that makes *you* feel like a stranger because, I suppose, you are. I was, at any rate. I held up my hands and counted out my good friends in London and realised to my horror that there were spare fingers, and that made me feel even more alone. I was sat on the sofa at the time, the sofa which doubles up as my office, and I slumped back, hands clenched behind my head, and said out loud to no one in particular, 'Dave, mate, you need someone to be lonely with.'

But how the hell am I going to meet someone? I live in London, which is, well, probably the hardest place in the world to meet someone. Strange that, isn't it? Millions of people, a good chunk of them single and looking, yet it's not easy to find them. Come on now, that's ridiculous; it can't be that difficult, can it? Really?

Well actually, that all depends on the situation. I work from home. I have a five-second commute from bed to sofa. During the day I leave the house only if I need to stock the fridge, and I do this no more than twice a week. Instantly, I am deprived of a working community, and as a magazine article once told me that 60% of relationships are started through a work connection, my odds are vastly shortened unless I time a good wave out of the window at the post lady. And as the post lady is actually the post*man*, I might be in trouble. Being cooped up indoors all day does give me extra incentive to make evenings and nights more social, but at some stage hanging out with your mates limits the option of meeting new people, or more specifically on this agenda, new *women*. Ultimately your friends only have so many friends, so once you've been introduced to them all and remain single and unattached another potential partner store is exhausted.

And then what? You're simply left with strangers, or chance. Give me a common point of interest with a girl and I'm fine, but as you know already, I'm rubbish at picking up women in bars, I've never been able to do it and unless I spend months learning *The Game* this isn't going to change. I'm not alone in that I have an innate fear of rejection, and perhaps wrongly this has manifested itself into an excuse; I don't like approaching strange women and asking for their number because I don't believe women want to be approached by strange men. Of course, this is utter bollocks. Women don't like to be approached by *strange, drunken, leery* men who use chat-up lines like 'ooh, I like your tits,' or, 'are your legs tired, because you've been running through my mind all night...' So my point is, I don't have the balls or the chat to *a)* approach a strange woman or b) convince her fairly sharpish that I am not, indeed, strange, drunken and leery; mainly because even if I did build up the courage to go for it I'd be so sure of getting the brush-off that my confidence wouldn't have a leg to stand on. So now we know that I'm not going to meet anyone through work, or through friends, or in a pub or a club, I think we've established that while it may be quite sad for me to be sitting alone on a sofa in South London thinking really hard about the girls I can't get, it's not exactly surprising that I'm doing just that.

It seems logical that a man who spends his days alone with a laptop might eventually decide to meet girls by sitting on his sofa, using a laptop. Until my friend Alice had asked me to write a profile for her on a site called MySingleFriend.com the idea of dating online had never crossed my mind. I'd visited the link she provided, written a couple of hundred words about her, filled in my details and pressed Send. That was it, there you go Al, good luck finding a digital man and all that, but it's not for me.

Fast forward a few months, though, and I had a different frame of mind. I was browsing on Facebook when an advert popped up in the bottom left of the screen – *Single and Looking? Try Facespin*. I clicked the ad and it took me to a demo screen for an online dating site called YesNoMayB. The concept was basic, but simple. Female faces would dizzyingly spin onto the screen one at a time. In addition to their image, five words or phrases sat to the left and right of the picture, under the categories *About Me*, and *What I Like*. Beneath the face were three buttons, *Yes*, *No* and *MayB*. If I liked the look of them and clicked *Yes* or *MayB*, they'd be entered into my *Black Book*, and the next time they signed on the system would surreptitiously spin my profile onto their screen. If they chose me as a *Yes* or *MayB*, we had a match and could then message each other through the site. I was intrigued, it was a great idea and what's more, it was free. With nothing to lose and at the very least a new experience to gain, I began to register and set about filling in my profile.

Now, I had to think about this. Effectively, I'm entering myself into a marketplace. I am now a product. I stared at the screen for a while, typed something in, deleted it, stared some more, typed something else, deleted it, and then went to make coffee. As the kettle whistled away, I had a think. They were asking me to fill in two boxes entitled *Looking For* and *More About Me*, seemingly ordinary categories but blindingly difficult to comprehend. I basically have to sum up my life in just two paragraphs, and I'm not sure I can. Should I be serious? Should I try to be funny? Or should I just close down YesNoMayB and learn to chat up chicks in bars?

Coffee made, I settled down again and eventually found some words. Finally, I was asked to upload at least one picture. I shuffled through my computer and went for an image of me in a white t-shirt, looking quite moody and possibly thoughtful. I should probably tell you here that I'm a redhead, more rusty red/strawberry blonde than orange, but still... The obvious answer was to turn the image black and white because no colour will almost certainly increase a redhead's catchment demographic. I cropped the picture to my neck and shoulders, and clicked *Upload*. Finally, after two hours of intensive brow furrowing and thorough self-assessment, I had my first online dating profile:

> **Age:** 28
> **Height:** 5'11"
> **Living In:** London
> **Looking For:** Honestly, I'm not really sure. I'm single, and enjoy it, but also think life is at its best when you're sharing it with somebody you care about, and who cares about you. Winter is drawing in and it would be ever so nice to find someone to cuddle up to! I'm looking for someone who is secure and comfortable with who they are, has a wicked sense of humour,

keeps healthy, has a lust for life and appreciates the power of a good hug!

Relationship Type: A Date. Email/Chat. Friendship. Serious Relationship.

Motto: If you're going to regret not doing it, then do it.

Personality: Easy going. Confident.

A bit naughty. Creative. Ambitious.

Loves about Life: Cooked breakfasts. Waking up happy.

A good cuddle. Cheese! Achieving big goals. Laughter.

A comfortable bed. The cool side of the pillow.

More about Me: Hate doing this! I'm independent and driven, but life's too short to take things too seriously and I'll always put happiness over money. I've just finished writing my first book which was a real labour of love, but I'm not going to tell you what it's about, not here anyway! I love sport, travel, learning new things and going on adventures. And I really like autumn and winter, it's so nice to wrap up warm!

With the easy part done, I decided not to wait for girls to come to me, it was time to Facespin. And in they spun! These female faces, all different shapes and sizes, colours and creeds. *No, No, No, No, No,* I tapped my mouse impatiently, feeling incredibly judgemental for rejecting all these women but immediately realising the value of attraction. When you fall for someone, and I mean *really* fall for someone, it's not their looks that get you, it's chemistry. Your personalities bounce off each other, you laugh, you make each other tick, yet if at any point there comes a time when you don't want to rip each other's clothes off with your teeth then the pair of you should probably just be good friends. Human beings are born to mate and physical attraction is a natural precursor to two people getting together. It's not the be all and end all, but it is important, and I realise as another lady spins onto my screen and I click *No* without a moment's hesitation that two things are going on here. Firstly, I'm not being shallow by saying cheerio to a girl purely based on the impression of a picture. I'm not pretending that I know them, or saying that they're not nice or good company. I'm not judging them, I'm just looking for somebody that I'm attracted to. Secondly, there are hundreds of people on here, so we can afford to be picky. Why click *Yes* or *MayB* for a girl that I simply don't fancy, when just around the corner there's bound to be someone who makes me sit up and say, 'Hello!'

Eventually, the faces stopped spinning. Four girls sat in my Black Book; one blonde, three brunettes, all with nice faces and articulate profiles with no spelling mistakes. You could sit Angelina Jolie in front of me and if she couldn't differentiate *your* from *you're* then I'd kindly show her the door. Call me a word prude, but good first impressions count, and out of one hundred and sixteen London-based women between the ages of 23 and 31, four of them had left a good impression. Now, I supposed, all I had to do was wait.

That evening I received an email telling me I had a match on YesNoMayB. She went by the name of Holski and had a devilishly cheeky grin, and now we had both *MayB*'d each other we were free to chat. Brilliant! But oh God, now what? This is almost as hard as writing your own profile. I composed myself, had a look at her write-up, which seemed lively and expressed a love for Zubrowka, and then decided to go with the friendly option, with a mention of something in her profile so she'd know that I'd actually read it:

> *Hello Holski! So...nice to meet you (virtually), and thanks for the mayB. Fancy a Polish vodka and fruit juice sometime? Or...if that's moving too quickly for*

> *online dating (hopeless with etiquette) then fancy an*
> *email chat?!*

Fifteen minutes later…

> *Sounds good to me ;)*
> *You seem tres charming haha*
> *Just about to RUN outta the office so will check my*
> *little black book for a possible Zubrowka rendezvous*
> *:)*
> *TTFN*

Ok, so punctuation isn't her strong point and I have no idea what TTFN means, but she thinks I seem charming, this is the first online dating message I've ever received, and she was obviously in a rush because she spelt RUN with capital letters, so I'll let her off. I jot a quick note back:

> *Lovely! Look forward to hearing about the spaces in*
> *your little black book…*

And then I wait. A day passes without reply, or without any of my other three remaining choices adding me to their *Black Book,* and although I keep going back to Facespin it doesn't look like anyone else has signed up to the site. I'd give anything to have just one face twirl into picture, even if I had to say *No* to it. Anything, please YesNoMayB, give me something.

In fact, YesNoMayB had given me something, I just wasn't aware of it. Not ten waking minutes had gone by since I completed my profile without me thinking about the whole process. I was intrigued by the notion of online dating but more than that, I was excited by it. Even though I didn't know this Holski woman beyond her cute photo and eccentric typing, I got a buzz when she sent me that first message; it turned her from just a strange face on a screen into a girl with whom I now had something in common. I had no expectations or perceptions of her, this was a girl who I might like or I might not, but there was a glimmer of potential because we were both on the same online dating site and what's more, we were allowed to talk to each other, which is quite important. It was the online equivalent of a strange woman at a bar being introduced to me by a friend, a friend who would tell me what they're about to do and give me a chance to put my thumbs around a drink, and not into my cowboy trousers.

Perhaps I'd been spending too much time on my own, but I realised I wanted more of this. The thing was, by now it had been two days since Holski had written to me, and still nobody else had signed up to YesNoMayB, and I was starting to get a little bit impatient. *Maybe it's just a new site*, I thought, *maybe in a few days thousands more people will have registered, maybe I should just bide my time and hang around.* But I couldn't. You see, I'm not very good at waiting, for anything. So it seemed sensible to take a little look at some other dating sites, just to see what they offered. And because I'd been there briefly for my friend Alice's sake a few months earlier, it seemed natural that the first one I went to was MySingleFriend.com.

THREE

Meet Dave

In early 2005, I hit a quarter-life crisis. In addition to the gut-wrenching final months of a three-year relationship in rapid decline I was unhappy in my job, very unhappy. I was not, it had become highly evident, very good at working for others. I was a graphic designer responsible for laying out poorly compiled newspapers and advertising brochures, and I was quite sure that there was more to life than disrespecting myself with every, feeble click of a mouse.

Yearning for a new challenge, I needed a change of tack. A family holiday in the French Alps gave me another realisation that I wasn't entirely comfortable with; I was crap at snowboarding, but God I loved it. Riding a board down a hill gave me a buzz of electricity that wasn't dampened even with a regular and possibly horrific face-plant into a snowdrift, although I would have preferred to spend more time standing than laying on my back. On the gloomy bus ride back to Grenoble Airport I felt like I'd wasted a week and several hundred pound coins, so I made myself a promise that, quite simply, the next time I went snowboarding I'd be better. The best way to achieve this, I felt, was by taking up a board sport at home, so when my brother handed me a magazine in the departure lounge I realised just what that new board sport would be. There, in a small corner page advert, was a picture of a long skateboard with two wheels, beneath the headline: *The Tierney Rides T-Board: Rides like a snowboard, on tarmac.*

One week later I was the proud owner of a T-Board, and at the tender age of twenty-five I set about teaching myself to skate for the first time. I had been living in the same town for six years and suddenly my perspective changed. I rolled along streets that previously I had only walked and cycled, and suddenly everything was new to me; a hill meant something! So did a smooth surface, a kerb decline at traffic lights, the cycle path bordering Swansea Bay. I was skating around a wonderful new world, and it was all down to this board. Two weeks later, at around the same time that I broke up with my girlfriend, I woke up and decided to make a change. I needed to stop lying to myself and I needed to start living. Rather than continue doing things as I was expected to – by doing a job for no reason other than to pay the bills - I decided I was going to live according to how I felt. In fact, I was ready to attempt to make a living doing something I was passionate about, and as I liked longboarding and travelling, I decided there and then to go on a journey, on my longboard.

Things started to happen quite quickly. I quit my job and founded an initiative called BoardFree. I had decided to push a longboard across Australia, from Perth to Brisbane, and I realised that if I made it to the east coast of Oz then the journey would break a new world record. I was on a mission. I lived off my savings and planned for months, designed a website, drummed up media coverage, sought sponsors and slowly started to build a support team. Barely a year after stepping onto my first board, I became the first person to skate the 900-mile length of Britain from John O'Groats to Lands End. That was a warm-up. Two and a half months later I flew to Perth, Western Australia, accompanied by a team of seven people who had given up their jobs to help the cause and follow a bloke on a yellow skateboard. It was a little bit like a cult.

It took five months to skate across Australia - it's quite a big place. I managed to break the world record for the longest journey ever skated as we passed through Sydney, and then I pushed onto Brisbane, finishing on the South Bank amidst a crowd of people having skated 3618 miles in less than half a year. Every day people would ask me questions about how big my legs were and whether I got bored, but they were missing the point. Thanks to my team and countless generous souls along the way the journeys raised almost £20,000 for our three charities, and some cracking media coverage meant that other people were inspired to go off and do the same in the following months, meaning more money raised for good causes. After all, if a skinny ginger bloke who had never skated before could get across Australia, then anyone could do it.

Getting that longboard in March 2005 had changed my life, and I wasn't about to rewind the clock and re-enter the nine-to-five world I had grown to loathe. Life was for living and new experiences were there for the taking, but they weren't going to come to me so I had to go and find them. Before I flew back to the UK a lady named Barbara called me. She was an editor at a London publishing company. 'We've been following your journey', she told me, 'and we'd quite like your book.' I was so excited I almost peed my pants. Writing had been a big part of my life since a nineteen-year-old me had started scrawling in a travel journal in Uganda, and in the absence of any vocational passion had you asked me at any point in my early twenties what I really wanted to be, I would have replied with two words: 'Travel Writer.'

Now, thanks to a wholly bizarre two years, I had my chance. I flew home, signed my first ever book deal, sold my house in Wales, rented a room in North London, set up my computer and started typing. On the rare occasion that I did venture outside, I found that when people asked me what I did for a living I didn't really know what to tell them. 'I'm a long-distance skateboarder' didn't seem to cut it, and I felt slightly uncomfortable saying, 'I'm an author,' because although I had one book on the way, I wasn't exactly Bill Bryson. I was just an average bloke who had done something a bit odd that people might want to read about. I was in no man's land with some cool stories to tell but nothing solid to call my own. I had no identity but I wanted to make a go of the writing so I could clutch a different book under each arm and say quite confidently 'Hi, I'm Dave, I'm an author,' without feeling like too much of a chump. Although the first book, *BoardFree*, had opened up some doors I didn't want to become typecast as someone who went on quirky geographical adventures just for the sake of writing about them. Instead, I wanted readers to be able to relate to whatever subject I was covering, and in turn I wanted to get my teeth into my work.

As a writer, you write what you know, so you either take knowledge from your past, or you totally submerge yourself in a new existence that requires you to completely reassess who you are and what you believe in. As long as it's carried out honestly, this self-critiquing can be life changing, and if a writer can articulate his or her findings in the same spirit of honesty then potentially the resulting book has some worth. The skateboarding project had totally changed my outlook on life and taught me some everlasting lessons; about behaviour, setting realistic but not constricting goals, surrounding oneself with good people and taking the positive fork in the road. I had begun to see every cup as half full, and then I started drinking the rest. All very well, but where did I go from here?

The answer, I soon realised, was right under my nose. There are countless Internet Dating websites, all offering their own unique take on matchmaking. Dating Direct, Plenty of Fish, Guardian Soulmates, Match, eHarmony and many others, but immediately there was one that stood out. MySingleFriend, or MSF as it's known to the cool kids (who don't have girlfriends or boyfriends), is a revolution in online dating. The site is based around the avoidance of all the difficult factors that usually put people off dating online. The main clue is in the title. Rather than spend hours trying to write about yourself in a clichéd box, something YesNoMayB had already taught me wasn't a simple affair, your profile is actually written by somebody else, someone who knows you very well. In short, you are their SingleFriend, and it's their job to pimp you out. Not satisfied with just one flash of cunning, the site pushed the boat out a little further. Most online dating sites require you to enter a username, like Beachboy or Foxychick69. MSF, on the other hand, went for the simple option: they let people use their own names. Genius.

Immediately, with two simple moves, MySingleFriend developed a reputation as a place you could go to date online with confidence and security. Yes, it cost about twenty quid for three months, but there was much less to hide behind. Profiles written by friends just didn't seem so desperate, and knowing the name of the person you were trying to woo was so much easier for both parties - far more personal than trying to chat up BladeRunner113. If you were looking for trust from a dating website, then MySingleFriend seemed to be the way to go. After a quick browse I realised that there was nothing to think about, so I dropped my friend Amanda a line offering to cook dinner in return for a very generous profile. She had never tasted my cooking, but she said yes anyway, poor girl.

What Amanda neglected to tell me was that she was very, very hungover, so as I toiled excitedly with a stir-fry in the kitchen, she was next door tapping away on my laptop with a pair of shaky hands:

Dave

*28 year old straight male looking for a female aged between 23 and 29 recommended by **Amanda***

Children: *none*

Drinking: *weekend good times*

Education: *university*

Religion: *none*

Height: *5ft 9in to 6ft*

Area: *London, Clapham*

Smoking: *no*

Employment: *self-employed*

Build: *athletic*

Summary: *a confident sort, a hard working person, an outdoors type, creative, enthusiastic about life, intelligent, laid back, loyal, sporty and well travelled!!*

__Amanda__ has this to say about __Dave__

Dave is currently in the kitchen cooking me dinner so that's definitely a plus point (obviously no bribes involved here!). I've known him for a few years now and he is definitely one of the most interesting people I know – he is also incredibly passionate about everything he does – when he has an idea he runs with it and he never does things by halves.

Dave is definitely an outdoors kind of guy – no challenge or adventure is too big or overwhelming for him to have a go. Having said that he also is a big fan of going to the pub and having a cheeky drink or three. He is very local and supportive friend and will be there with a listening and understanding ear if needed whilst making you see the funny side of things and having a drink to make you smile about life.

There are a few key facts about Dave that immediately spring to mind – he has been on some incredible journeys recently (geographical no emotional – don't worry!) however I've been told I'm not allowed to mention these specifically so you'll just have to meet him and find out for yourself!

So thats Dave – he is lovely, funny, interesting and would suit someone a bit adventurous with a good sense of humour and, most importantly, someone who doesn't take life too seriously and is up for a giggle – give him go!

I couldn't quite believe my eyes, the grammar monster in me decided to burn Amanda at the stake. Of all the mistakes anyone could make, I'm not sure calling the bloke you're trying to advertise 'local' is the way to go. 'Local' means 'Retarded', 'Stays at home a lot', 'Nose like a little piglet'.

'You know, Mand, if I don't get any dates out of this I'm going to whoop your ass.'

'Yes, but if you find one that you fall madly in love with then I'm going to have to be a bridesmaid.'

That's the thing with Amanda, she can't stop thinking about weddings. One downside to MSF is that once your friend has written your profile, you can only accept or reject with no amendments allowed. What she'd said was very nice, but would potential dates read it and wonder why I got my seven year-old friend to write it? This was not a good start but I had to roll with the punches, and as all MySingleFriends get to add a little paragraph to their friend's gushing appraisal, I had to think fast:

*to which **Dave** responded:*

Firstly, I have to say that Amanda was a bit hungover when writing this, and she always struggles on second paragraphs anyway, bless her. Suffice it to say, don't judge me on my friend's spelling, I think she meant loyal, not local! Cheers Mand!

I guess I'm just looking to meet someone who is comfortable with who they are, has a wicked sense of humour and believes that life's too short not to have fun. Other essential knowledge is that you appreciate the power of a good hug!

If that sounds like you then let's go and have a coffee, or do something a bit more inventive!

I uploaded the same black and white moody picture I'd used on YesNoMayB, and sent the profile off to get verified.

'In less than twenty-four hours,' I said to Amanda, who was sipping a glass of red wine and reading a magazine article about wedding bouquets, 'I'm going to be a dating man. It all seems very simple, doesn't it?'

'It's as simple as you make it,' she said, and as it turns out, she was right.

The problem was, I wasn't going to make it very simple at all. The next day, as I passed the time waiting for my MSF profile to go live, I started to run some tests. MSF has a pretty restrictive search engine in comparison to other sites, but there were still choices to be made. *Sex?* Yes, I think I'll search for women. *Location?* I live in London and it would be quite handy if I didn't have to go to Northumberland to meet a girl for coffee, so girls in the capital it is. *Only show profiles with pictures?* Well, yes please, it would be nice to know what they look like. *Age?* Blimey, how old do I want a prospective girlfriend to be? How young, even? I'm 28 now, and although girls mature faster than boys I'm not sure I want to date anyone younger than 20. Or 21. Or 23. Where does it stop? If I start my age search at 23 am I missing out on the 22 year-old love of my life? Bugger it, if it's meant to be it's meant to be, I'm going to start at 23. And then how old? My age, or higher? Let's go for 29, I'm not sure I'm ready to date someone in their thirties.

So those were my criteria: Women living in London between the ages of 23 and 29, with a picture. That should narrow it down a bit.

Search.

Oh. My. God. There are thousands of them! Pages and pages! And more pages! I had no idea online dating was so popular, I don't know where to start. Are there really this many single women in London? And this is just one dating website out of goodness knows how many. I feel like I've just opened a door at the back of a wardrobe and instead of a massive snowy forest with funny walking goat-people and small boys with swords, there are just women. Loads of women; all kinds of women.

And then, as I scrolled through the pages, looking at the things that people had written about their friends, clicking on Emily, 25, and Sophie, 28, and Jemima, 29, an act that felt sleazy and voyeuristic yet liberatingly legal, an idea began to form, an idea I really should have quashed there and then. But I couldn't, it was gripping, I'd just discovered a whole new world, which, with one click of a button, I could be a part of. 'There might well be a book in this,' I said out loud with an enormous grin.

But it's been done before, hasn't it? Pop into Waterstones or Borders or WH Smith and there are shelves of books about relationships and love and sex and marriage and dating, is there honestly anything left to write about? Well, maybe, just maybe, there is.

FOUR

A Short History of the

Women in my Life

Even before a restless night at the age of nine led to an accidental yet arousing discharge that shot fire into my belly, curled my toes and made me wonder just how my pyjamas had gotten wet, I'd been fascinated by relationships. Men and women (back then they were just boys and girls) and the attraction between them, and the politics of kissing (a very young me once refused to snog a girl behind the Youth Club because, I told her, I didn't want AIDS). As time went on these interests became complicated yet sharpened by the unexplained phenomena of chemistry and love.

Not long after that fateful first ejaculation, which, by the way, occurred in the highly erotic surrounds of a Thundercats duvet, I started to eye up the ladies. Across the street was a girl named Sonia, who was two years older than me and had a moon face covered in delightful freckles. She wore these tiny little shorts that hugged her bottom in a way that made me shiver, and from those shorts sprouted long, tanned legs that were quite possibly the most amazing things I'd ever seen in my life. We were playing one day on our road and Sonia was struggling to climb a tree. Her legs were flapping about uncontrollably and I think she was starting to cry because her torso was wedged in between two forks of the trunk, so when she asked for my help I did the first thing that came into my head. I reached up, planted both hands on her buttocks, and pushed as hard as I could. It did the trick, Sonia was now firmly in the tree, but there were repercussions. Even as I had been pushing I went through the conflicting emotions that adulthood was going to start dishing out on a regular basis a few years later. I was thinking two things at once; *Wow, this feels great!* and *Oh no, I really shouldn't be doing this*. I had never touched a girl's bottom before and I was flushing with a balanced mixture of glee and embarrassment when Sonia, now settled in her elevated position, turned and glared at me so fiercely that I had no choice but to run away. We lived on that road for another fourteen months and I never built up the courage to go and play with Sonia again. It became the story of my life.

Bar Sonia and a wispy Norfolk farmer's daughter named Stephanie Fletcher, I had two other brushes with females before I turned ten. The first was with one of the most attractive girls I had ever met. Ashleigh Morgan had blonde hair cascading to her waist, blue eyes with lashes so long that they held her dark framed spectacles so far from her eyes that they kept slipping down her nose, which was like a perfect little button. She was seven. One morning at the end of break time Ashleigh Morgan ran up to me and said six words that made me drop the tennis ball I'd been kicking around.

'Will you go out with me?' she asked. I picked up my ball and stared back at her, shocked. We had never spoken before.

'Ok,' I said.

'Cool!' She shrieked, and ran away giggling.

The next day I went into our classroom stationary cupboard to have a rummage. When I turned around Ashleigh was there, looking glum.

'Hi,' I said.

She looked at her feet.

'I'm not sure this is going to work out,' she mumbled.

I looked at my feet.

'Ok,' I said.

'Sorry.' She walked away, and a solitary tear fell onto my brand new textbook.

What I had yet to realise was that to have a girlfriend I needed to communicate with her: 'Ok, Hi' and 'Ok' was just about as far as I got with Ashleigh Morgan, and it just wouldn't do.

The next time I got a girlfriend I made more of an effort. We were both eight and we sat on the swing in my garden kissing each other with our mouths closed. Sometimes my Dad would come out the back door and ask me if I wanted to go and play golf, and I'd tell him in no uncertain terms that I was busy. I wasn't going to let Shona Ness slip through my fingers just because sport was on offer, and I was also a bit pissed at my Dad for shaving off his moustache. He'd had it all of my life and now he looked like a different person, I wasn't even sure if he was really my Dad at all.

Despite the interruptions Shona and I had a brilliant time for two weeks and then one day I went around to her house. I distinctly remember the path through the woods with trees swaying and yellow leaves on the ground, then pushing open her back gate to find her sitting on her own swing. Correction: she wasn't sitting on the swing; she was sitting on another boy who was sitting on the swing. That boy was my best friend Andrew Ball, and he was kissing my girlfriend with his mouth open. I picked up a lump of mud from a nearby flower bed, threw it with such force that it landed closer to me than them, and then I ran away.

After that, the thought of getting close to another woman was too much to bear, so I played a lot of football, buried myself in novels and tried not to make any male best friends just in case a girl came along that they could steal.

I must have been about twelve when I wandered into the kitchen after a game of football one warm summer evening. Dad's back was to the door and my brother, only eight at the time, was facing him, all wide-eyed at the conversation they were having. For all my naiveté I instantly knew that they were talking about sex, and I paused at the door for a moment, taking it in, before experiencing what can only be called a jealous flush. You see, I had clearly walked in upon a Birds And Bees lesson, which in itself would have been fine. But my brother was eight and I was twelve, and I hadn't yet been fed this information from either of my parents. Had they forgotten about me? Or had that picture of Pamela Anderson's bare chest cunningly folded in my bedside drawer convinced them that I was an early starter and already knew all there was to know about getting jiggy? Had they asked, I would have assured them that I knew absolutely bugger all about the subject, and that they better spill the beans before I turned thirteen and automatically became embarrassed when they spoke to me.

Not long after that my Dad asked me what I thought about prostitution.

'I don't think it's very good,' I said, screwing my face up.

'What about sex?' asked my Dad.

'I'm not sure I'll ever do it.'

Such a sweet, innocent boy.

After a while, through no fault of my own, I was sent to a boarding school on a hill in the middle of Surrey and for two years managed to have just as little luck with girls as I had previously. When I was twelve and a half a common cold managed to develop into pneumonia and there I lay, resigned to a bed in sick bay as the rest of the school continued unabashed on the floors below. It was my first day in there and I was woken from a sickly slumber by a girl in my year. 'Dave,' she said, 'I want to ask you something.' Sophie Smith was stunning with long brown-blonde hair and a faultless olive complexion; I had fancied her for weeks. 'Do you like me?' she asked, and I stared back at her with rheumy eyes, looking much like a rabbit with Myxomatosis.

'Yes,' I said, 'Do you like me?'

She nodded.

'Shall we go out, then?'

'Sure.'

'Great.' And she bounded off, much like Ashleigh Morgan had done on the playground five years earlier.

One week passed and my pneumonia had gotten worse. I was a rake of a child, skin wrapped around bone, the heaviest part of my body was a gigantic shock of ginger hair. My face was peppered in acne and I wore thick NHS glasses that spanned from cheekbones to hairline, and because my lungs weren't working very well I spent much of the time sleeping and the rest hacking ferociously. I wasn't, you might say, a very sexy boy. Sophie popped in now and then but not being in much of a position to woo her I usually pretended to be asleep and because I was very tired then actually drifted off, and when I woke up it was almost always in a sticky puddle of dribble. I was on top form for the ladies and it was only a matter of time before Sophie came in and uttered the immortal words, 'Dave, I just don't think this is going to work out. You're dumped.' I couldn't really blame her for leaving, I wasn't exactly a catch, she'd stuck with me for a whole week and in that time I'd been either catatonic, or vomiting. An early marriage had never been on the cards but even so, I started to wonder whether girls just go out with boys so they can dump them. I became wary and then, coincidentally, sicker.

A couple of months later I was back in school, no more cough, no more dodgy lungs, still no girlfriend. I had the odd dalliance, wrote love letters to the pretty girls and found them torn up in the common room bin later that day. Chatted one morning to Gloria Kitchen who was the form bicycle, and couldn't quite believe it when she put her hand on my crotch and told me I had a big dick. 'I could suck it if you like?' she suggested,

'Nah, I've got football in a few minutes,' I told her, shaking with fear. I think she's got about seven kids, now.

What haunted me most about my time at the Duke of Kent School, though, was my inability to kiss a girl. I was petrified of the whole thing and had no idea what I'd do if I got into a kissing position. Even talking about kissing was beyond me, so although on paper I had girlfriends for a few days at a time, it never turned into anything more than getting asked out and then getting dumped.

School did, of course, throw up a bit of excitement during break-times, although it was a rarity for me personally during the impromptu games of spin the bottle or pass the polo. To this day I'm quite sure that Matt Bell fixed every game we were involved in – I lost count of the number of times Caz MacGregor, Nat Lane and Sarah Blackshaw literally squealed with delight when the bottle slowly revolved just past me and pointed straight at Matt's already pouting lips.

Years later during a school reunion I was chatting to my old primary school beaus Sarah Fuller and Vicki Barnes, when Vicki made a startling revelation. 'Do you remember how Sarah and I used to go out with half of you each?'

Sarah looked just as amazed as I felt. I'm sure I would have remembered having *two* girlfriends at once but, sadly, I didn't. Neither did Sarah, she was looking at me like I was a right slut.

'Which side did you have?' I joked, but Vicki was deadly serious.

'I had the left, Sarah had the right. We drew straws.'

'God, I feel like such a commodity.'

My early relationships were summed up right there and then, I may have had the opportunities but I just didn't realise it, and if I had, I still would have had no idea what to do. Despite a lack of sexual progress at the Duke of Kent I loved the place, and it was a very sad day when the time came to be shipped off to secondary school. There, again, I was a boarder, but this time, tragically, it was in an all-boys establishment. For five long years I was kept in the dark, far too withdrawn to take advantage of the High School girls across town, utterly sans kiss until A-Levels had been completed and my gap year was grasped with both hands. It was time for a little bit of the real world, and it couldn't come a moment too soon.

FIVE

Being a Grown-Up

Contrary to the story so far, I haven't been a complete failure when it comes to relationships. I was eighteen the first time I fell hard for a woman. I was doing the most menial job in the world, cleaning dishes and wiping ovens in order to earn money to escape to Africa, and she worked with me. We were both fairly ordinary: I was spotty, introverted, untouched, unkissed and unloved. But most of all, I was bored shitless. I may have been hanging tightly onto the bottom rung of Lothario's ladder but I wasn't stupid, and I wasn't overly happy with the droll of washing pots and pans for six months. I was there because I had a mission, to earn enough so I could go to Uganda and grow up, have something to talk about, maybe kiss someone. But rising at 6am and walking across a dewy golf course in tight blue flannels to scrub pots for ten hours on end reduced me to tears regularly, and had the aforementioned woman not been around to make me laugh like I'd never laughed before then I may well have flown to Entebbe in a state of serious depression. Luckily, I didn't. It was a totally unconsummated relationship and I'm not sure I could even call it love, perhaps obsession is a better word, but either way I'd never felt quite that way about a female before. I was pure as a day of deep snow and my gut melted each time Sarah looked at me. Still, it was never going to work out, her being married and all.

I'd like to be able to report that I popped my cherry on a tour bus as a cocky teenager with three naked groupies. But it didn't happen that way. I was nineteen years old, pale and skinny and in Kampala, and there she was, Jessica, all ravishing beauty and cherry-popping Latin fire. Head over heels and round and round she turned me. Oh yes, I was in love. I was so in love I could think of nothing for nine months other than Jessica. My world revolved around this girl, so much so that after our African adventure I followed her out to Colombia to meet her family. Not many weeks later Jessica sat me down somewhere in the middle of this vast and apparently dangerous nation and told me that we weren't going to work out. I was bemused, befuddled, confused and upset. Not to mention a bit lost. So I went to Ecuador and managed to get involved in a quite horrific traffic accident. Somehow I escaped unscathed but in the midst of a scene of bloody carnage I realised that I'd been given another chance. Right then, right there, looking over the Amazon jungle with the truck I'd just been riding on somewhere down a steep verge, I decided in a very lucid kind of way that there was nothing more important to me than love, so my only option was to go back to Colombia and win the girl back. So I wandered around the jungle for a while just to make sure that I wasn't crazy, and then flew back to Colombia. When she saw me stood there outside her Bogota house wearing a quite ridiculous blue poncho Jessica collapsed in a pile of tears and told me I shouldn't have returned. I suspected she'd already taken someone else up, but here's a tip for all you boys; if you're trying to win a girl over for the first, second or even the third time, dress smartly, and not like you've just come home from a Pablo Escobar Theme Party. With Jessica's tears comprehensibly dispatched, I wrapped my heart up in my poncho and flew back to the UK, where I spent the best part of a year with a big lump in my throat writing love poems to no one in particular.

After Jessica came Amy. I'm not overly sure why we were ever together in the first place, but I put it down to two things. One, in the early noughties I was going through an odd stage of character development – 'The Hippy Stage', some might say. I wore long, shoulder-length hair, which earned me nicknames such as Simba and Aslan. My face went from moderately to heavily bearded and back again. I wore very stripy trousers. And smoked a pipe. Amy studied the same things as me and liked me a little bit, so getting together seemed like the right thing to do. The thing is, if the sole reason for anyone losing his or her single status comes down to a whimsical thought such as *it seems like the right thing to do*, then it probably isn't the right thing to do.

So why did I do it? Well, Amy was my second serious girlfriend. The first one had plunged her beautiful little fist into my chest and thrown my heart into a frying pan alongside several different types of South American plantain, and after that I simply wasn't ready to risk getting hurt again in such a brutal fashion. So I went for Amy because in all reality she was never going to hurt me, not as much as Jessica, in any case. At the time this wasn't a conscious passage of thought on my behalf, I only realised what I'd done years later when thinking in depth about relationships and how they begin, and how they end, and how bloody awkward they were sometimes. After heartbreak an automatic preservation system kicks in, and instinctively I focused on a safe bet. All that said and done, I loved her; she was wacky, super sharp, had lovely blonde hair and she cared for me very much, which was pretty cool considering my abysmal dress sense and poor grooming habits. She even bought me chickens for my twenty-first birthday; I named them Tikka and Korma. After a while, though, the false reasons for our unification started to bubble to the surface and we parted company, very, very slowly. Yes, it was one of those break-ups. There was no clean incision; if our two sides were paint then they were wiped apart by a very dirty sponge. There was much overlapping of colours, and the final result was less than pretty. Which actually summed up the pair of us in the first place.

And then there was Natalie. We met and moved in together pretty much in the same couple of hours. She was gorgeous and funny and caught my eye as soon as we started to work together in the University Students Union. First, I started to accumulate my belongings in her room, which was near our mutual place of work. Then, a few months later she moved across town into my house; I quickly shipped the upstairs tenants out and we started to do things like decorate the living room and get a cat. I did what all men do in such a situation, and started to make a den. I called it a study, but in reality it had a big TV, a Playstation, two sofa-size bean bags, a shelf full of DVDs and a computer that was hooked up to the Internet. Basically, we lived like a married couple for three years. During that period we both moved jobs and started to change, because people do change when they're young. We were twenty-two when we got together and by the time our twenty-fifth birthdays passed we had started to look at each other as best friends who said 'I love you' to each other before we left the house. Eventually the thing we most looked forward to was getting some friends around and settling down on some beanbags to watch the *Lord of the Rings Trilogy: Extended Version*. We both started to wonder whether this was it, whether we'd ever have sex with other people and how we'd managed to act like grandparents without being remotely close to having our own children, and when you start wondering these things it's definitely time to move on.

But it's not easy to make the break when you've been with someone for three years. We were partners, my friends didn't refer to me by just my name anymore – they said things like 'I wonder if Dave and Natalie would like to come out...' I was one part of a gruesome twosome and I spent about two and a half years getting my head around it whilst we were sleeping in the same bed, eating in the same room (sometimes) and going shopping together in the local Sainsburys. And unbeknownst to me, Natalie was thinking along exactly the same lines. We were both bloody miserable but couldn't talk to each other about it on the off chance that the other didn't feel the same way – the potential upset was too horrible to bear. So we kept quiet, grew grumpy, settled for what we had and started to stagnate. It was a sad state of affairs, so sad that the happiest I'd been for about half a year was when she pushed open my study door one Sunday in March 2005 and told me she was leaving. I loved her and I didn't want her to go, but she did anyway, and although I wept for a while in the sanctuary of an enormous purple bean bag at the top of a three bedroom terrace that I now lived in completely by myself (except for Kiwa the cat), I knew it was for the best because we'd been getting over each other since mid 2004 and now we had our lives back. I am about 105% certain that she felt exactly the same way, too.

It sounds harsh, writing it down like that, but we all know it's true. If you've spent several years partnered up with someone you lose some of your identity, and when the parting finally comes the real pain exists as the remnants of your ex slowly inch their way out of you. Those parts, now foreign bodies which don't belong, become deep, agonising aches. It feels as though they've left little fishhooks in each muscle, under each lobe, with a special dollop of extra sharp spikes in your aorta, ready for the most ironic pumping action of the year. Have you ever been so cold you feel as though your life was slowly ebbing away, and then you made it to somewhere warm and all at once your relief at being in a place so potentially cosy is countered by utter agony as the cold is ushered away from your core and out of your extremities? The cold, like the exiting partner who glances at you one final time before pulling the door shut behind her, takes as long as it bloody can to completely disappear, but when it does it's the most wonderful feeling; *'Oh, hello Dave, it's you again! You've grown up, thank God all that's over, eh? Blimey, better late than never, fancy a pint?'*

I've always thought that the blues are not so much about missing someone else, than missing yourself. When you're getting over someone you're actually in the process of becoming *you* again, regaining the individuality that simpered away into the jointly-owned rug and that cleverly worked compromise that invades every long-term relationship at some point, the second TV.

Until that relationship ended, I'd never really played around. Single once again, I rebounded like a huge ... no, *giant*, elastic band. I partied hard, drunk too much, all reaffirming everything I'd doubted about myself during the final, stale months of my dying courtship with Natalie. Eventually, though, I fully regained my individuality and realised that I couldn't carry on like this for much longer; I missed being in a relationship and longed for a familiar warm body to wake up besides, but until someone came along who was going to give me butterflies I suppose the short-term chase continued begrudgingly, little morsels of company filling a hole that was a bit too large for anyone to make any difference to. We've all had relationships, flirtations, affairs, kisses and maybe even a bit of spooning with someone we're not 100% about, but after a while you just start hating yourself. It's not cool to feign attraction, for you lie to everyone, including yourself.

Later, there were other relationships, one that even threatened to go all the way but, of course, it didn't. It was a traumatic break-up that at least confirmed my heart was still capable of cracking a little bit - it had been so long! It was confirmation that subsequent relationships can rival the first love; for passion, and sadly, for the pain that comes after it's lost. It was one of those splits where we battled for ages before the emptiness, but at least I could see her face as it was happening. Once she was gone I agonised for months; missed her, doubted myself, picked up the phone to call and then used my spare hand to lever the handset to safety. I was fighting with my own hands! There's an unspoken element of competition that has the power to lift past feelings to the surface, even months after both parties go their separate ways. Yes, she moved on before I did. What a kick in the teeth that is! Even if you've been fine, mellow, perhaps even playing around a bit; convinced that finally you're past the worst of it. And then Facebook goes and tells you that they've found someone new. *Thingy Majiggy is in a relationship.* I become John McEnroe all of a sudden and shout at the screen;

'Are you serious?! Noooo, she pressed the wrong button on her profile didn't she? Must be a mistake. But it's not a mistake, is it? No. I'm a loser!' All those lonely nights with chocolate and films with no romance in were worthless, the feelings bubbled up again but now in a different guise. Anger. How dare she move on before me, surely that's not fair?! Bet she didn't even love me in the first place. Lies! I hope she's happy, because I'm a nice person, but she better not be too happy, that would be unfair. Even if there's no chance or will to reunite with your ex, that moment when you realise that they've moved on is a nail in the coffin. Suddenly the past becomes unobtainable, there's no going back; regret is utterly desperate and final.

But it could be worse. My friend Bree's ex, Bodie, bought her an engagement ring one Christmas but freaked himself out so much that five days before the proposed proposal he sat her down and said:

'I love you, you're perfect for me and if I stay with you I'm going to marry you, but I'm too young for a long-term relationship, I'm leaving.' Six months later Bodie met another girl, and her name was Jodie. In Bree's words:

'It was hard enough as it was, but when his name rhymes with hers it just takes the piss. I mean, change one letter and they're basically the same person!'

Eventually, one morning in 2007 I woke up from my own personal crisis and thought to myself, *Oh, hello Dave, it's you again! You've grown up, thank God all that's over, eh? Fancy a pint?* I didn't have a pint, it was morning and things hadn't been quite that bad, but I did spend the rest of the day thinking about how different I felt now compared to five or six months earlier, and one thing resounded again and again. I'm single, very settled, happy with the place I'm in, and am pretty sure that I'm ready to meet someone. Yep, I'm ready to find a girlfriend.

SIX

The Hundred

I'm quite sure it is no coincidence that I began to write around the same time that I fell in love for the first time, and I put it down to those long teenage years of suffering when females were so far removed from my life that I could never envisage myself kissing one, let alone having anything more meaningful. My girlfriends were in FHM and Maxim, clippings of buxom beauties stuck (with blu-tac) to the walls and ceiling of my enclosed bunk at boarding school. Going to sleep each night with paper versions of fantastically unobtainable women was not good preparation for the real world, and boy did I know it. But even as my teens slipped into twenties and I started to distance myself from that shy, spotty, bespectacled character of my youth, a part of him remained and still does, indivisibly, to this day.

When I first fell in love I fell hard. If I spent a week away from her I would write a poem for each day we would be apart, and leave them all beneath a pillow for her to find later. I loved her so much that I believed she would never leave me because it would be impossible for any other man to feel as strongly as I did about her. The sex we had was unforgettable for me and quite forgettable for her, I'm sure, but at the time I didn't know that, and I was fully aware that if I had to choose between losing the sex or the love, I would have kept the love every single time because it made me feel more complete than anything I'd ever experienced.

As years and relationships came and went, I filled notebooks and journals and loose sheets of A4 paper with my feelings about love and sex and losing it and finding it again, the endless discovery of something new making my appetite for the topic insatiable. And as the notes grew I realised that some day, one day, I would write a book about relationships that would show that men could be caring and compassionate. That yes, they were capable of laziness and loss of judgement and outlandish immaturity, but that at heart they were sensitive creatures who craved love and security. Even for a male homosapien, life isn't all about following your penis around like a panting dog.

In short, I had a hunch that men and women were a lot more similar than we give them credit for and the differences between the two lay mostly in who's interpreting them. But how I was going to explain it all on paper I wasn't quite sure. Maybe a novel? Perhaps a collection of short stories? Or who knows, one day a woman might swoop into my life and change the way I think about everything. That's the thing though, you can't tell when you're going to fall in love, it never happens the same way twice and there is absolutely no formula you can use to predict it. But wait just a minute. Here I am scrolling through hundreds of pages on a website, looking at thousands of women who are single - or at least claim to be - and an idea is forming. Books have already been written about dating, but look at all these people, all varying shapes and sizes, each one with a different sense of humour and a unique set of facial tics. With all of these strange women all waiting to meet the man of their dreams, and little old me sitting here on a sofa just a few miles away from all of them, surely there is a story in there somewhere? I'm just looking for someone to sit on the sofa with, that's ok, isn't it? I picked up the phone, and called my friend Will.

'Muthafucker!'

'Hey Will, fancy a drink?'

'Sure dude, everything ok?'

'Possibly more than ok, I'll tell you all about it in a bit.'

When Will and I first met we were nineteen years old, in Uganda. We fought like cat and dog for months. I thought he was a pain in the ass and I have no idea what he thought of me, quite sure it wasn't pretty, though. Either way, as time went on we didn't so much as work out our differences as forget about them, and now we live about fifteen minutes walk away from each other, which is relatively handy because he's my best mate.

We meet at The Railway on Clapham High Street because it's closer to his house and I'm on my longboard. I buy the pints and we perch on a bench outside.

'I signed up to a dating site yesterday,' I told him.

'A what?'

'Online dating, a website, I've joined one.'

'What for?'

'I think I'm ready to meet someone and thought I'd give it a shot.'

'What about...' he paused and stared across the road, 'what about ... thingy?'

'Well ... I'm not exactly sure who you're talking about, but, well, you know, I'm ready for something serious.'

'Right, and you asked me to the pub to tell me that, did you?'

He knows me quite well, Will does.

'Not exactly, it's just that I was on this site earlier and I thought that maybe I could write a book about it, what do you reckon?'

'Been done before, hasn't it?'

'Well, yeah, but there has to be a different tack, surely?'

'Ah, I don't know, mate.'

'Here's what I want to do,' I continued unperturbed, 'there are thousands of women on this site, thousands more on others, what if I try and date loads of them and write about the experience?'

'That would take years, mate, and anyway, I thought you said you wanted something serious.'

'I do, I really do. Don't you think that the more women I meet the more chance I have of finding someone?'

He thought a little bit about that, and started to nod.

'Yeah, I suppose. But it's still going to take ages, when are you going to Oz?'

Ah, yes. Book Number One was due to launch Down Under in the New Year and I was going to promote it. He had a point.

'You have a point,' I told him, and then we sat there quietly for a bit. I started working it out in my head, not why we were sat there quietly, but how long I had until I went away. It was early October, and I was due to head to Australia at the end of January, so that gave me just over three months. *Hmmm, what can I do in three months? Maybe a date a week? That's around 14 or 15, that's loads. I've never even been on a date before, not sure I could handle that many...*

Then Will piped up,

'I thought you wanted to write books about endurance journeys, anyway.'

'Well, now and then maybe, but there's a lot more to life than being Forrest Gump.'

'True. What about speed dating, or endurance dating?'

'Ooh, good point, I could do a dating marathon, like ten people in a week.'

'Not much of a marathon, that.'

'Fine, what about a hundred dates?'

'Dude, you're going to Australia.'

'Well, I have about three months, I could date one hundred women in that time.'

Will looked at me sideways.

'Sure you could.' He didn't mean it. 'Want another pint?'

'Yes please,' I said, deep in thought. Endurance dating, blimey, that sounds quite hard. But then so was skateboarding across Australia. So this next book could be about relationships, but in a sense it could also be a long-distance journey. And then, just as Will thumped a new pint down on the table and some beer dribbled through the slats onto my left leg, it came to me.

'I know what I'm going to do,' I announced, triumphantly.

'What's that then?' asked Will.

'I'm going to date one hundred women in one hundred days.'

'You're a nutter. Bet you don't get past fifty-seven.'

'I'm not betting you because this is about more than just a challenge, but I bet I will, anyway.'

'Well dude,' said Will, raising an eyebrow, 'you better get going then, you don't have very long.'

SEVEN

The Dating Game

'You're going to do what?'

'You heard me.'

Amanda had her arms crossed and was shaking her head. I waited for it.

'You're going to die.'

There we go.

'I'm not going to die, it's going to be an adventure.'

'A bloody hard adventure.'

'Yes, well, it wouldn't be a challenge if it were easy.'

'Dave,' she said, adopting that superior pose that women do whenever they're lecturing men about other women, 'do you know how many women one hundred women is?'

'Erm, I'm going to hazard a guess, about one hundred?'

'No, seriously, think about it. One bad date is hard enough, one hundred will honestly kill you.'

'Mand, I'm delighted that you have enough confidence in me to believe that I'm only going to have bad dates, but I'm actually really excited about this.'

'I am so glad I know you,' she smirked, 'you are going to be an emotional disaster in a couple of weeks. It's going to be hilarious.'

With friends like Amanda watching my back, I was going to be just fine.

The weeks ahead were littered with potential potholes and I wanted to create a bank of rules to cover every possible eventuality. Knowing from the off that I was going to be writing a book put me – and the girls I was to date – in a potentially compromising position, so I needed to make sure my objectives were fair. If people read the completed book and thought *oh those poor girls* then I would have failed; it's hard to get across that guys can be sensitive and compassionate by having a one hundred day shag-fest, so here's rule number one; I am dating first, writing a book second. After all, this is legitimate for me; I'm single, free, and most importantly I'm ready to meet someone. I'm bored of messing around, engaging in non-committal flings that are merely small-fry substitutions for commitment and security. I want the real deal, I want love, not sex (but both would be nice). I want someone who knows me inside and out, will put up with my foibles and trust me even when one of my Cornthwaite moods makes me distant and uncommunicative. I can't quite explain it, but something in my blood tells me I'm ready to hand myself over and reciprocate all of the above.

Up until recently, I've had an open fear of certain areas of commitment. The mere idea of marriage and kids worried the heck out of me, not because I couldn't see myself being a father – I'd love to be a father! – but because throughout my young adult life I'd displayed one constant reaction to being enclosed or trapped - I'd run. From relationships, from jobs, even from myself. During a relationship I've yet to discuss with you, I began to realise that the girl I was with meant it when she told me she was built to love, and that there is nothing better than sharing your life with somebody who loves you completely. I just couldn't see it at the time, not clearly, but whether she knew it or not she'd planted a seed in my head. When we broke up the circumstances were so confused neither of us knew what was happening, and I was torn between two counteracting forces: no girl had ever loved me like this one, she was my best friend, she was beautiful in and out, and if I couldn't make this work then I didn't stand a chance in hell of finding love then keeping it for more than a couple of years, so what was I doing letting her go? And weighed up against this I was being magnetised by my instinct, which told me that although a part of me wanted desperately to keep the girl, another part of me wasn't sure, and if I wasn't sure then it just wasn't going to work. So I went with self, let her go, immediately regretted it, and paid my penance when she cut all ties. The needles of the blues started inching their way out of me so, suffering from an inordinate amount of pain, I occasionally sought comfort in others to make myself feel better.

The internal battles weren't welcome, but eventually they bore fruit. That seed in my head had been growing like a baby, and without knowing it I was due in early October. Finally I was content, my life was going well, and it was exciting, really exciting. So exciting, in fact, that I felt like the only thing I had missing was someone to share it with. The commitment bubble that had thwarted me for years suddenly burst and out of it popped a rather simple realisation: it wasn't that I was afraid to commit, it was just that I was afraid of doing it with the wrong woman. Having kids, although not something I planned on doing immediately, suddenly didn't seem like such a gross invasion of my personal freedom anymore. Aye, maybe I was getting soft, but for years I'd rushed into relationships, acting totally on impulse, spontaneity, instinct. Move in with me. Go to bed with me. Kiss me. Sometimes in that order. And where and what has it got me? A first class ticket on the pleasure train to Nowhere, via Nutty Fruitloop and a quick change at Emotional Heartache. I shan't spend hours scouring relationship websites checking the Yes box of every women living in London who might appear to have a pulse. I'm not going to let my standards slip just because I need to shovel in these dates. I want funny, articulate girls, attractive yes, but I'm done with half measures. No, this time I'm going to do it properly, take my time and be sure. So, with an apparent maturity and a very open mind I decided, with a fair degree of intensity, to put myself back on the market.

But first, back to the guidelines. I had a little think and wrote down some ideas, and then some more, and finally the conditions of my new endurance project lay before me, like a modern-day Ten Commandments:

The Rules for Dating 100 Women in 100 Days

1. Always, whatever happens, put dating first, then writing second.

2. Only date women who are total strangers, or those I have met only very briefly before.

3. Only date women who I feel I may be attracted to. They are potential partners, not numbers in a challenge.

4. Women met online must not know of the challenge before the date, otherwise their behaviour may change from the norm. In the purpose of fairness and trust, friends of friends who are single and looking may know in advance about the challenge – but they must also fulfil Rule 3)

5. A date must last for at least 30 minutes. Speed-dating does not count.

6. Follow-up dates are allowed, but they do not count towards The Hundred.

7. Multiple dates on one day are permitted.

8. It is not necessary to tell each date about the challenge; use judgement wisely.

9. If things start to heat up with a date, I must be honest about the challenge before any form of sexual contact commences.

10. Kissing is allowed, and does not constitute sexual contact.

There they were, my Ten Commandments. All I needed to do now was find some women to date, and as soon as I went on the first one the one hundred days would begin. I planned to find most of the dates online, but supplement them by finding the odd date using other methods; maybe by getting a friend to set up a blind date, or I could even approach a single-looking lady on the tube, or a bus, or in the lingerie section at BHS. Probably wouldn't do that last one, though. However the dates were going to come, I teetered on the verge of a brand new experience and skipped around the flat pulsing with excitement, wondering just what was going to happen over the next couple of months. What if I meet the girl of my dreams on Date Four? Then what? Four Dates in Four Days doesn't exactly sound like the meatiest book title. Or what if I get to Date One Hundred and I have three hours to go, and she stands me up? What if they *all* stand me up? Am I willing to go through depression for this book?

What really kept me going, though, was the fact that pretty soon I might meet someone who made my heart go *ba-boom*. I imagined positioning one hundred women in a row and walking down the line with a clipboard; you'd think that from one hundred there would be at least a few of them who were girlfriend material, and if not then let's face it, if I couldn't find a girlfriend after going on one hundred dates then there was absolutely no hope for me. I was trying to push that possibility out of my mind when a text came through from Will: *Fancy going speed-dating tonight?*

Speed-dating was another one of those quirky city things people do when they're single, and although it wasn't going to count towards The Hundred it would be good practice for the real thing. Four minutes with a woman might be enough for some men but who knows, I might even meet a couple of girls who I could then take on a proper date. I had a look at the website Will sent me, apparently there would be up to twenty women there, all single, all looking, all potential dates. Later that evening, I pulled on some jeans and a jumper, and wandered up the road.

'She's cute,' said Will, nodding towards a lone girl sat cross-legged on a stool in the corner.

'And with ten minutes to go until this thing is meant to start, she's the only female in the joint,' I added, as two city boys strutted into the bar, suited up to the nines. And so it started; my senses began to fine-tune, I was mentally preparing myself to dive headfirst into Dating Mode. Every girl or pair of girls who walked into the bar was noted, every other male who looked like they were here for speed-dating was ranked. I looked at the clothes on show, made a judgement on how nervous or confident they seemed, even started to pair off likely couples based on initial flirtatious glances and levels of attractiveness. Almost overnight I had changed, and now, casually leaning up against a bar with a gin & tonic, I felt uncomfortably like I was a loose part of a pack, always on the prowl looking for indicators that might predicate a chase. This was the lower end of the Singles Marketplace, where everyone was openly stating their availability yet kept their price closely to their chest. And then we were ushered upstairs, into the pit, and once everyone had settled down it became clear that there were ten men and only seven women, and that my first speed-dating event was going to be an almighty disappointment.

The set-up was muddled, to say the least. A not-exactly-circular format required the girls to keep to their seats and after a four-minute chat the men were to move on to the left, or diagonally across the room had they just finished with Girl No. 5. At intervals there was a chair for a man who was to spend four minutes alone, and I took the chance at each of these three empties to consider exactly why I had spent £20 to meet twenty single women, when in fact I was spending most of the night by myself. Luckily, when I was placed in front of a human, there were two girls to each tiny square table and I developed a cunning knack of listening to the next girl's statutory dating answers, courtesy of Will who preceded me. Then when the bell rang I'd shuffle one seat to the left and cut straight to the nitty-gritty, astounding the woman in question with how perceptive I was about her.

Girls 1 and 2 were pleasant, but there was no spark. Number 3, who was so plain and lugubrious I started digging my nails into my leg in order to stay awake, was memorable only for her rudeness. 'Hi,' I said as I sat down opposite her, 'how're you finding this?' I tipped my head back, rolling my eyes towards the room.

'It's a bit shit.'

'Ah. So, er, where are you from?'

'North London.'

'Whereabouts?'

'North London.'

'Anywhere specific?'

'I'd rather not say."

Your personality is endearing, but you could tell me your house number and postcode and still be reassured I'm not going to stalk you.

'I'm going to be up front with you,' I said, looking her in the eye, 'I'm not going to stalk you.'

'That's good.'

'You really don't want to be here, do you?'

'Not really,' she looked sideways at her friend, who was talking to Will about trains, or something, 'she wanted to come.'

'Are you actually single?'

'Yeah.'

'So why not make the most of it?'

'Can't be bothered.'

Little Miss Life Is Fun and her friend left at the half-time break, just as Will started telling me how crap he was at speed-dating.

'I can't go two minutes without ranting about the Northern Line,' he said, his head leaning against one hand, which in turn was propped up on the bar, 'it's weird, it's like a switch goes off in my head.'

'So let me get this straight,' I wanted to understand him, 'you get four minutes with each girl, and you've talked about the tube with each of them?'

'Not talked, Dave, ranted. I've actually been ranting. I think I've pissed off every girl I've met so far.'

'Well you certainly put No. 3 off men for life.'

'Oh God, she was long gone before I got to her. What does your score sheet look like?'

DAVE CORNTHWAITE

We'd been given a piece of paper to make notes on each date, and showed them to each other. Mine was blank.

'There's only seven girls here, I think I can remember enough not to make notes,' I said, 'although I should probably write something for No. 3.' I clicked a biro and scribbled *Would rather stick a poker in my eye.*

'That's the spirit,' said Will, 'keep that up and you'll easily get a hundred dates.'

'Whatever, train boy.'

It's Friday, and I spend the morning on MySingleFriend: my profile has now gone online and I'm not sure what the hell to do next. It's all very well saying you're going to date one hundred women, but in the cold light of day even writing to one seemed difficult. Each girl has a profile consisting of between one and four pictures, a write-up from a friend and a response from the single girl herself. There were other characteristics like where she lives, what her job is, age, level of education, whether she smokes or not, how many diseases she thinks she might have, etc. Beneath these stats are up to ten words or phrases, things like Well Travelled, Sporty, Pub Lover, Marriage Material, Deep Thinker, Ghastly Lover, and more. Also shown is the age-range within which her potential suitor should fall, and after clicking through a few profiles a pattern begins to emerge. I do a quick search pretending I'm a woman looking for a man, and my suspicions are confirmed. A study has just been released to the wider press claiming that the ideal age difference between partners is fifteen years, that is, the man should be fifteen years more mature than the woman. Several reasons are cited, but it's food for thought seemingly backed up by an almost unanimously consistent age-range selection by the folks on MySingleFriend. The women are all looking for men their age or older, and men are seeking women their age and younger. I double-check my own profile and sure enough, I've done the same. Taking the study in hand, I'm not entirely comfortable with the fact that my ideal partner is apparently a twelve year-old girl.

Once a boy hits his twenties his pubescent fantasies about older women start to wane and adjust as an innate search for firm, developed flesh takes hold. For women, it's the opposite. Girls in their teens realise very quickly that they have a power over boys, and in some circles lucky lads barely into double figures (age-wise) are used as practice dolls by adolescent females keen to experiment with their blossoming bodies and advanced sense of worth. But once they reach their late teens girls start to look forward, dreaming of an older man, someone who can teach them a thing or two, offer some equivalent maturity and with that, security. Whether or not a fifteen year age gap is pushing the boat out too far, there is an indisputable truth that women seeking serious relationships are more likely to go for older men, and it is largely due to the inescapable tick tock of the body clock. However old they are and whatever path of life they choose, whether they are sportsmen or accountants, Christians or atheists, soldiers or circus performers, most men will one day find themselves in a position where they are faced with a fairly critical decision: either stay with a woman for life, or leave, because perhaps they haven't had enough sex yet. Women have the same feelings, let's not be misguided. Women enjoy sex just as much as men do, but the female of the species is designed to procreate and if at some point a baby is going to come along then preferably by then there should be a stable man at her side. And more often than not, it would be quite nice if he were the father, too. So ask yourself this question, who is likely to be more stable; a 23-year-old with the wind in his sails, or a 35-year-old with a slack jib and a realisation that his playboy days are soon to be gone?

I have one hundred and six days until I fly to Australia. I need to get on it, now. Above each girl's picture there are some buttons, and one of them reads, Send A Message. I find a pretty girl with blonde hair and a humorously grumpy pout, open up the message screen, and stare blankly. I am a total dating novice. I have no idea how any of this works. What do I write? Should it be a paragraph about me? Should I be quirky and make a little joke? Or should I just write *Hi, you sound lovely. Fancy a date?* Surely it's not that simple?

Actually, no it isn't, not all the time anyway. There is no way of telling from a couple of images and a few words just how different girls will react to the same message, so the key, I reckon, is just to be myself. If I crack maybe a slightly flirtatious or edgy pun, then any girl who can't deal with that probably isn't the type I'm looking for anyway. So I start bashing off a few clumsy messages, and as in my first message to Holski from YesNoMayB I added in a little joke or comment referring to something from each girl's profile, just to get some familiarity going. If there wasn't anything particularly inspiring to pick out, I'd write something like this:

> Hi!
> I think yours is the only profile on here that doesn't involve the words 'very comfortable staying in and watching a DVD.'
> If you fancy a coffee sometime, or something stronger, then I'd like that very much.
> Dave

Online dating was a new world to me, and I needed to learn fast. I had no idea whether I'd get a response from any of the messages I'd sent out, but after I'd typed about twenty I needed a break. In three hours I'd looked through about 100 profiles and I couldn't help noticing that most of them were just horribly generic.

> My friend is just amazing. I can't believe she's single. You better be quick because she won't be on the market for long. She's fun, intelligent, is looking for someone tall, dark and handsome, and she's just as happy having a night out with friends as staying in with a bottle of wine and a film.

Hold on, let me get this straight. Sometimes she likes going out, and sometimes she likes staying in? That's ... just ... *groundbreaking*. I don't know what to say. Oh, yes, I do. Why? Why write that down? You may as well put:

> *My Single Friend also has a head, two legs, a similar amount of arms, occasionally she's happy and other times she's sad, and now and then, and by the way I know this is going to blow you away and make you want to marry her instantly, but now and then she breathes through her nose. And sometimes through her mouth. You'll just love her, she's SO normal! And of course I'm not biased, I'm only her best friend.*

Ok, perhaps I'm reading a little bit too much into all this, but I've always been of the mindset that if you're going to do something then it should be done properly. If you're writing a profile for someone on MySingleFriend, you should treat it as though you're selling yourself, too – I have a theory that the initial attraction on MySingleFriend is actually to the person writing the profile, so make an effort! If you're promoting your friend then make them stand out; sell your single friend, people, sell them! And don't, whatever you do, don't write anything about her being equally happy staying in or going out. At one point I clicked into the profile of a girl who had a quite delightful smile, and her brilliantly supportive friend had written the following:

> *My friend is great. And she's single. Did I mention that she's great?*

That was it, it all fitted onto one line, so forgive me for thinking that the poor Single Friend probably hadn't had justice done to her by that profile. I was tempted to write half out of pity and half because of her smile, but was put off by the Single Friend's response:

Yep, that pretty much sums me up x

Dear Lord. Yes, I was starting to take this seriously, probably more seriously than any other single person in the country currently signed up to an online dating website, but what can a boy do? I'd embarked upon a project now, and for me that means total immersion, which I was never able to completely take advantage of when I had my day job. The idea of having a career and working for someone else day-in-day-out for thirty years gives me earache, but all over my body, like I'm one big human-size ear just screaming at the pain of being told what to do. This was perfect, I had no boss, and in a way my job now was dating!

Luckily, after a food shop that involved a smashed jar of pickled onions and twelve obliterated eggs, there were some emails waiting for me. There's something glorious about receiving a first notice from MySingleFriend:

Hi there Dave. You have mail ... go and take a look!
GOOD LUCK AND HAVE FUN!

My fingers twitching nervously I logged in, wondering just which of the twenty girls I'd messaged earlier had replied. In fact, it wasn't any of them:

how is your day been ??? not sure what to write but like your profile and your out look on life and would like to find out more drop me a email if you fancy a chat ;))

A total stranger had written to me, and in her excitement she'd forgotten to use punctuation and grammar. I wrote back, using capital letters and full stops:

...So, how would you feel about having a drink sometime? Email tennis is great, but there's no substitute for meeting in person. Tempted?

And I actually meant it. Yes, it would be super to go on a date with a real human and not my keyboard; she seemed like a nice person and I couldn't judge her just because she'd used an emoticon. What is it with emoticons anyway - for instant messaging I could understand them, but has a man ever got anywhere with a woman just through inspired use of a colon? Don't answer that.

The day drifted on and slowly girls from all over London started to get in touch, evidently proper work wasn't very important on a Friday. By 4pm I had managed to convince two girls to go on dates with me,

When's good for you? I asked them both.
How about Saturday lunch? replied the first.
Saturday afternoon coffee? suggested the second.
Saturday sounds fine by me, I confirmed to them both,
It's a date!

EIGHT

It Begins

I'm about to go in. Nothing makes a man change his mind more than dealing with females, so I'm not going to risk losing my daily thoughts to hindsight or confusion. From here on a diary begins, and in beginning it I hope I emerge at the other side with my faculties intact.

Saturday: Day 1
Date No. 1

It's a beautiful day. I didn't sleep brilliantly because foxes were mating in the garden, but I still have a spring in my step. Walking around the flat just doesn't do justice to the sun filling the front room so I skip around, in a fairly masculine way, of course, and can't help but wonder what I'm about to embark on.

Questions fill my mind, like what happens if I fall for someone early on, and how on earth am I going to afford all of this? Hypothetical ponderings aside, what am I really looking for from this project? I stand on the sofa and peer out the window. The street is quiet. The workmen from next door are absent on a weekend and the portable loo stands lonely at the roadside; it could probably do with another toilet to keep it company. I clamber down from the sofa and turn to face my own upcoming predicament. I'm alone. I'm not necessarily lonely, but it feels like it's time to find someone willing to stand beside me. I'm ready, I'm open to love again, finally. How do I know? Well, like all things love, and men and women, and sex and chemistry and birds and bees, the answer is instinctual. It's just time, it's something that has to be done, can't be ignored, needs to be sated. It has been ever so long since I felt romantically nervous and if I had to sum up why I'm about to do what I'm about to do in just one word, it would be 'butterflies'. I'd like to quite fancy them, please. I want someone to take the bottom of my stomach and flip it upside down, inside out, make me feel dizzy and light-headed and confused about where it all came from but glad at the same time. No, more than glad - ecstatic, endlessly smiling. I want butterflies. I want them to flutter about making me feel alive again. I might find them today. And if I don't then surely at some point during the next 100 days?

What should I wear? Fully consider dressing like a tramp because it might be worthwhile getting through a few dates without making a good impression, but I suppose I have to do what The Rules tell me to do and be as normal as possible. I slowly pull on jeans that are coming apart at the bottom, then slightly ragged lime green trainers, a white t-shirt and rather worn yet debatably smart-casual olive sweater, pausing for a second before each item to contemplate whether it is right or not. I wonder if this dressing rigmarole will continue throughout the project. In an instant I become self aware, this is the first time in my life that on a social level I am fully conscious of the impression I am about to give. I've just spent ten minutes in front of the mirror checking myself, getting closer to inspect pores and misplaced hairs and too-shiny forehead. Even in anticipation of an almighty hunt for a woman, am I just turning into one myself?

I'm five minutes early and lean up against a bike rack outside the tube station. I can't ignore the fact that there is love all around; a man gives his girlfriend a piggyback across the road, other couples hold hands, a small oriental man is selling heart shaped balloons. One woman is holding her dog like it's a baby. And she just kissed its face. Oh, come on! There are other people standing and waiting outside the station, too, but I don't recognise any of them. There is a lot of watch checking and I can't help but think watches should be left at home on a weekend. Are all of these people meeting friends, or are they dating as well?

I turn just as Date No. 1 leaves the station. We clock each other immediately. She's shorter than I thought she'd be; five six, five seven. 'Hey, how are you?' she asks brightly in a strong Australian accent at the same time as wrapping her earphones tidily around an iPod.

'Good thanks, did you get here ok?'

Clearly she did, because she's here, and she's on time, and she's smiling. Don't ask silly questions, Dave. She nods, I kiss her cheek in welcome, and we head towards the Common with small talk and the occasional grin. She has wide, sparkling eyes, a kind face, jet-black hair dipping below the shoulders. 'I have to dye it,' she tells me later, 'I found my first grey hairs at fourteen.'

We park up at a bench beside a glassy pond and talk non-stop for an hour. She's very candid and tells me about a recent bereavement in her family. In just a few messages on MySingleFriend we shared a lot of information, but hearing the same stories in person puts an emphasis on what's important – a smile, a laugh, hand movements, all so significant. I look at her eyes, wide and tired. Sometimes they look like eyes that have been grieving, but now and then they flash with colour.

I like her. I wish she'd stop being so nice and open, so honest and … well, likeable. Bar the seesawing of new questions, we're chatting like old friends on a catch-up. Her body language is positive, far leg over the near one, shoulders towards me. I'm slouching, my legs and torso aimed straight ahead, the only clue that she's drawing me in is my left foot crossed over my right. I turn and study her face, her hair, trying to work out whether the small wrinkles beneath her eyes are from tiredness or loss. Tiny money spiders are lowering themselves from the branches above and I watch as she patiently picks them off her chest, her jeans, her hair,

DAVE CORNTHWAITE

placing them safely on the bench beside her. She's a sweetheart and I already want to see her again, but at the same time I'm overcome with guilt. It's not deep and organ-wringing, but it's there all the same, mixed with the realisation that I may have to go through this not one time, but one hundred. She's so sincere – so *together* – that I realise I don't want to write about her, I want to write about how she makes me feel.

I could give her a pseudonym and not mention any personal details, describe her so blurrily it could be any Australian girl in London. But without knowing it she is making it very clear that I've just set myself a near impossible task, that there is a very great chance that at some point I'm going to break, unable to see out this challenge because love and trust means so much more than the aim of a book. She keeps talking and I like her more and more, and I slowly begin to realise that I'm only going to learn more about what I want to learn about if I see her again. And I know that creates its own problems, but what the hell: dating is dating, and I'll have a few hours here and there to see people for a second time. For a third time. *Oh god, stop thinking like this, Dave. You can't automatically line up No. 1 for a follow-up.*

So I start nitpicking, trying to find a fault so saying goodbye at the end of this date will be easier. I begin convincing myself that this girl isn't the one for me. I'm not necessarily attracted to her physically, but as she talks I become more so. We're warming to each other, this could be a disaster! One Date in One Day. Brilliant story. Nice one.

We've moved now, walked around the Common and found a bench at a pub, and she's talking about her passions: 'I like cars, I like riding motorbikes, I'm a real revhead,' she says. Brilliant, there it is! I don't even have a driving license. This will never work.

Finally, after almost two hours, we've found something we don't have in common. Maybe my lack of passion for driving isn't such a big deal, but surely it's a deal breaker, isn't it? I can just picture the phone call, 'Hi there! It's Dave. Listen, I liked you and all, and you're really nice, but I don't drive, and you do, and I can't see how we can get around that…'

And then she pays for lunch…

I'm not sure what that means. I got the first drinks, but lunch is a different matter, lunch is a big deal. Isn't it? I mean, she's buying food for me! Is this her way of ensuring that there's a second date? Does she somehow know that I'm doing this challenge and she's trying to corrupt me? Doesn't she realise that food is the way to a man's heart, that ultimately we all want to be looked after by someone who enjoys feeding us? I can't just say goodbye and never call again now, can I? Date No. 1, paid for my lunch, got written about. Doesn't seem fair, that. Oh bugger.

I pretend to read the papers when she goes to the toilet, but I'm not taking any of the words in. Our bench is surrounded by other benches and they're all drenched in sunlight, it's a lovely day but such an extraordinary one at that, because I'm on my first ever date and in two hours I have my second one, and I'm not even sure if it's the right thing to do. A haze hits me, a wave of tiredness that pressures the temples and forces my head down. I have an instant need for sleep, or perhaps escape. I put my sunglasses on and try to rationalise what is happening. I like Date No. 1 but she's not my type. Yes I'm looking for excuses not to like her, but why am I doing that? Physically there's no spark, but does that stop us being friends? And if we're going to be friends at some point I'm going to have to tell her about The Hundred, but God, how do I do that? She comes back from the toilet and I open my mouth to speak but the words don't come out, and then the food is in front of us and the chance is lost. It's as though there's something stuck in my throat and I need to keep it in to avoid embarrassment, but spit it out in order not to choke. I decide to choke, because maybe I deserve a bit of discomfort for embarking on such a ridiculous challenge anyway.

After lunch it's time to say goodbye. I walk her to the station and we hug and kiss cheeks. I'm sure the moment lingers just a little longer than when we first met. 'I'll drop you a line,' I say as she walks away, realising what I've done as my words chase her down. But I want to drop her a line. I want to. She turns and flashes a smile, a beautiful smile. A very nice smile. Yes indeed, I think as she slips through the gate, that was actually a pretty good first date, but goodness me my head hurts now.

Date No. 2

Exactly one hour after Date No. 1 disappeared into the ground, I'm in a bar near my house. I've changed top and shoes, it felt kind of dirty wearing exactly the same clothes two dates in a row. Date No. 2 is five minutes late and apologises, but I don't mind at all. Our online messages were fun and flirty, both of us learning how to correspond using this strange new medium:

> **No. 2** - *How long have you been on here? Any advice for a first timer*

> **Dave** - *Not sure I have any advice, but I think we could find out more about each other over a coffee than over goodness knows how many messages. Should you be the messaging type, I'd advise completely random questions. For example: assuming flying time and money wasn't an issue, where would you go for a long weekend?*

> **No. 2** - *Coffee is a damn fine idea - let's do that - this email tennis is already more than a little overwhelming. You're the only person to suggest coffee instead of copious amounts of alcohol - that's a definite positive! And... for the record, Boston in 'the fall' – not done it yet but it looks beautiful and a long weekend would probably be just enough. You?*

Dave - *Don't get me wrong, I'm not averse to copious amounts of alcohol, but a coffee seems … well, a bit grown up. Boston in the fall, good answer! I would go to Zanzibar, because the seafood there is probably the best in the world. You're probably allergic to seafood, aren't you…*

Had she not recognised me I'm not sure I would have put this girl and her profile photo together, and I know instantly and instinctively that romance is never going to be on the cards. Thank God, I might just get through Day One without falling in love. I'm not attracted to No. 2 but there's something disarming about this girl. She's very frank, has wonderfully flamboyant lips, curling this way and that as she talks. I can't help but wonder how good at giving head she is, but check myself – *you must only think about bad things, Dave.* I could see us being friends, even after she recoils in terror as a spider scuttles towards her chair. Her right boot is up and down like a pneumatic drill, resulting rather brutally in a fairly flat spider. I look at it and think of people who compress dead butterflies in notebooks.

'I hope you don't love insects,' she says, not giving a fuck whether I love insects or not. Date No. 1 wouldn't have done that. Date No. 1 would have picked the spider up, stroked it for a while and knitted it a small coat before sending it on its way. And Date No. 1 would also have known that a spider is an arachnid, not an insect.

Despite her insect brutality, No. 2 and I chat for an hour and a half quite comfortably, so much so that for a moment I consider letting loose my secret. She's open-minded and I'm sure she'd be interested in The Hundred, but I bite my lip and try to be strong. I can't work out whether this urge to tell my dates about what I'm doing is a desire to be honest, or a need to unburden. Nothing is going to happen with this one, I doubt I'll ever see her again. But I'm glad I've met her, and evidently she's glad she met me. 'You're my claim to fame now,' she announces, curling her blowjob lips before she pretends to talk to an imaginary friend, 'I once went on a date with someone who was in the Guinness Book of Records.' I make note of the fact that she used past tense, and appreciate that the lack of interest is mutual. We walk fifty metres down the road and say goodbye. This is my stop.

It takes about half a minute to walk home, but it's enough time for me to realise one thing, that already I can't wait for this to be over. Despite insisting with myself that I'm not going to let the challenge affect the dating, I know deep down that The Hundred is going to have an impact. As I dig in my pockets for the door key, loud imaginary noises shrieking at me from every corner of my brain, I look forward to this all being over. Because when it is, if I'm still single, I'm going to be able to date in peace.

Sunday: Day 2
Date No. 3

Her MySingleFriend profile photo is almost side-on. Pretty face, delightful nose, curly blonde hair threatening to reveal the base of her neck. She's sipping a drink and looking quite stern, and the image is a little dark so I'm not sure if I'm getting the full picture. Her profile promises that body type is slender but there are no other images, so whether I'll recognise her is anyone's guess. Plus, she hasn't written back. We agreed to meet on Sunday. I suggested 2pm, and then nothing. It's so early in this challenge yet it feels like Date No. 3 is never going to happen. A fruitless day-saving text message flurry with a girl from YesNoMayB ends when she says she'd rather not meet anywhere but Ascot High Street. Ascot! Her profile said she lived in South West London, not Reading. Are they all liars, on these sites?

Amanda meets me for a drink. 'You're never going to get a hundred dates,' she says, openly delighted at my current failure and rubbing her hands at the prospect of witnessing my slow emotional decline as the days go on. As I'm thanking her for her concern, my phone rings, it's a strange number.

'Dave! I'm so sorry!' It's the MSF girl with a side-on profile. Breathlessly she apologises for not getting in touch sooner. Her Internet's been down and she has an abysmal hangover from the Rugby World Cup final last night.

'Do you still want to meet?' she asks, and tongue-in-cheek I say something about squeezing her in before meeting friends later, instantly regretting it.

'Ahh, nice get out clause if you need it!' she says, before promising she'll be as quick as she can. It's ten to two.

I'm not dressed for a date at all, just coffee with Amanda. I stroll to our meeting place slightly nervous about turning up with my longboard, a big fluffy beanie and dark glasses. Possibly disconcerting to a stranger, I'd imagine. A slim girl looks as though she's waiting for someone and I try and match her face to the picture on the website. As I stare she looks my way and cocks her head. It's her.

'Nice disguise!' she says. And we walk.

She's beautiful. Tanned neck and shoulders open above a well-cut woolen top. I'm sure she has a hickie on her left collarbone but try not to concentrate on it; she doesn't seem to be a hickie kind of girl. She doesn't have much make-up on but is naturally very pretty. Well-spoken too, a real catch. I wish I'd dressed a little better. We find a pub and quickly sink into a now familiar situation. I like this girl. She's shy, shyer than the first two, but there's something about her. A little chuckle now and then, the occasional chuck of a beer mat in my direction when I'm cheeky. There's a chance after the third flying mat that either she had anger management issues or I was being too cheeky for my own good, but I shrug off the missiles and take them as a sign that we're getting on. In fact, we've got so much in common I'm not sure how we've never met before. We went to Africa with the same gap year company. She's passionate about her work. She once had a ginger boyfriend, so she's not a hair-racist.

She's very up front and I can't imagine her taking any shit. I don't want to tell her about the challenge because I think she'd hate my guts. Or punch me. Saying that, by the end of our first drink I'm quite taken by her and want to stop The Hundred here and now and see where this goes. She's clearly unsure about online dating and what she's going to get from it and I can't help but look at her arms, always crossed in front of her chest, shielding herself. I want her to open up and show some signs that she's attracted to me, but instead she says, 'you don't look anything like your photo.'

I have no idea what that means, and she can't really explain herself. But it can't have been so bad, because later she asks if I want another drink. And then she suggests food, and as we walk to another pub I sneak a glance at her legs (I'm allowed, right?) and then, briefly, at her bum as she walks in front of me where the path is too narrow for us to be side by side, and I am so attracted to this girl I just want to see what she looks like naked. Now. Please. Please? We eat and talk and watch the big TV as Lewis Hamilton loses out on the Grand Prix Driver's championship, but it doesn't really matter so much because No. 3 is quite wonderful. It's dark when we leave the pub and I walk her to the bus stop. We share a very hasty and nervous cheek kiss when the bus comes but in the process forget to hail and it just drives straight past. No. 3 and I look at each other with blank faces and to fill the space she leans in to kiss my other cheek. I'm really not expecting this and think she's after a hug, so I wrap my arms around her shoulders and she pulls away abruptly. Bollocks! I'm such an idiot. There's no sign of another bus and moments later she decides to walk home rather than wait. We say goodbye and I put a hand on her waist as we turn in opposite directions, but it's getting cold and she has her arms crossed, hugging herself. I want to give her my hoodie and tell her to give it to me next time we see each other but instead whisper, 'I'd like to see you again.' She smiles and pirouettes, and as I walk away I feel quite sure that I'm not going to get through 100 dates. I'm just not sure I can do it.

Later on I email No. 3 saying I had a great time, and I give her my email address so she has every option available if she wants to get in touch, and then, exhausted of options, I tuck myself up in bed and regret not giving her my hoodie right up until the moment I close my eyes.

Monday: Day 3
Date No. 4

This was always going to be a strange one. Date No. 4 wrote to me on YesNoMayB two weeks ago:

hey

That's all she said, which I thought was remarkably thoughtful for a first contact message. What bugged me, though, was the fact that there was no punctuation. No capital H. No full stop. Just *hey*

She'd filled her profile with ten very similar images showing a slim, smiley black girl with curly hair and a wide, toothy smile. In two of them she wore a Burberry peaked cap. She really wasn't my type, but despite my editorial fury at her capital letter failure I wrote back, keen to employ a similar amount of detail in my message:

Dave - *Hi! You seem very nice.*

No. 4 - *I am a very nice person. I like your profile…*

For some reason I started to get the impression that this was going to take a while…

Dave - I like yours... So what are you looking for on this site?

No. 4 - a man with all or close enough qualities, personality, looks as l desire.....my dream guy...does that answer your question?......l honestly like your pic....it makes you look so....so....aaahh...so masculine...you have very strong facial features...l like that in a man

And that's how it started. Eventually we agreed to meet. Last night, a text bleeped through:

No. 4 - Wat tym do u wanna meet 2morrow?

Dave - What what do I want to meet tomorrow?

No. 4 - tym

Dave – Ah, right. How does 7 sound?

No. 4 - Wel da ting is I aight feelin so good, can we reschedule?

Dave - How is 'I aight' shorter than 'I'm not'? And why did you ask me what tym you wanted to meet if you're ready to be sick on me?

I have two options now; either try and persuade her that she really aight feeling so bad that she can't come out, or surrender to the grammatical monster in me that just can't stand the text mess. I realise, with most of my frontal lobe still thinking about Date No. 3, that I don't have the energy for this one.

> **Dave** - *Ok…hope you get better soon.*
>
> By noon today she changed her mind…
> **No. 4** - *Hi Dave I suppose we can meet up for a few drinks if u stilup4it…*

Oh, bloody hell. But she used a capital letter once so I thought I'd give her a chance. So there I am, perched on a bench outside a pub in East Dulwich. It's half past eight. She texted an hour ago to ask if I could delay from 7pm to 8pm, which was no problem, but as the minutes ticked by I started to laugh. What am I doing? This girl clearly isn't going to turn up. Another cancellation. Another date to make up. Passers-by look at me curiously as I swing my legs and laugh now and then for no reason, I really am on a silly mission, waiting in a strange part of London for a strange girl who can't spell and is twenty minutes late and possibly not going to turn up at all.

And then she calls and minutes later she walks around the corner, a tiny girl with a wide smile, incredibly pretty and well presented. I wasn't expecting this.

'I feel over-dressed,' she says, and I have a pang of guilt for not making much of an effort and try to tell her that she looks great and that it's all my fault. She pretends to take it to heart and we go inside and settle down shoulder-to-shoulder, chatting away but with an occasional forced silence that suggests we don't have a huge amount in common, which, frankly, we don't. At the same time there's a strange spark, it's all a bit touchy-feely and flirtatious, arm strokes, a brief hand hold. It's all very strange and I drift off, thinking about Date No. 3 and how different this date is from that one. I'm brought back to reality when No. 4 pats my chest.

'Are you feeling me up?' I joke, but she doesn't quite get it and withdraws, which makes things a little uncomfortable.

'Would you like another drink?' she asks eventually. I nod, and No. 4 just sits there, waiting for me to go to the bar. I laugh and mutter,

'Cheeky thing, aren't you,' under my breath, but there's some conflict now. This girl is twenty-one and I'm sure means nothing rude by expecting me to buy all the drinks – maybe that's the way they do it in Lewisham - but it ticked me off, just a little bit. There's a contradictory naiveté about her, she talks the talk and tells me about her studies and her passion to be a dentist, which seems an incredibly well thought out plan. But then, almost in the same breath, she'll spurt out something ridiculous, like how she hates dogs, is terrified of flying, and bicycles, aeroplanes, boats. And yet I still quite like her, her youthfulness, her looks, her attitude. What a shame she can't bloody spell.

I got the drinks anyway, because I'm a boy and had been staring at her lips for a while. They're coated in that glittered lip balm which makes them sparkle and shine, and despite all of the bad signs something had come over me and I just wanted to kiss her – not because we were compatible, but because I wanted to feel what it was like to kiss those lips. This girl and I were so far from a match made in heaven but sexual energy was zipping to and fro between us, and I was caught between wanting to lean over and kiss her neck and a need to leave, because I had to clear my head. I'm not one of those letchy men who sit by themselves in pub corners leering at pretty young girls, but all of a sudden I've become a single man with a high sex drive who has consciously put himself in a position where any kind of physical contact transforms an innocent date between two like-minded people into an almighty complication. I can't go kissing girls all over the place. I don't even want to think about sleeping with them, this whole project would just fall apart if my penis was writing the book. But it's not, and I'm in control; it's just that every girl that sits across from me has something attractive about her and that feeds temptation, especially when it's not in a state of satisfaction.

I need to take my mind off sex, at least for six seconds, so I start asking her random questions and when she answers I stare into my gin and tonic, at the paintings on the wall, at my palms, anywhere but at her lips which by now she keeps licking seductively for some totally inconsiderate reason. Maybe that lip-gloss has a nice flavour, but all that licking isn't fooling me, she's testing my resolve because she's twenty-one years old and is just discovering what certain things do to men. Then, in a curious act of karma, the enormous pub dog decides to come and lie down under our table and No. 4's allure abates as she begins to tremble. 'I need to crap,' she says, four words guaranteed to dissolve a man's scrotum, 'but with that thing there I'm not going anywhere, I'm going to scream.' And with that she covers her mouth with both hands and begins to hyperventilate, whimpering through the holes in her fingers. Tears build up and pool on her mascara'd lashes. I don't know whether to laugh or cry, and watch No. 4 as she edges off her seat and dashes to the toilet, causing a few people to look over in my direction to see what I'd done to elicit such a departure. I shrugged at them and pointed at the dog, which in hindsight wasn't a good thing to do because the dog was under the table and I just looked like I was pointing at my crotch. I am never coming back to this pub again.

I wait with No. 4 at the bus stop and even then, even after all of the palaver with the bad spelling and the phobias of everything and the dog situation and her cobwebby purse, I still wonder whether we're going to kiss, because it's not her lips' fault that their owner is a bit weird. But there's no kiss, there's barely a peck on the cheek, and the 187 takes No. 4 back to Lewisham, where I'm quite sure she's going to stay for the rest of her life because the big wide world is far too terrifying.

Tuesday: Day 4
4 Dates so far

I've dropped a day. No dates today, just a few messages on MySingleFriend and YesNoMayB and a couple of other sites I've signed up to. I feel a little empty without a date and get a little edgy when no new message notifications arrive. I'm excited about everything that's happening, I am, but although another day is lost it does give me some breathing space. I suddenly have time to ponder what I'm doing and how I'm doing it. And then I start thinking about Date No. 3 and how long I can hold out without seeing her again. I'm worried about it and fluctuate between knowing that there was a little chemistry and then trying to convince myself that I'm imagining it, that there was nothing there, that it's just her shoulders I'm thinking about. Seriously, I've met this girl once, I can't even picture her face when I close my eyes, and yet I'm analysing how I feel about her. I'm a weak man for beauty and maybe it's clouding my judgement here. When two people meet on a dating website there is more than a suggestion that both are looking for a relationship, and if the first date goes well there should, theoretically, be a follow-up. I think there's a good chance that at some stage Date No. 3 and I are going to go on a second date, and that means we're one step closer to a relationship, one step closer to me telling her what I'm doing – and when that happens it goes one of two ways: either she accepts it and we continue as we were, and that puts the challenge – the book! – in jeopardy. Or she's angry, or upset, and she doesn't want anything to do with me. I want to write this book, I'm determined to see it through, but I don't want to lose somebody who might just turn out to be *somebody*. Perhaps it was always going to take a day without a date for me to realise that. Most importantly, for the time being, I need to chill out. This dating thing is filling my mind, and I'm thinking about it too much. Perhaps after the second date No. 3 and I both realise we're not such a good match, and that's that. Just keep the dates coming, Dave, and it turns out how it turns out, there are few things more dangerous than a man who thinks too much about stuff he doesn't understand.

When I get home I set up an anonymous Facebook profile, and call myself Joe Date. I create a group called 100 Dates in 100 Days, and prepare for the backlash. I then spend the evening on the sofa watching Manchester United. Does that count as a date with eleven? And then my phone vibrates. On the screen it says Jo Date, and it scares the crap out of me, surely the karmic retribution hasn't begun, already? Then it becomes clear, I've been chatting to a girl called Jo on My Single Friend, she gave me her number a couple of days ago, and we're lined up for a date on Saturday. Her text reads; *Fancy being traditional, I'm feeling chatty tonight...*

So I call her. And within three minutes she's telling me that her only impression of public schoolboys is that they play a regular game of soggy biscuit, which involves communal wanking over a digestive. The slowest to expel their fluids then has to eat the biscuit, which by then is, quite simply, very soggy. Picture the scene. I'm sat on my sofa, typing frantically on my laptop as I speak to a girl for the first time, and she's going on about wanking. On biscuits. She swears like a trooper, flirts like a dog on heat and has an incredibly dirty laugh. I initiated the contact with Jo a couple of days ago, having read a line in her profile stipulating that all potential suitors must at least match her six foot stature. I couldn't resist sending her a message: *Hey Jo, You sound lovely. But I'm only 5'11 and don't look so good in heels.* She replied, promised to wear flats on our first date, and that was that. Meanwhile, our telephone conversation is still zipping along and once I've given her the nutshell version of the skateboarding story she yelps, 'Bloody hell you're half-famous! If you sign my tits on Saturday night I promise I'll never wash again!'

Wednesday: Day 5
Date No. 5

Date No. 5 is the only girl so far to make the first move. Well, the first online move. In doing so, she made me realise that a courtship email doesn't have to be drawn out, or funny, or anything but simple.

> *Hello Dave, Your profile sounds cool..... if you like the look of mine, be great to hear from you.....! x*

So straight up, so definite. And hey, it's always nice to have a cool profile. I can't make a physical judgment from her pictures. One of the shots is of her on a mountain. In a group. Quite far away. On a cloudy day. So, basically, I have no idea who I'm going to meet as I stroll from Charing Cross to Covent Garden. She's petite, slightly mousey, slim and shapely, and has an amazing mass of curly hair. And when we finally find a bar she can't make head nor tail of my skateboarding exploits. I can tell because she has lots of lines in her forehead when I'm talking. And I can barely see her eyes she's screwing them up so much.

I try to read body language and just like her profile can't work her out. She leans in and leans out, shows cleavage and bra and then covers it up quite pointedly in equal measure. I love her hair, it's so ... so, curly. She's telling me about her job and I'm wondering what happens when her hair gets wet, what it would look like in bed, sat there on top of a naked No. 5 all cute and curly. She scratches her hair quite often, like she's got nits. Or maybe she's doing that thing when girls play with their hair when they're flirting. It's vigorous scratching, but a bit playful, too. Can't work her out.

She likes the outdoors, hiking and walking. She once had a seven-hour scramble in bad weather over a Scottish mountain, but she's surprisingly lacking interest in other sports. She lived in Bondi for six months and didn't surf because she couldn't see the point. She didn't even try. Excuse me? Not even once? Not once. I can't work her out.

We talk about why we're dating online and I skirt around the subject of whether I've been on any other dates. It all seems a little taboo and frankly I'm not sure she's ready to hear that she's my fifth date this week. Later, as we're walking to the tube, I realise she's taken my coyness to mean that she was my first date. 'You're a real sweetie,' she says to me, and I'm so taken aback that I bow my head and go 'awwww' as though I'm gurgling at a baby in a pram. We say goodbye not long after that, unsurprisingly, and although No. 5 and I are far from a perfect fit I do reserve a special place in my heart for her hair, because tonight something has clicked in me. I'm not a straight hair Nazi by any means, but I like curly hair, I really, really like it. Perhaps this is another way for me to convince myself that a date isn't working; 'sorry love, your hair is just lacking a certain ... waviness.'

Thursday: Day 6
Date No. 6

I'm twenty-eight years old today. The significance of birthdays always lessens as you grow older. It's like swearing, the more you do it the less force it has. The first text of the day is from a girl on MySingleFriend. She wishes me Happy Birthday even though we've never met before, which is very nice of her.

Later I'm meeting someone different, Date No. 6, who is also very excited by my birthday. So much so, in fact, that yesterday she sent me three emails and four texts, and each one of them included the words, *'hello birthday boy'* She doesn't use punctuation, and she clearly likes cooking rabbits, but her keenness ensures that I have a date on my birthday and I'm not sure I can ask for more than that. I meet my friend Mette for brunch. As I skate across Clapham Common towards Battersea Rise it starts to drizzle. Although the summer was practically non-existent, October has been a dry month, and now it's raining for the first time in weeks. On my birthday.

'They say that you've been a bad person if it rains on your birthday,' Mette tells me over eggs benedict, 'it's a karma thing.' I'm not sure that I have done anything untoward, not recently anyway, but dear Mette is here to bring me down a notch or two, she tells me, and she has succeeded fabulously. I don't feel miserable, but as I sit below a glass roof splattered with raindrops, poached eggs before me all sunny side up and looking as pretty as food possibly can, I'm starting to feel the pressure of The Hundred. I'm doing nothing illegal, and I'm far from expectant for every girl I meet to fall madly in love at 'Hello', but emotions can run high when two single people meet and I'm not yet entirely comfortable with my actions, mainly because I've had five dates and haven't yet invited or been invited to a second date. This is totally normal, I realise, but I wonder whether I am unknowingly being controlled by my book and everything I might want to write in it.

The day rushes towards 4pm and I realise I'm about to meet Date No. 6 in exactly the same place as I met Date No. 5 twenty-two hours earlier. She's cowering under a hood, glasses and a smiley face. 'I don't want to get my hair wet,' she grins,

'As long as you're not pretending to be a stalker, I'm fine with that,' I say, and we wander off toward Leicester Square.

'Oh, Happy Birthday! Birthday boy!' She says,

'Umm, yeah, thanks,' I look at her sideways, 'it doesn't really feel like my birthday though.'

'But…' she says, stopping, 'it's your birthday, you have to enjoy it.'

'It's not that I don't,' I say, 'it's just another day though, isn't it?'

She tells me off for being an idiot and not being excited about my birthday, so I suggest that she's just put herself down as I'm spending some of the day with her, and she giggles and pulls the hood tighter over her head. I'm not attracted to her but she's a giggler and once we settle in a pub we chat about why we're dating online, and where we've come from and what makes us who we are. It strikes me that maybe

I should already be getting bored of the routine, it's so similar to arriving at school or university for the first time and facing similar questions from a mass of strangers, but so far it hasn't been hard at all. It's nice being able to relate to different people in different ways and although we've met under slightly arranged circumstances there is no pressure on a first date because if it doesn't work we both know there are a thousand more people waiting to meet us. Online dating isn't the taboo it used to be, but all the while it does seem a little contrived. For someone wanting to meet one hundred women in one hundred days it is ideal, but is it *too* easy these days to meet a complete stranger? And does the ease of communication lower people's standards? I'm not suggesting that I've lowered my standards to meet Date No. 6, but she's a couple of years over my proposed age threshold and is going through a divorce, and whatever I tell myself I ordinarily wouldn't be dating her. So why am I?

You might expect me to own up, to say *Yes, I needed a Date*, but I'm not so sure. You see, why shouldn't I meet this girl? Her marital status doesn't necessarily point to an automatic failure, she might be three years older than me but does that matter? No, it doesn't. *It shouldn't*. For all I know, my efforts to meet a wide range of girls might just open my eyes to a bigger picture, to the fact that I shouldn't be compromising my chances of meeting someone special just for the sake of using a search engine. I don't mind what job they do, I don't care how much they earn, I'd rather they weren't happily married with kids, and I probably wouldn't date a midget or a giant, or a girl who used to have testicles, but still, personality counts for a lot and you can't get hold of that until you meet them in person.

And actually, Date No. 6 is growing on me. Or rather, she's growing closer to me. Her eyes bright and her laugh infectious, she tells me she's learned her lessons and isn't looking to fall into the same traps of commitment all over again, which suggests she just wants a shag. As the clock passes five I return from the toilet and the work crowds have lessened our space. Suddenly our legs have closed in from knee to knee to knee to crotch, and for the first time I notice her physically. She's in good shape and although she's not my type and my interest is still far from blossoming I'm not afraid of our proximity. At half six we walk to the tube and as I thank her for meeting me she wraps her hands around my head and begins to kiss me. The crowds mill around as we embrace, on and on and on, and I quickly relax and realise that there is nothing wrong with this, that I'm allowed to kiss her, and that maybe I'm allowed to enjoy it, too! And I do, she's passionate and it's comfortable and I realise that it doesn't matter who it's with, a good kiss is a good kiss, and it makes you feel warm inside. It does the same job as a hug, but feels like you're being hugged from loads of different angles. And besides, her grip was so tight on the back of my neck that even if I'd wanted to escape I couldn't have. When we finally break apart I grin and say, 'well, it looks like I did finally get a birthday present,' and she looks up at me with questioning eyes,

'How do you mean?' she asks, and I realise she's lost the joke and thinks I mean more than a kiss. Oh god. She thinks I just told her that I've found The One. We kiss again, more hastily this time, and I give her a friendly little shove as she moves through the crowd and down into the underground.

I ride the Northern Line back to Clapham with Date No. 6's strawberry lip balm circling my mouth. It's time for birthday drinks and no doubt a bout of date-related storytelling. I meet Amanda and Alice and sip G&Ts for a couple of hours. I know these girls, they're my best female friends and I open up to them, sharing my fears about making mistakes, going too far with some girls and creating hurt. It all comes out and I realise that before all of this began I was on top of the world and now I'm overcome with worry. The one thing that potentially stands in the way of what I'm doing is ironically, women, love, and sex. My three biggest weaknesses rolled into one, and for months now I have no escape. If anything is going to stop me doing what I'm doing it's the right girl. I'm terrified of meeting her, and potentially losing her because of what I'm doing. I'm going round in circles.

'Don't think about it so much,' Amanda tells me as she leaves, 'you're not doing anything wrong.'

'But am I doing anything right?' I ask, feeling better anyway.

'Let's go to Firefly,' I say to Alice, 'it's speed-dating tonight and there might be some singles milling about.'

I've twisted her arm, and we walk. Outside Firefly I recognise a girl from MySingleFriend, I'm sure her name is Natalie, and it just so happens that we have a date lined up for Sunday morning. She clocks me as I walk in and I turn from the bar to see her and her friend mouthing my name. I trot outside and grin,

'Hello Nat!'

'I knew it was you!' she giggles, and then tells me that she's been looking at my website, and that the skating thing was amazing. Beside them, a scruffy looking chap was listening intently, and then spoke for the first time;

'You skated across Australia, on a longboard?

I look at him, realising he's heard about the journey from a different source, 'Yes mate, it's a big place!'

'This is mad,' he says, 'you dated my friend last night.'

Firefly is separated from Clapham Common by a main road, one of the busiest in South London, but there are no cars there now. Suddenly the noise has been switched off. The girls' hair struggles in the wind. There are no sirens. No chatter from the bar. Everything is quiet. Tumbleweed rushes quietly down the road.

'Dave! Are you a serial dater?' asks Beth, Natalie's housemate, and I look at her, and then Natalie (who has one eyebrow raised) and then at Alice because she's just coughed up the ice from her drink, and finally I glare at the scruffy guy, who introduces himself as Johnny, yet still seems completely oblivious to what he's done. I take a breath and address Johnny.

'What was your friend's name, again?'

'Jo,' he says, and I grin. I didn't date Jo last night, I spoke to Jo on the phone Tuesday evening, and she asked me to sign her tits. I'm dating her on Saturday night, just a few hours before I'm dating Natalie. My phone rings, oh thank God for that.

On the screen are two words; Jo Date.

You're fucking kidding me.

I excuse myself and wander away, wondering what I've done to deserve this.

'Jo!' I growl down the phone, instantly realising honesty is the best way forwards, 'you will not believe what has just happened...' And I tell her...

She finds it hilarious, mostly because her friend Johnny has met me before she has.

'It's all quite funny really, isn't it!' I giggle, 'I should write a book about this!'

'You so should!' says Jo, 'but you have to give me a credit.'

'Can't see that that would be a problem,' I say, 'I reckon you'd make a great character.'

One minute later Johnny's phone is ringing, and then it's being passed around from Johnny to Natalie to Beth and even to Alice, who can't quite believe what's going on and is the only other person involved who knows just how funny this little cameo really is. I suppose there was always the chance that six degrees of separation would force two girls together who I've recently dated, thus destroying my secret research programme, but I've only had six dates so far and it's already catching up with me. Johnny is quite bemused at the fuss that's being made, Beth is chatting to Jo and tells her I'm fit, but that her friend Natalie wants me, and Johnny is clearly a little perturbed that he's no longer the centre of attention. He had met Nat and Beth during speed-dating earlier that night and now speed-dating has been forgotten, so Johnny puffs out his chest and turns to Alice and I,

'You know what,' he says, 'a long time ago I fucked Jo.'

Some gin and tonic goes up my nose. Alice looks at me, wide-eyed.

'I'm sure that was nice for you,' I say.

'Yeah. She's got a great rack.'

I sidle over to Beth, who is chatting away to Jo like they're old friends. 'Hello,' I say into Beth's ear and the phone, all at the same time. Beth hands the phone over and Jo, who I suspect has had a little to drink, is gushing,

'Dave, I am just so intrigued by you now, I think we're going to get on like a house on fire.'

'Well don't put too many eggs in one basket, Jo darling, it's not time to get down on your knees just yet,' I say, getting cruder by the second. But if I have a match in that department, it's Jo.

'Oh I shouldn't think it would take too long to get to that stage,' she cackles.

The rest of the evening is a blur. I have a short chat with Natalie, wondering whether this counts as a date or whether I should try not to talk to her too much and still see her on Sunday. We laugh at the scenario and agree that if you're dating online then it's all fair game, it's accepted that you might be seeing other people at the same time. She's a lovely girl, great eyes, sensible and funny. And she doesn't even mind when I sweep a glass of gin and tonic all over her. Somehow throughout all of this palaver, the simple fact that I'm going to be dating Jo on Saturday night and then Natalie on Sunday morning has been bypassed. What an unbelievable birthday.

Friday: Day 7
Date No. 7

I don't know how to say it, but Date No. 7 is a little bit funny looking. Her profile photo was slightly elfin and she didn't have any problems with her punctuation, so along with some clever banter I figured she'd be worth at least an afternoon slot. Thing is, she wrote yesterday and cancelled. Her flight from South America was delayed and she told me she wouldn't be back in time for our 1pm date. Bugger, another dateless day. But then, at about 11am this morning, a message comes through, she's back in the UK but just wanted to apologise for cancelling before heading to bed. I wrote back, chancing my arm:

If you change your mind I'm free up until 5.

She took the bait.

I'm going to try and battle through so can meet at 3pm if you like.

So we did. And my god she was boring. Ok, maybe she was a bit jetlagged, but still, a twenty minute monotone ramble about organising conferences and how bored she was with her job was too much to take. She's the type to grow old with hundreds of cats at her feet, and as much as I like cats, there's no persuading me with this one. Not once did she ask me a question, not once. She was bored of herself, bored of her job, bored of her life and bored of me. I kept checking my phone, cunningly watching Sky Sports over her shoulder when she searched for clarity in her lemonade. I willed the minutes to go by, realising that a watched date never ends. As the thirtieth minute passed I tightly clenched my fist beneath the table in celebration.

'Do you want another drink', she asks soon after, and I sigh. If there was ever a moment to use the most damning end-line in history, then this was it.

'I'm afraid I've got to go and wash my hair,' I said, 'birthday dinner tonight...'

'Ah ok, that's cool,' she said, astoundingly accepting my reasons.

It was perhaps the most uneventful forty-five minutes of my life, but outside I sucked in the crisp, dry October air and felt glad to be alive and perhaps more importantly, making haste in the opposite direction of the excruciating Date No. 7.

Saturday: Day 8
Date No. 8

Today is potentially very busy. One mid-morning coffee date, one game of football, and then an evening date with Jo. I jump on my board and skate across town, having apologised to Date No. 8 in advance for turning up in pre-football dress. On MSF, this one's photo is terrifying. I'm not sure if she's talking to a crowd or sending a prisoner to the chair, but I can see gums, lots of them, and a seriously furrowed brow. This lady is a high flyer, and she clearly means business.

Our messages on MySingleFriend are quite formal, very few exclamation marks, lots of talk about her walls, which she's currently painting herself. She's articulate, as should be expected for someone who works in the country's higher echelons, and we get on surprisingly well after a slightly unsure start. She looked at my longboard sideways in utter confusion as I apologised and explained the football situation. I always skate to football, it's a good warm-up, but on a soggy morning a mud-covered longboard probably isn't the best dating accessory.

We're not even close to a chemical fizzle but she's good company all the same. Our lives are different in almost every respect yet the conversation never lulls, as we tuck into muffins and coffee. When she laughs her gums smack me in the face and the table shakes quite considerably, drawing glances from the waitress who clearly can't work out why the man in jeans and a hoodie with a dirty skateboard was sitting with a woman in a Gaultier business suit. I wasn't overly keen on No. 8 but I'm glad I met her, even if a second drink was never on the cards.

Afterwards, as I head to football, I receive a text from Jo, she's cancelling our date tonight as her removal man has stood her up. I graciously accept defeat and make a joke about getting the hint, but behind the banter I'm a bit disappointed. She stresses that she still wants to meet up, but I am actually looking forward to dating Jo and the disappointment of her pulling out is genuine, rather than figures-based. We'll rearrange, but in the meantime it looks like I'll be home alone this Saturday night...

Sunday: Day 9
Date No. 9

It's a lot easier waking in time for my 11am date with Natalie than it would have been had I been out with Jo last night, and I'm ready to get back on the horse, as it were. Nat and I broke the ice on Thursday after our coincidental rendezvous at Firefly and were straight into chat like old friends. She's a pretty girl but reminds me of my Mum, and that's never a good start, whatever Freud says. Like my Mum, Nat's a midwife, too, and her passion for baby popping is evident. There are echoes of my Mum's mum in her too, which is even more worrying; a family obsessed with animals – her parents have a lizard, dogs, cats, a tarantula. I know quite soon that this isn't going anywhere romantic but something twangs in me. Maybe it's because we've met once before and Nat was so understanding about the whole multiple-dates thing, or maybe it's just because I like her and can see us being friends. Whatever it was, for some reason I decide to tell her about my challenge.

'Umm Nat, ok ... I'm going to tell you something...'

She looks at me, a bit worried, and I blurt it out, 'I'm writing a book about you. No! Not you, women! Loads of them! Hundreds!' I compose myself and try to explain, just a bit more clearly this time. She looks at me, stares at me, and then...

'Oh my God!' she says, 'that's a really good idea!'

This is a breakthrough and relief surges through my body. From the beginning I've been terrified about revealing the plan to any of my dates, almost totally through a fear of inciting anger, or violence, or even worse, rumour - don't want girls starting to pace the town, telling all other singles that there's a serial dater called Dave on the loose, do we?

So, having finally blurted it out to someone, and them accepting it, my shoulders subside as Nat asks me what would happen if I met someone I totally fell for and what number she is, and on and on. I feel an affinity to her now, that rare feeling of being able to completely let go, I have no secrets and she tells me she's glad that I was honest with her.

Later on she texts, says she'd like to go for a drink sometime, and that she thinks the book is a great idea. 'I'd read it,' she tells me. And that's enough for me.

Date No. 10

The rest of the day stretches away like a desert road, frustratingly empty for a Sunday. I sit on my couch, playing on the Internet, chatting to a couple of girls, including a new one I haven't seen on the site before. Her profile picture doesn't paint her in the best light, but she's cheeky and has just moved to Clapham, so I try my luck. *Fancy a drink a bit later?*

She does. We meet in a bar local to us both, and she seems quite excited. 'You're the first person I've spoken to online, the first person I've met too, and I can't get over the fact that we're neighbours,' she says, giggling, and we slump into a couch shoulder to shoulder and talk non-stop for a couple of hours.

I didn't dress up for the occasion but as soon as she walked in I was a little taken aback. She's very attractive, confident, affable, and I feel like there's something between us, a little crackle of electricity. As we talk I follow the line of her face, the cut of her top, she has remarkable breasts and the way we're slouching next to each other I know she knows I can see them. Tease. For the second time since I started dating I think about seeing a girl seriously for a second time, but there's a catch; the pleasant surprise of meeting someone is then dulled slightly by the fact that it's a complicated situation, and that at some point I know I'm going to have to tell someone I care about that I'm on a challenge. It's a risk, and while telling Natalie this morning was easy, I'm fearful of the reaction of someone that I want to see again romantically, because suddenly I'll have something to lose.

I feel with Date No. 10 that at some point I may have something to lose, and that worries me. I watch her legs as they cross and uncross, I try to read her body language. We're both very tactile, and discuss it, and I become distinctly aware that I'm wearing white socks and curse the broken heating in my flat – I washed my darks this morning, you see, and now, strangely, it matters. I want to make an impression on this girl, and I'm thinking about my socks. Jesus. No. 10 is very well-spoken, she rides horses, she even went to Africa with the same gap year company as me, which reminds me of Date No. 3 with the wonderful shoulders, and I'm thrown slightly. I wasn't expecting to enjoy myself this much tonight, and now I have another dilemma on my hands.

So where does this put Date No. 3? I've thought about her frequently since we met a week ago and earlier today we arranged another date for Tuesday; it'll be my first follow-up date. Although I'm almost forced to think about her less (my senses are naturally dulled as time goes on and I meet more girls) I'm still intrigued about what might happen, and then what might happen if something does happen, if you know what I mean. And now, I truly, sincerely feel that now it's not just about Date No. 3, it's also about Date No. 10, and perhaps a few more girls from the 90 I have left to see. How the hell am I going to manage all of this?

Date No. 10 and I have had a good time, and we tell each other so. 'I expect we'll be in touch a little more,' she says, a glint in her eye as we say goodbye,

'I am sure we will,' I say, turning with a little wave. That was most unexpected.

Monday: Day 10
Date No. 11

Holski was the first girl I ever spoke to on an online dating site. Back when I first logged onto YesNoMayB, back when it was all romantic and exciting, there was Holski, writing to me. It was a wonderful feeling.

And now I'm back, leaning against the bike racks outside Clapham Common tube. I'm not the only bloke there; in fact, there are six of us, all mid to late twenties, all looking around, all acting in a remarkably similar way. A thought crosses my mind: what if this Holski chick has played a trick and told all of these blokes that she'd meet them, same time, same place? How easy would it be to do that? How long would your average guy wait for a date? Could a girl really be that sadistic? Ten minutes past the hour, we were all still waiting and I was starting to get the impression that my musings weren't far off the mark. And then she's there, a slim, dark-haired girl with a very big smile, bounding across the road, grabbing my arm and telling me that I was waiting with a look exactly like the one in my profile picture. 'I thought I saw you over there,' she said pointing across the road, 'but obviously, it wasn't you!'

We settle in a nearby bar, supping on some 'surprise' cocktails rustled up by a bearded Canadian waiter, and we get straight to a conversation about life, and who we are, and what comes next. She's the philosophical sort but amidst all of the tell-tale signs of maturity and personal security, I get the feeling that despite her wanting to set up a life-coaching business she's not quite sure exactly what she wants from her own life, yet. She talks in long, drawn out clichés, often tailing off at the end with a pronounced sigh. This isn't necessarily a bad thing, and in all honesty if she wasn't one date in a hundred I probably wouldn't have read too much into it, but unfortunately this is me now, one slender hunk of analysis and questioning. I check out her body language, and whatever language it was the body is bloody good. She's friendly and open, but she's been single for four years and I can't help wonder why. She's an attractive girl; articulate, funny, openly tactile. She touches my hands across the table when I'm least expecting it, so what's wrong with her? I can understand someone being single for one year, two, even, but four? That's a long time by any standard, especially for a good-looking girl in her mid-twenties, so I try to get to the bottom of the situation and in answering my questions she starts to contradict herself. She likes living with all of her friends but would love to have a place of her own. She loves travelling and for years has been promising herself to learn other languages, but she hasn't yet got further than English. She used to be a vegetarian, but gave it up because, in her words, 'I just couldn't live without meat.' I am thoroughly confused because I'm very attracted to this girl, but in the contradictory spirit of the evening I'm unsure whether I want to go on another date with her.

At the end of our date we wrap up warm and venture out. We walk side by side to the bus stop and I tell her I'll wait until the big red thing comes along. 'You're only waiting if it involves a hug,' she says, and I oblige. Three minutes on she realises she's at the wrong stop and we walk slowly to the correct one, just slowly enough to let her bus pull away. 'That was mine,' she says, not at all distressed. She turns to me, smiling, and wraps her arms around me. Her next bus is in 12 minutes and it takes me about fifteen seconds to realise that you can't hug a complete stranger for 12 minutes without having a kiss, because otherwise you just feel like a blanket. It's a strange situation, this. This girl is lovely, and attractive, but I don't think there's enough chemistry to warrant a second date and I don't want to give out the wrong signs. But physical proximity brings out the caveman, and while I know these are the last ten minutes we'll spend together it becomes obvious that they are going to be very pleasant indeed. Her fingers wriggle their way under the back of my shirt and she starts to rub my waist, and when we start to kiss I'm caught between two completely separate emotions: dismay at the fact that her mouth is fixed in a whole-orange eating position, and amazement at how soft her tongue is, and if I'm honest, how exploratory it is too. Kisses should be soft, with matching lips and gentle, teasing tongues, if you're lucky, but suddenly I'm standing at a bus stop with a girl I met two hours earlier, and she's practicing dentist-like manoeuvres. It was one of those kisses where I had to open an eye to make sure no-one was looking, because if they were they would have wanted to step in and rescue me, but I didn't really want rescuing, because it was actually quite nice. Date No. 11 is extremely sensual and for someone who has been single for four years she's remarkably fun to lock faces with. Practice makes perfect, I suppose.

Her bus finally arrives and we squeeze hands and wink at each other. It's dark and winter is coming, just the kind of season that threatens to make lonely people feel lonelier. Surely, after a fun date with a quite splendid if inquisitive ending, I shouldn't be walking home with a slight hunch, wondering whether kissing her was the wrong thing to do. Since when does a bloke have qualms about kissing an attractive girl? Exactly what is wrong with me?

Tuesday: Day 11
11 Dates so far

A quick peck on the cheek. Perhaps a little longer than the one we shared the last time we said goodbye, but just as awkward, and still on the cheek. The bus is leaving and she needs to get on. 'Maybe see you sometime soon?' I say as she walks away, and she turns and barely nods. Quite non-committal, I thought. Right. Brilliant. What the heck is going on there then?

Date No. 3 and I have just been on our second date. It doesn't count towards my total, but I don't care. I didn't care. I've never cared about that. I hadn't even thought about it. I just wanted to see her again. So we had a drink, and then watched a film (Atonement), which had a hugely erotic and lengthy sex scene with Keira Knightly and James McAvoy. We're on our second date and a graphic bout of love-making up on the screen doesn't do much for the pressure of the situation. Two things could happen, either one of us just takes a chance and leans over with puckered lips, or we do what we did and sit there all nervous hoping the film stars stop having sex so we can breathe again.

I've been talking to an actress on MSF, not Keira Knightly, and today she messaged and told me she was in Atonement and where in the film to look out for her. At this point, I should point out that I had told the girl I was going to the cinema, but hadn't told her I was going with a date. So there I was, staring at this girl on the big screen who I know I'll be dating in a few days time, then looking sideways at Date No. 3 wanting to tell her that I know that person up there, then realising I can't because it's just not cool whispering in the cinema, and it's hard to justify mentioning another girl you've been talking to on an online dating site. Instead, I bury my head in some popcorn.

After the film we found a bar and sat outside under a heater, and thus began The Deep Stuff Conversation, about things like love and relationships and destiny and reincarnation. This is the juicy bit, where man and woman reveal their innermost secrets and nature confirms that they're meant to be together by a loosening of collars and a nearing of feet, but not at one point did Date No. 3 show she was attracted to me, which left me a little dazed. I'm still attracted to her, and although I couldn't see her shoulders tonight (she was wearing a business suit) there was a bit of plunging neckline and her skin is just phenomenal. Yes, I still would like to see her naked. Now. Please. But there's nothing showing from her side and I feel like at some point I'm going to have to stop thinking about her and draw a line under it.

When women are above a certain level of attractiveness do they become more aloof, more aware that they're deserving of a man of, say, higher physical quality? Or when lesser men - and yes, at least physically I consider myself one of these - are in the presence of beautiful women, is it *our* behaviour that changes? Do we play it safe, dumb down, under-perform even, purely because we know deep down that beautiful women are capable of breaking us into a thousand little pieces, heart and all? A natural shield, defending the uggers against heartbreak! Date No. 3 is very pretty, sure, she has an amazing complexion, a wonderfully shaped body, but I don't feel like I'm being anything other than my normal self.

Flirting a bit, talking openly as I usually would, but there's little from her. There's the odd smile, a cheeky sideways glance. But not as much as I'd usually expect from someone who has been willing to spend so much time with me. In total we've spent between nine and ten hours together but so far there's not been a hint of mutual attraction. Not a hint. Unless, and this might be clutching at straws, unless beautiful women show that they're attracted in different ways to lesser mortals...

Yep, I'm clutching at straws. The simple fact of the matter is, Date No. 3 seemed like she wanted to see me again and yet I don't feel like she wants it to go anywhere. Maybe she's just always wanted a friend who's got themselves into the Guinness Book of Records? Or maybe she does want it to go somewhere, and she's always been trained to only start flirting on the third date. Or maybe it's just because my hair's getting a bit long and I don't really know what to do with it and she feels sorry for me, and secretly she's glad she got on that bus because it means she doesn't have to look at my head anymore. I'm so confused. But partly relieved too, because in the back of my mind, having kissed Date No. 11 yesterday and with a potentially tactile date lined up with Jo tomorrow, I'm now not in a position where I might feel guilty about kissing three different girls three nights in a row.

Wednesday: Day 12
Date No. 12

I was hanging around outside Clapham South tube, pretending to read a copy of TNT and glancing with a slightly furrowed brow into the station. Of all my meetings so far, none has had such a build-up. Jo Date, as she is now called, is obviously going to be taller than me, and her personality, I think it is safe to say, is even bigger than she is.

And Lord, this girl is big. She's not wide, just tall, skyscraper tall. On her dating profile she made a joke about short ex-boyfriends being on a level with her breasts (not that they were too bothered), and I feel as though I've joined a select band when she walks towards me. It's eerie, I'm 5'11, and apparently Jo is just an inch taller at 6ft, but I feel like she's a whole foot larger. I've never been side by side with a female who makes me feel like a dwarf, until now. I get the constant feeling that we're on a pavement with a camber and I'm on the down side. I'm struggling with every sinew to stop myself feeling small, weak and unmanly, straightening my back for all I'm worth, bracing my shoulders; it's an incredibly weird sensation. But what can I do, pop on some raised shoes? Bugger that, let's have some wine.

We perch under a palm tree in Gigalum and with all aspects of height removed we hit it off. Jo's moving up to London after a break-up with her boyfriend, who she claims she's not bitter about but still has a few choice nicknames for - 'lying cheating bastard' among them. She has long blonde hair and breasts that just don't belong in her shirt, and my God she can talk. After half an hour I'm not sure that there's anything she hasn't told me, I know about her ex-boyfriends, the holidays she's been on, where she grew up, the rather embarrassing fact that I added her sister Nina to my Favourites on MySingleFriend. I know that Jo likes karaoke, wine and cooking Pad Thai, I know that she doesn't like infidelity and small willies. When it's my turn to talk she buts in with a regular, 'Oh my God, babe!' and the occasional 'that's so funny!' and once the second bottle of wine is on the table her hand starts to creep over and massage my wrist and lower arm.

She's not the invasive type, just very, very flirty, and as the white sweeps through our systems we slide into a booth and she struts off to get a third bottle of wine, swinging her hips hilariously. Somehow, though, I don't think she's putting it on. I shake my head and text some friends with one, simple message, *Fuc. King. Hell!*

This is it. This is the date I was worrying about, the one where I tell the girl that I'm doing something ridiculous and writing about it and she's a part of it and, oh please, don't hit me. I steady myself with both hands on the table, ready for a new step in the project, one I feel like I have to make because we're both very drunk, there's another bottle of wine on the way and frankly, if Jo Date decides she wants something from me there's no way in hell I'm going to be able to fight her off.

'Jo, I have to tell you something,' I say when she's back.

'Oh really?' she says, flicking her hair like there's a fly around.

'I'm writing a book...' I start to tell her about it, my reasons, the rules, the dates so far, even the last two-minute panic I've endured. And then, out of nowhere, she leans over and kisses me. It's like a dark cloud has descended without warning, the light is blocked out, there's a tongue down my throat, and I have absolutely no choice but to kiss her back because, frankly, she's very attractive for a giant, and I'm also rather drunk.

'You've had some practice at that...' I grin when we finally separate, and she smiles back,

'Maybe I have...'

The rest of the night flies by. We chat and kiss, then chat some more. This girl doesn't sit on the fence, she keeps saying, 'Oh my God, Dave, I can't believe you're writing a book! I think it's fucking brilliant, but I really don't want to be in it. I definitely don't want to be the first girl you fuck!'

A mouthful of wine goes all over the table.

'You do though, don't you. Want to be in it, I mean?'

She looks at me, wide eyes twinkling, and shakes her head. And then the dark cloud descends again.

I'm beyond control now. Wine, a ridiculously flirty and attractive girl and a back-catalogue of sexless weeks has me ripping up my dating rule book. I knew tonight was going to be interesting but truthfully didn't want to get to the stage where I was out of control, but it's too late! Jo knows she has me but is now slyly putting the stoppers on. 'Babe, I just couldn't go home with you on the first night, you've got, what, another ninety women to date, I might get jealous!'

'Oh don't give me that, it's so irresponsible thinking you'll get a second night when you're treating me so badly!'

'Well, who says I'd want a second night...?'

I put my hands on my hips and pout, imitating her. 'Well, you won't know if you want a second night if you don't take advantage of the first.'

By now I'm slurring my words and know it, but there's a stage during a man's drunkenness when embarrassment is no longer a valid emotion, it's basically that point when the brain is too drunk to function and the penis is drafted in as a replacement. All sense is gone and one urge is overriding, so please Jo, come home with me. Somehow, women in this situation always seem to hold the upper hand, and written on that hand in thick, dark marker pen is a word so desperately cruel the ink leaps through space and smears itself all over the man. Tonight, that word is 'NO'.

She hails a taxi, snogs me roughly as it pulls in, and then she drives away, sticking her tongue out through the window. I stand there all wobbly on the pavement with hands deep in pockets, grinning and wobbling some more. I wandered home knowing I'd regret the wine the next day and then, wondering exactly what repercussions would come from this date, I was about to jump into bed when my phone rang.

On the screen were two words, *Jo Date*. I brought the phone to my ear, 'Hello babe,' she said, 'What's your address?'

Thursday: Day 13
12 Dates so far

I'm totally and utterly furious at myself. Jo came over last night and she was lovely, and great company, but we both felt cheap as chips when she left for work this morning. I had no self-sympathy when a neighbour I had never met before came knocking sharply on the door to ask if 'I wouldn't mind keeping the noise down next time I had a female over'. From cheap to cheaper in a mere sentence, not only have I acted like a total slapper, but I managed to bring home the one girl whose bedroom vocals could make a braying horse sound like a mute's rendition of Silent Night.

This wasn't in the plan. Not that there was ever a plan, but I was certainly not intending to bed down at the very first hint of a chance. I'm sure my nether regions very satisfied, but my other brain is squeezing itself to death. Now what? If someone special comes along during this stupid challenge how is she going to feel, knowing I've already slept with someone in my 'quest for love'? She'll just feel like a number, surely? I can't blame the alcohol; I put that in my own mouth. And I can't blame the challenge for making me horny, because that's my doing too. And I certainly can't blame Jo, even though it was all her fault. Speaking of Jo, she calls mid-morning to tell me not to worry about last night. 'I think you're great,' she says, 'but I know we don't fit together like that.' She pauses, then cackles, 'well, not all of the time!'

I'm dateless today, but meet Will for a drink. Last week he joined MySingleFriend and yesterday went on a date with a girl who I've also been talking to on MySingleFriend, who stopped messaging me without warning despite an interesting first flurry. Will says she has bad skin, but beautiful eyes.

'Did you kiss?' I ask,

'She went in for the kiss and I tactically turned my head, upper hand mein Freund, upper hand!'

There's such a game on show during these initial encounters, to kiss or not to kiss. Usually, if there is attraction a boy would opt for the kiss, but my challenge has begun to teach me that I can afford to be restrained. A rich comment after last night, I know, but there are so many women out there, now more accessible than ever thanks to the internet, that no-one needs to take a kiss for the sake of it... I'm happy that Will is getting out there, his Dad died suddenly last week and he needs something to take his mind off the hurt. 'He'd want me to be doing this,' he tells me, 'he was a right cad in his day.'

Friday: Day 14
Date No. 13

I'm going on so many of these bloody dates that I'm actually referring to them as 'bloody' dates. I don't mean the women, just the occasions. I'm still enjoying myself, I love meeting these girls, except maybe the really boring ones, but as Date No. 13 sweetly chatted away this afternoon in Covent Garden I couldn't help wondering whether part of me is holding back on these dates because individually they have less meaning than they usually would. Dates are supposed to be sacred, things you go on because you're hopelessly single, your friends are supposed to cross fingers and hold hands in the hope that you're going to come home and declare that you've fallen in love and proposed already. But in reality, my friends couldn't really give a hoot about my dates anymore because I have one a day. Sometimes two, even. And I'm sure at some point I'll have three. So what does that mean, does my 'schedule' have its own repercussions, or as usual am I just over-analysing and as soon as the right person comes along I'll realise that actually I do take each date as seriously as the next, it's just that most of them weren't with someone that I found totally extraordinary. And if I am being over-picky and therefore unknowingly making it harder for myself to accept that any given date is a potential partner, what's to say that if I wasn't writing a book, if I wasn't doing a challenge, that I wouldn't be just as wound up about a date, only for different reasons?

I bring this up here because Date No. 13 is positively delightful. She's an actress (the one from Atonement), and a struggling one at that, and there's something ever so romantic about someone with an artistic talent who is determined to make a living from it, whatever the cost. Her Dating Profile suggested anyone who dates her would have to deal with being beaten at Mario Kart:

> **Dave -** *Hello, is the offer of a Mario Kart challenge still on?*

> **No. 13 -** *Of course, although I have to confess that my skills have been hyped up waaay too much, my friend is stuck in a time-warp that means she perpetually thinks it's 1994, when I was Queen of the SNES.*

> **Dave -** *Do you know how hard it is not to make a joke about women drivers at this point?!*

She's humble and grounded and funny, yet I know from the instant we meet that it's not going to work. She's pretty, has an amazing smile and a very cute hat, but there's no chemistry, not a hint of it, and I can't explain why. So I have to start questioning myself, don't I? I'm sat here really enjoying talking to this girl, but instead of thinking about her as a potential partner a thought starts to prey, a realisation that I wish more dates were like this one but that even if they were there would still be no guarantee that I'm going to meet somebody special during this challenge of mine. As Date No. 13 talks she looks left and right as if she's constantly being distracted. She's so endearing and as she laughs at herself for the umpteenth time I feel a sense of emptiness, as though with each date I'm taking a step closer to happiness, to finding someone, but intangibly, almost as though I'm searching through a haystack and this girl is just another straw to look beneath.

When we say goodbye she says she'd like to see me again. It catches me, because while I would like to spend more time with her I know that we're not going to go anywhere. There was no chemistry between us, we could become good friends; we're both creative and have plenty in common. But I'm looking for more and maybe she wants more from me than I can give her. 'Drop me a line,' I say, an end-of-date sentence riddled with non-commitment, and we hug goodbye.

Date No. 14

Four hours later I'm on my second date of the day. Date No. 14 is 31 and we met on MySingleFriend, which is proving to be rather productive so far, and after some cheeky online banter here she is in person, texting away beneath a speed camera on Clapham Common South Side. It's fireworks night and the bar is incredibly busy, but we get drinks and make it outside just in time for the display. In reality, we don't watch the fireworks. She's a pretty girl with one of those faces that draws you in, a mischievous smile with a touch of mystery. I'm pleasantly surprised. Maybe it's because I've been dulled by the sheer intensity of the dates so far, but when I do get on with a date I find myself helplessly thinking it through as we talk, questioning why we're getting on so well, which of course just reduces the meeting's effectiveness. This is just a momentary thing, but it's there, and I can't help but worry, I'm just not sure what I'm worried about.

At about 10pm I get a text from Date No. 3 asking whether I want to join her at a pub in Clapham Old Town. I'm tempted, I really am, but I'm on a date, and one I'm quite enjoying, at that. But still, the fact that Date No. 3 wants to meet again says something to me and I want to explore that possibility. Tonight, though, is not the night, and my attention returns to No. 14. There are no awkward silences, no signs that this shouldn't go anywhere, but as usual I start to watch her body language. She is a totally different breed of 31 year-old than Date No. 6, who left me with a mouth full of strawberry lip balm on my birthday. She's very articulate and doesn't seem to have any baggage, although she has been online dating for almost two years. 'My friends tell me I come across as aloof,' she says, but I can't see where they're coming from. The only hint of a suggestion is a lack of tactility, but this is countered by a lot of honest talk about her past, her family, her friends. The only sign she gives me of a possible attraction is when she looks at me coyly as she drinks through a straw – if that's not suggestive, then what is?! Still, that's all I'm getting. When it comes to saying goodbye No. 14 turned away from me, so my cheek kiss actually turned into a neck kiss, far more sensual than intended. I pulled away and stood back bashfully, the two of us looking at each other with cheap grins. 'I enjoyed tonight,' she says.

'Me too,' I say, 'let me know that you get home ok.'

Saturday: Day 15
Date No. 15

For a couple of days Date No. 15 has been a bright, witty conversationalist on MySingleFriend and we've organised a breakfast date just down the road. As I leave the house she texts to tell me she might be a little late, and that she'll be wearing a green dress and curly hair. *Not that I don't look like my photo!* She adds. And it brings up an important topic, the Online Dating Profile Image. Do people look like their pictures? To a degree, of course they do. But is that a recognisable degree? A first-rate 2D image can never replicate meeting in person, and although you may be able to get a sense of looks there must be an expectation of the unknown. And let's face it, when you're uploading a profile to an online dating site you're going to choose the best picture ever taken of you, and if that means it was taken five years ago then so be it! At first glance I don't recognise this one at all, but there's more unknown in the profile than just looks, this girl is speaking in a South African accent and for some reason it stuns me. I enjoyed our pre-date messages, a few jokes, all with perfect punctuation and delightful sentence structure, but it was all in English. Date No. 15 hadn't mentioned that she was from South Africa though, and the two-pronged attack comprised of looks – she has strangely large ears - and the accent, left me feeling as though I was having breakfast with a total stranger. It's a ridiculous thing to say, because she was a total stranger, but there's a build-up when you meet online and I suppose basic preconceptions can't be avoided.

Still, we got on, we laughed, we chatted, but there was nothing there, and I skated away to football afterwards feeling a bit dejected; I'd been looking forward to that one. Will texts with news of a date he had last night, *She was absolutely gorgeous but, dare I say it, a little dull!*

I bet he sees her again.

I spend the evening with Mette, who's an ever-faithful date replacement. And thank god she's around, because I'm bloody miserable. Being exhausted and aching from football doesn't help, but the one-two combination of a great day of dating yesterday and then a fairly non-eventful one this morning flings moral dilemmas around. Is it fair to meet people and then not get back in touch, even if they don't get in touch either? Am I being fair on myself? Is this 100 Dates thing actually going to be worthwhile? I've been out with fifteen girls and my heart hasn't exactly been wrenched out yet. Before all of this, had you lined up a variety of women, fifteen of them to be precise, I would have said that I'd get on with at least ten of them, and that amongst the 15 there may well be one person minimum who would be relationship material. And perhaps that has turned out to be true, judging by the regularity that No. 3 pops into my head. But here's what I'm worried about, to date I'm pretty sure I haven't met The One. And what if the next fifteen are like this fifteen. And then the next fifteen. And the next. And then I'll be on Date 60, still loveless, knowing that having seen 60, the chances of finding someone special in the last 40 might seem so much slimmer. Yet again I'm worried, I'm tired, I've even got a bit of man flu, but I feel lonely. And I feel guilty about sleeping with Jo on Wednesday, because I didn't have to, I did it because I enjoyed her company. But I don't for a minute think Jo and I are going anywhere on a relationship level, and I'm 99.9% sure she feels the same way. I've gone a bit too far, I feel, and again I worry about the impact of it if I do meet someone on this challenge who turns out to be special.

As I'm learning to behave at the end of dates thanks to the growing realisation that dating shouldn't be a desperate situation, I'm thinking more and more about the differentiation between sex and love. They're not the same thing, obviously. I know my sexual tastes. I'm not averse to casual relationships, not one-night stands, but sexual relationships with women who become friends. Sex should be enjoyed, and when it's between two adults who have a mutual attraction and have underlined their consensual boundaries sex can be blissful even if a formal relationship is not on the cards. But these can only last so long. In the past I naively believed that as long as the rules were laid out at the beginning, there would always be an understanding that a relationship was not going to happen and although we were friends and enjoyed each other's company, emotions weren't going to run away with themselves. But physical relations can't function for long without emotional collateral, at some point feelings emerge, and when they do 'casual' is no longer the defining term for the relationship. You see, men are fairly simple creatures when it comes to sex. They think they're being honest and open by laying down guidelines with words, but that's just because sex is external for men, as is the penis. The physical act of sex is easy for them, even if getting it isn't always as simple! There are always exceptions to the rule, but it's emotionally harder for a woman to allow somebody inside of her than it is for a man to just, well … stick it in!

There is, however, one urge more natural to humans than sex. The need for companionship is forever ticking over in both men and women; it's just that men show it differently. A single man would be happy for the same woman to come to his bed five out of seven nights while still fighting any suggestion of commitment. He has the companionship he craves, but without the tightening of the noose which his penis can't stand. The male mind works in simple ways but his dick is never fully in control, whatever the rumours say. Men chose when to use their will power and when not to, and it's this inconsistency which fools everyone, even men themselves. After time, a single man will become tired of seeking carnal sex for sex's sake and that's when they become emotionally available.

I need to be straight with myself here: I miss being in love. I haven't lost my sexual appetite, which might explain my eagerness to have Jo stay over the other night, but although we were both single and did nothing wrong I do feel guilty, mainly because while no-strings sex can be enjoyable, it's not all that fulfilling. I want to be able to commit, but I won't settle for anything less than butterflies in my tummy and the more I look the more frustrated I become. Butterflies, especially in the winter, seem very hard to come by.

Sunday: Day 16
Date No. 16

I've been a bit under the weather for a couple of days and desperately need to lessen the pressure on my sinuses, but weekends are critical for credit-building and this Sunday is no different. To my penance, though, I'm about to have something very large and heavy dropped on my foot, I am about to be very male, and be punished therein.

You see, when a girl on MySingleFriend writes to me and seems very keen to have a date, I am usually tempted, obviously! But when the girl is Brazilian my heart starts to beat quite quickly. Brazilians are just the epitome of beauty, aren't they? She has to be very good-looking and therefore our date is going to be very enjoyable. I'm quite convinced that even when she's in South London she walks around in small bikini bottoms and a yellow top with green trimmings. I know she can play football better than me, dance better than me, she's definitely not the type to stand at a crowded bar and be overlooked. God, she's way out of my league! Even though she hasn't uploaded a profile photo yet I don't really mind, because she's Brazilian. *They haven't arranged a photo because I've only just signed up*, she tells me and I'm happy to go along with that excuse. Happy even when I have to wake up at 9am on a Sunday. Happy even with my man flu. Happy even descending into the depths of the Underground with leftover vagrants of a past Saturday night. Happy, in fact, with everything, until I walk through the gates at Tooting Broadway.

Because there, stood in front of me in the pre-arranged yellow top, is Date No. 16. The Brazilian girl. The one who was supposed to be gorgeous, amazing, breathtaking. She looks very much like Eddie Izzard, and I suppose I deserved that.

Don't get me wrong, I like Eddie Izzard, I think he's a very funny man. But he's a man, and that is kind of a problem for me. 'Why don't you date a few gay guys?' my friends have asked me, and although maybe it would be interesting it just doesn't appeal, mainly because I'm straight and looking for a woman. This Sunday morning, however, might just be an exception. We make small talk en route to a coffee shop, very small talk. In other words, I ask questions, she answers in as few words as possible and then looks away while I wonder why I'm in Tooting when I could be in bed. It was the second clock-watching date I've been on, but by far the most uncomfortable. She didn't want to be there, I didn't want to be there, the people around us probably didn't want us to be there. She had a nice smile, granted, but Eddie Izzard is a comedian so that's no surprise. God it was awful, and it lasted 31 minutes. Final slurp of coffee and then we both stood up in the first instance of common understanding we'd shared. We raced to the front door and I beat her, just.

When you meet a date for the first time you're hoping there's going to be a connection, a bit of chemistry. If not, then maybe you'll have a nice chat and become friends. But until now, I didn't think there was such a thing as negative energy. I'm a personable bloke, plenty to talk about, love listening. But Date No. 16 and I were opposite poles, content to keep it civil (even when she went on a rant about the war when I told her my brother was a pilot in the RAF) but struggling to get beyond the starting blocks. I'm not sure a date could be more painful. Again though, I thoroughly deserve it, and on the train north make a promise to myself never again to have a blind date with a Brazilian.

Date No. 17

I did have a 1pm organised with a girl who sells maps, but she cancelled yesterday, and in a way I was relieved. Cancellations are frustrating at the best of times, let alone when you're trying to fit the dates in, but today I needed the rest so arrowed for my sofa and set up dating headquarters.

I've been having a weird and wonderful online chat with a Park Ranger who wrote to me out of the blue a couple of days ago asking which I thought would win in a fight, a polar bear or a crocodile (I chose the polar bear, although did think it would depend on the bout's venue). We hit the ball back and forth, talking about ourselves and always including a random question at the end, and although I couldn't quite get a reading on her pictures the chat was enjoyable and I was quite pleased when she agreed to an early evening Sunday meeting.

She texts before meeting saying she's had an utterly ridiculous day involving a lost dog, an RSPCA officer who hates her and a police anti-terrorism unit, but she arrives in Clapham Junction on time, and then she speaks.

Now, I think I'm a bit of a snob. I'm not at all posh or belonging to high society, but there's something about certain accents that makes my willy droop. Date No. 17, unfortunately, owned a strange accent that I couldn't quite place. She was British, I think, but I had to lean in and lean out regularly in order to give her voice definition. It was a date that confirmed to me that there should be a place on an Internet dating site for a voice file. Looks-wise, I wasn't attracted to her but we lasted an hour and a half before I wandered home. She was pleasant, but there were awkward silences and she laughed a little bit like a beaver on helium. Still, compared to the Brazilian this morning I'd just dated a supermodel-raconteur.

Meanwhile, Date No. 5, she of incredible curly hair, sent me a text this evening and says she's been thinking about me a bit and wonders whether we should meet up. I ponder this for a while, slowly realising that the only reason I'd want to see her again is because of her hair. And I'm tempted, because it was amazing hair. But ultimately meeting again just wouldn't be fair; not on her, not on me, not on the hair. This is the first time I've been faced with a situation where I need to reject someone. She's been good enough to get in touch after the date (apart from Date No. 3 and Jo, I haven't had a peep from anyone) and I'm not going to ignore that, but am also not sure how to actively turn somebody down. If it clearly didn't work out on our first date then I don't think either party is required to do the dirty work, but if one wants a rematch and the other doesn't then we have a potentially awkward situation. Eventually I text back, saying I wasn't sure that we had the spark, and soon after she concurs, saying she'll probably stay away from the first dates for a while. Just like surfing, then.

Monday: Day 17
Date No. 18
When men are ill, they're pathetic. I'm pathetic. I feel all weak and unloved, and I can't help thinking how nice it would be to have someone to bring me cakes. I get a text from Will.

He's feeling guilty about kissing a girl who paid for his food and drinks on a date last night. Thing is, he's got several other dates lined up and he's damning his guilty conscience. I feel much the same, except in two weeks I've dated six times as many girls as Will has. Maybe that's why I'm coming over all pathetic.

I'm now comfortable with messaging strange women. Only about 4 from every 10 I've messaged have replied, but once we get chatting I've so far arranged dates with about 3.5 out of every 4. I don't mind how long we exchange messages, but with time I feel like I can tell earlier and earlier whether they are comfortable with me, and then I spring the question: *can I tempt you with a drink? Fancy meeting up sometime?* On the other hand, if I ever felt like I was replying to a message just for the sake of it, I'd wind the conversation up and let it lie.

The last thing I felt like doing was dating tonight, but it's not like I have a choice. I meet Date No. 18 in a Clapham pub. She's late, Scottish and much plumper than her profile photo suggested. I suppose it's the intensity of my dates, but for the first time in my life I'm realising that I'm incredibly picky. I'm not exactly a supermodel but we all have standards, and it feels like there's been little or no physical attraction on three quarters of my dates so far. Date No. 18 adds to the list, and although we chat along quite happily her body language shows she feels the same. We're on a sofa and she's squeezed so tightly against the far arm I'm worried about her hip bruising. There's nothing going on here and we're about to leave when a chubby but ever so smiley bloke wanders up to our table brandishing a piece of paper.

'Pub Quiz?' he asks with a raised eyebrow.

Date No. 18 and I look at each other, it's 50-50. 'Come on, let's do it,' I say, and she grins then, quite unbelievably, spends the next hour flirting shamelessly with the quizmaster, who is admittedly a very likeable chap, but still. I'm sat there with my arms crossed, my head darting between the two of them as they eye each other up. She goes to the toilet at one point and actually puts both of her hands on his chest, I can't believe my eyes. It's not like this guy is really trying it on with No. 18, but she can't seem to get enough of him.

The quiz comes to an end and I scribble a team name at the top of our sheet, *MySingleFriendDotCom*.

'Are you two on a date?!' asks the quizmaster when he sees it, and I nod glumly.

'Blimey mate,' he says, 'she's a goer!'

I mumble something about her liking meat on a man then sit there perhaps more amazed than at any other point during the night when *MySingleFriendDotCom* is announced as the winner of the quiz. Date No. 18 and I share the £25 pot and I offer to walk her to the bus stop. Halfway down the road we're joined by none other than the quizmaster, who seemed to appear as if by magic from behind a lamppost. Massive lampposts, in Clapham.

Frankly, I wasn't sure what to do. I bumbled along as Date No. 18 and the quizmaster walked just ahead of me, gently barging each other's shoulders and making jokes about foodstuffs. 'See you soon,' I say to them both at Clapham Common, a farewell directed more at the quizmaster than the girl; it was actually quite a good quiz and I think I might take more dates back there, just for fun.

On the way home Jo calls me and we have a good old natter, as per usual, and after I delight her with the quizmaster story she relays tales of what she's been telling people about our date... 'I met this dude right, and he told me he broke a world record, and my knickers slipped down!' This girl's one in a million. She checks herself as we talk, remembering that I'm writing a book, 'I'm sure there must by some copyright on this shit,' she says, 'I want an embargo.' I ignore that and ask her how her dating is going and she says not too well.

'Cheers Jo!' I say, teasing.

'Oh shit yeah!' she laughs, 'well look, out of three dates one was a psycho stalker, one was a mute and one was writing a book on me!'

We talked a little more about how our date ended. She's wonderfully funny and open and makes it clear she knows exactly where I'm coming from, and that she feels the same.

The simple fact that we're still talking shows it was a bit more than just a one night stand. It seems accepted that we're not going anywhere romantically (we're not exactly couple material) but that's fine, she is a breath of fresh air, and I'm ever so glad I met her.

Tuesday: Day 18
Date No. 19

Will and I have a sneaky drink half an hour before I meet tonight's date. I tell him about a 22 stone African American who is trying to pick me up on Dating Direct.

'You're not in a position to be picky here, mate,' says Will.

'But it's a man!' I said, before leaving hurriedly.

Date No, 19 is called Rhi and she's a friend of Sarah, who I went to primary school with. Whilst meeting Date No. 3 for the first time we were moving on from a first pub and bumped into Sarah and Rhi, who were having lunch around the corner. Date No. 3 nipped off to the loo and I quickly told the girls what I was up to. A few hours later Sarah texted and said that Rhi would be up for going on a date with me. So here we are, having a drink fifty metres down the road from our first meeting point two and a half weeks earlier.

This is my first date with someone who knows about The Hundred and in many ways it instantly cleared the air. It took about half an hour for the subject to come up and Rhi seemed focused on one particular question, 'what happens if someone really likes you, what do you do then?'

Until then I'd spent some time being a little pensive about causing upset to any of my dates, but when Rhi asked me her question I realised that the dating game is full of pitfalls, and whether I'm writing a book or not if the girl really likes me and I'm not reciprocating her feelings, or of course, if it's the other way around, then it's not going to work. The challenge or the book doesn't play a part in that. If there's a two-way attraction then it's a different story, and that's when it gets complicated.

'I tell you what is tricky though,' I say, 'it's remembering everyone's names. I've been out with two Katies, two Amys, a Kath, a Kate, a Caroline, you're the second Jo….'

And she looked at me sternly and asked, 'So how many Rhi's have you been out with?'

Oh bloody shit.

Wednesday: Day 19
Dates No. 20 & 21 & 22

This was always going to be a momentous day. Assuming no cancellations, I was about to have three dates in one day for the first time. Initially there was just one, in Covent Garden at 6pm, but then another got in touch: *I'm in Covent Garden on Wednesday for a friend's 30th, but her party doesn't actually start until 10pm. So if you fancy it I'll meet you for a drink before hand? I know that seems a little quick and I can't quite believe I'm writing this myself, but hey - as friend once told me - you've got to be in it to win it!!'*

Bugger. The second girl looked very pretty and her profile said she had been a backing dancer for Robbie Williams, and I've never met one of them, but I already have a date on Wednesday. Hold on. I do have a date on Wednesday, *in Covent Garden.*

So I typed back; *there's nothing wrong with a quick drink invite. Tomorrow night would be grand, how does 8.15 sound*? A few minutes later another message, this time from a totally different girl who also seems very nice. She wants to meet me on Wednesday, at 3pm.

And thus the marathon begins. Date No. 20 is tall, about my height, has jet-black hair flowing around her shoulders and sparkling dark eyes, which hide more than a little intellect. We wander around giggling and getting through the small talk as we trot, then settle on Café Nero. For two hours we sit opposite each other, separated by a small plastic table and nothing else.

'I've been on your website,' she tells me coyly, 'I hope you don't think I'm a stalker?'

'Only a little bit,' I grin, 'what did you think?'

'It's very interesting, didn't you get bored?'

I tell the skating story for the twentieth time and should be yawning inside, but no tale is ever the same if someone different is listening. Date No. 20 has a question for almost every sentence and seems genuinely enthused, but perhaps it was because we were getting on so well that I started to check out her body language, and then I started to analyse whether I was reading too much into her body language, and then I wondered if she thought I was staring at her boobs rather than her crossed arms, and after a while I'd gotten myself so confused I just listened in silence as she talked about her family. Then, somewhere in the middle of it all, she mentioned her sister and waved a hand in the air and said, 'oh you'll meet her at some point anyway...'

I might have misread the situation, but No. 20 seems to think that we've already begun a long-term relationship. She may be a member of Mensa, but even they know that two cups of coffee isn't enough to secure a lifetime of memories. I mean, I liked her, she was good company and conversation bounced around without so much as a whisper of silence, but it didn't mean I was ready to introduce her to my brother.

Is meeting Date No. 20's sister such a bad thing? I ponder the question as the Northern Line takes me to Charing Cross. I hover outside a nearby bar until Date No. 21 appears. Slim, short blonde hair, cute face. We settle downstairs and chat aimlessly. She tells me she had a date last night, which I thought was refreshingly honest of her. 'It didn't work out, though,' she said, chin on her hands, shaking her head, 'he knew exactly what he wanted and it was just question after question, it was like an interview.'

'God, I hope I'm not like that,' I said, slightly alarmed,

'I wouldn't have told you the story if you were,' she said, smiling.

And she has a very nice smile, but there's something about Date No. 21 that I'm not sure about. Maybe it's the total obsession with Alfred, her little dog? I can't work it out. Here, sat in front of me, is a girl I shouldn't really be having any doubts about, but I'm not sure all the same. What is wrong with me? Am I really ready to meet somebody? Has this dating game just brought out my ultra picky side? Or do I need to specify on my dating profiles that I don't want to date anyone obsessed with Highland Terriers?

'My cousin is coming down,' I guiltily told her earlier, not delighted with myself for the white lie but thinking it probably wouldn't go down too well if I told her I had another date. I mean, there's a date last night, and there's a date in ten minutes. We have a hug then go our separate ways, and as I'm waiting outside Covent Garden tube for Date No. 22 a text buzzes through from Date No. 21: *I thought I'd be brave and not wait for a response. I really enjoyed tonight and would like to meet up again, if you would?* I pop the phone in my pocket and have a think: this is new territory.

Now, I don't feel as much for Date No. 21 as I did for Date No. 3 (who incidentally I haven't heard from since I decided not to join her last Friday) and honestly I'm not sure that I would have initiated any second date with No. 21 had she not been in touch, but why not? Are first dates honestly enough to tell you whether you want to see somebody again? Is the first date situation too nervous or tetchy or pressured to really get an accurate feel for someone's personality? Is sitting across a table and chatting to a stranger really the best way to judge an attraction? Am I using my dating marathon as an excuse not to see my dates for a second time, or do I honestly know as soon as I meet someone that it is or isn't going to work out? I'm not so sure, so I text Date No. 21 back and tell her I'd like to meet again. And then Date No. 22 walks out of the tube station.

'Awight!' she says, a smiling face beneath a mass of blonde curls. She's tiny, has a killer body and seems incredibly friendly, but I'm taken aback by her voice. She's from

Croydon, and I'm not sure what to do with that. The snob in me is rearing its ugly head again. This lovely looking girl is less attractive to me because of her voice, there's no doubt about it. Is this *my* problem? Or are ticks like this beyond my control? I'm haunted by these thoughts less and less as the date goes on. We've both been through similar break-ups earlier this year, both run our own businesses, both are sporty and healthy, but I get the feeling that Date No. 22 isn't that interested in me, either. Maybe my voice puts her off? We get on, giggle a bit, have three drinks and then say goodbye. Nothing is said but it's quite obvious we're not going to see each other again, and whether that's down to voices or body language or personality or just the fact that she lives in Croydon and I'm in Clapham, I don't know. But that's that, and for all the questions, it's simple – there was just no chemistry.

I'm exhausted as I walk towards Charing Cross. Three dates is a lot to deal with and although it's brilliant making up numbers I can't help but feel that I've had three very different, yet lovely dates in the space of eight hours. What if things develop with one of them, can I then be honest and say she was one of three dates I had on the same day? Outside Charing Cross I pause. My mind is racing and the Underground isn't the best place for thinking. *You're in London, Dave, make the most of it*, I tell myself, so I carry on walking and stand in the middle of an empty Trafalgar Square, spinning round and round beneath Nelson's Column.

'What are you doing mate?' I say out loud to myself, 'this is all so fucking crazy.'

I think about my dates so far; a lot of them have been lovely, did they think the same about me? Admittedly I haven't been back in touch with many of them, do they deserve that? Or is it just as much on their shoulders to get in touch if they really do want to meet again? Is it fairer to write and say that you're not interested, or is not writing at all enough to say that it didn't work out? I hate the secret; it weighs me down. I feel a sudden urge to text all of them and ask them on a second date, tell them what I'm doing, get it all out in the open, but do those who I haven't spoken to since our first date want me to get in touch? Maybe they do, maybe they don't. Who bloody knows? I don't know these girls, not really. Apart from the couple of hours spent on a date, I have no idea what their life is like, who their friends are, what they do with their time. They could be on another date right now for all I know, and that's perfectly fine. There's so much unknown, is there really any point trying to get to know someone unless you *feel* something?

This is a big day for me, for this challenge of mine. A busker in tight leggings that stop just above the knee is strumming a Beatles song brilliantly and I drop some coins into his guitar case hoping he'll use them to buy some proper trousers. It's one of the last trains of the evening and everyone is packed in like little helpless fish. I catch the eye of a bearded guy who has an old woman's umbrella rammed into his neck, and we simultaneously raise our eyebrows. I drift off, thinking through the night's dates, but every now and then I look around the carriage and the bearded man is always trying to catch my eye. At Kennington the crowd thins out and the man shuffles over. 'Hey,' he says, 'good night?'

'It's been interesting!' I grin. It's always a surprise when a total stranger starts up a conversation on London transport; everyone usually keeps themselves to themselves, head down in a book, a phone, a newspaper. The man tells me he's just been celebrating a promotion, and slowly I realise that he wants more than just a chat.

'I couldn't help but notice you,' he says, 'you had a wonderful glow of confidence when you got on here.' He rolls his eyes around the carriage, which all of a sudden seems much smaller than it did a few seconds ago. There's a slightly sizzled look in his eyes, the odd drunken grab at a pole when the train jolts off from a station, and when his stop comes he looks at me and says, 'I hope you don't mind me saying this, but you're a very handsome man.'

I'm a bit taken aback, and stutter, 'oh, well thank you,' without looking at him. And then he walks away down the Clapham North platform, chin on his chest, having failed unknowingly in an attempt to become my fourth date of the day. People say that confidence is attractive, but by dating three women on the same day am I unwittingly exuding some kind of social magnetism, something that says *hey, talk to me, I'm open to everything.* Or maybe it's just coincidence that I've just been hit on by a guy for the first time in my life, just as I'm beginning to feel like I could sit down and strike up a conversation with anybody.

Thursday: Day 20
22 Dates so far

No dates, no nothing. But I probably need a break after three yesterday, anyway.

Friday: Day 21
Dates No. 23 & 24

At 4pm I meet Date No. 23, a very straight and well-to-do Indian girl who works in TV. She's intelligent, does a job she doesn't want to be doing, and wears her hair in little pig-tails, which seemed strange because she looked older than twelve. There's no attraction whatsoever. On these dates where nothing seems to be at stake it's so much easier to chat away about dating experiences, and this girl is another proponent of the not getting in touch afterwards if you're not interested, which makes it much easier for both of us when we say goodbye.

Two hours later I meet Date No. 24 outside Covent Garden tube. Petit, oriental and bearing a slightly chubbier face than her photo, No. 24 is half Korean, half Around-The-World, and has a thick and incredibly stubborn American accent. She's a tough nut to crack and I'm not sure where I stand with her for almost an hour, but we slowly start to warm up and I can't help but find her hilarious. She has a knapsack full of bizarre stories and thoughts and the uncanny ability to talk the hind leg off a rhino, so I let her chat and soak up some glorious titbits, some of which are too golden not to share. For example, she loves Spam. She *really* loves Spam (the meat, not junk mail), so much so that she once spent time in an African country and had Spam shipped in from the States once a fortnight. Spam aside, she wants to set up a business making artefacts in China, she tells me how odd she finds British bathroom sinks which have separate hot and cold taps, and says a friend of hers who felt the same way cut out some old soda bottles and tied them to the taps so the water came out in the middle, just so she felt at home. Genius! She prefers cats to dogs, but dogs to rabbits, and by the time she goes off on an endless sentence about how clouds sometimes look like people I spit out a mouthful of beer because I'm giggling so much. This girl is hilarious, and despite being unknowingly dappy she's becoming cuter by the second. She talks non-stop, which is annoying. She sounds and acts so American, so sorority house, so indignantly ignorant sometimes, I find myself grimacing. But she's funny, and cute, and remarkably good company, and despite the reservations I like her. We have dinner in an Angus Steak House and then I put her on a bus home, because a couple of drinks started to make her wobble a little bit. Almost before the bus pulls away she texts: *Hey I had a really good time tonight. We should get together soon. Glad I gave u a good laugh, hope you giggle for a while because of it!*

Saturday – Monday: Days 22 - 24
24 Dates so far

Three frustrating days. Two dates are cancelled and having a long, dateless weekend is a kick in my lonely teeth. On Sunday Date No. 24 sends me a text:

Tonight I walked slowly alone a busy street and just observed, first time in two and a half years. It was great. Wanted to share it with someone who might appreciate it.

Possibly she's trying to be genuine, but it feels almost rehearsed and it makes me even more unsure about her now. Let's put it this way, I don't have any dates, and still I don't feel the inclination to meet her again. How do I know whether or not I want to see a girl again? The same way I know anything. I ask myself whether I'm going to regret it if I *don't* see her again. All I want is to find someone I click with, and now!

Even in the middle of an extreme dating mission, I'm still human and need some shopping. I read somewhere that there's a supermarket chain in Australia where it's acceptable to chat people up if they've got certain products in their trolleys, nothing suggestive, just a brand of washing powder or a box of cereal. In the Tesco magazine section a young boy is throwing a complete tantrum, tearing things out of his Mum's basket and stomping his little feet with a sentence that will forever fill me with total joy, 'I WANT THIS ONE, I LIKE PINK!' Sometimes, however young, our futures are set in stone.

Will's been on a date this weekend, even if I haven't:

I went on a date last night with the girl that could've been quite pretty, but was very dubious from her photo. She actually turned out to be good looking, but conversation was quite hard. I ended up ranting about the Northern Line. I don't know what came over me, I think it was just the rage from the morning before when the fucking thing had been closed completely. See? I'm doing it now... Right, I'm going to stop before I can't get any sleep tonight with worry about my journey into work tomorrow...

On Monday, a week on from Date No. 18, I go to the quiz in the Calf with Will and Jo, who is now just a friend and nothing more. Towards the end of the night the quizmaster, who introduces himself as David, approaches and says, 'look I know this is a bit weird, but I really want to hook up with the girl you were here with last week.'

'No shit!' I say, admiring his front, 'you guys were getting on like a house on fire!'

I took his number and texted Date No. 18 from last week, asking her if she was interested … later she replied:

Ha ha! That's hilarious! How did you get on in the quiz?
Win again?!

Tuesday: Day 25
Date No. 25

Date No. 25 is Australian, and she's another one I'm just not sure about. I'm just a mean, ruthless dater now, if I'm not sure about them from the very start then there's not much chance at all. I'm not so desperate that I feel the need to find any old chick to be my partner, and with another 75 dates to go it's becoming glaringly obvious that there's no use settling for someone that doesn't immediately wrap my heart and head up in a ball of roses and other soft stuff. I haven't heard anything more from Date No. 3 and have now accepted that we're unlikely to meet again. We met 22 dates ago, and I can't help wonder whether I've let something good slip through my fingers because I've been telling myself I can't give one girl the attention that perhaps she deserves. Not one day has gone by that I haven't thought about Date No. 3, but looking back it seems fairly obvious that she wasn't that into me. Damn it!

Seconds after I agreed to meet Date No. 25 an email came through offering me a free place at a speed dating event in the city, which I would have much preferred, but a date's a date. It's not that she seems unpleasant, it's just that I'm tired of dating, and I'm not sure I can take another night with a girl that doesn't knock my socks off. Am I fussy because I don't want to settle, or because I won't settle for less than what I deem to be perfection? So here we are, Date No. 25 and I in a bar and that horribly familiar sense of clarity hits me between the eyes in seconds, there is and will never be any chemistry. It's almost like we're just friends, and I feel like she's interviewing me, asking about my past, asking about online dating, speed dating, my parents, how many pets I've had. It's the most platonic date I've ever been on and it seems totally reasonable to tell her what I'm doing, so I do. I explain The Hundred and my reasons for it, and even though she's very enthusiastic it just means she starts to ask more questions, and I end up with the feeling that she doesn't even realise she's one of the dates. We finish early and hug goodbye, and I realise that despite a distinctly average night I have learned one thing, that teeth are important to me. Date No. 25 is not unattractive, she has wonderful legs and glorious eyes, but you could drive a truck between her two front choppers and it's a rather distracting feature.

Wednesday: Day 26
Dates No. 26 & 27

Attentive waiters prey in a Victoria bar while I wait for Date No. 26, but as soon as she turns up they don't want to know. Bizarre. I lean in for a cheek kiss as she approaches the table but am a bit taken aback when she stretches out an arm. She wants to shake my hand. Problem is, I was already leaning in and she gently prodded my package. I straightened up again, quite hastily, but by then she was leaning in, so I did, and in the end I gave her a firm hug and we sat down all confused. Date No. 26 is 22 but very mature, incredibly well-spoken and clearly plays polo in her spare time. Her defining physical feature is a zit on her cheek that at some point is going to cause more devastation than Mt St Helens did when it ruptured in the 80's. Despite that wholly shallow observation, she is actually quite a pretty girl, in a pale kind of way. We get on, banter, draw out each other's back stories and chat easily. It's not an outstanding date, but not a disappointing one either, and I'm starting to think that maybe we could meet up again and see where it goes. She pays for lunch, and I tell her I'll repay the favour next time we meet, but did I really mean it? Following my usual instincts, I'm quite sure Date No. 26 and I are not going to go further than a pleasant coffee, so why say I'll see her again? Have I had so many sub-standard dates that I've gone full circle and now I'm pushing myself to like someone? Or did I really like her and it's such a rare thing that I can't even recognise it when it explodes in my face?

That evening I have another date. I arrange to meet No. 27 outside Clapham Common tube and again I find myself one of a series of guys and girls who stand like a mongoose on sentry duty, waiting for dates. I can safely say that before I started to meet people I had no idea I was surrounded by first daters so regularly, but already I'm becoming a weary veteran and can notice the signs immediately. Nervous sidestepping, occulting necks then a sideways bow, tentative first kiss, once on the cheek, maybe another on the other. The first thing that hits me about Kate is how very well-spoken she is, but within five minutes I realise she's the type of person I want to be around all the time. This happens sometimes. I have a very early feeling that it's not necessarily going anywhere in terms of a relationship, but the girl still draws me out of my shell and I begin to think that we're going to be very good friends, that we can enrich each other's life, somehow. In actual fact, as Kate talks about her experience as a PA, I get a weird feeling that perhaps I need a PA (just to organise my dating schedule!), and Kate could indeed be the one, because she's quality through and through. She's my age, 28, and tells me she can't understand why people are on dating sites in their early twenties, 'it just seems so desperate and shows that these sites aren't just for people looking for long-term relationships.'

'Either that or the young are too desperate to meet someone, soon,' I suggested, like an old person would. Either way, online dating does lend itself to being quite formal in the pursuit of a partner and the age ranges that people are looking for are a great indicator of whether they're after love or sex.

Kate and I get on very well, chatting and laughing and moving from bar to bar, the last of which is the Clapham North, where Jo happens to be dating a Kiwi bloke right next to the door! Typically she's so far into her drink she doesn't notice me, and with hindsight winking at her date as if to say *I know what you've let yourself in for* probably just freaked him out.

Kate and I settle at a table towards the back of the pub and she tells me about a guy she dated who went to the effort of calling her just to say it wasn't going to work out. 'You know,' she said, 'I'd rather he just hadn't have bothered.' She tells me about another date she went on, with a Greek man. It was a mediocre date, he was Mediterranean and loved his mother, but nothing was ever going to happen. A week later he sent her a text – and at this point in her story Kate delights in scrolling through her phone to show me the message – which read:

> *Hi Kate, I enjoyed the other night but I've been thinking and I'm not ready for a long-term relationship (I thought I was), but if you fancy a bit of fun some time get in touch.*

This girl is right on my wavelength, and as she visits the bathroom I work up the courage to tell her about The

Hundred. This is maybe the fourth time I've told a date what I'm up to but the nerves, if anything, have increased. I have no idea how they're going to react, whether they'll be angry or intrigued, so by the time she's back from the toilet I've worked myself up into such a lather that I just want to burst.

'Kate, I have something to tell you,' I told her.

She looked at me, knitting her brows, recoiling and straightening her back. Her hands, once open and available on the table, shrink into her lap.

'Ok?' she says.

She's nervous. Nice one, I've made her nervous. Save the situation Dave, save it!

'Oh no, you don't have to worry, just bear with me.'

So close.

Even though it seemed to work the first time, I continue to punctuate each sentence with 'bear with me' as I tell the story and eventually Kate comes back to life, leans in a bit more, starts asking questions. By the end of the night she seems totally fascinated by the whole thing. Thank god, I still haven't been punched by a date. Before we go she wags her finger at me, 'Next time you're telling a date exactly what you're up to don't start with 'I've got something to tell you.' It's horrible. I was thinking, *he's married*, or *he's gay*. You're not doing such a bad thing, so don't act like you are!'

Thursday: Day 27
Date No. 28

Date No. 21, who was the sandwich in last Wednesday's day of three dates, has been writing and suggesting a second date. I'm game, but have held her at arm's length a little, because the girl I dated two hours before her also wanted to meet up again. This morning I skated over to Clapham Junction to meet No. 20 and share breakfast in a brilliantly named café, Boiled Eggs and Soldiers. No. 20 was the one who told me out of the blue that at some point I'd meet her sister. Surely she assumed that we had something in common, a little bit of fire, and perhaps I'd missed that because I knew that I still had two dates to go that day and was blindly attempting to be as non-committal as possible. Still, I'm intrigued by No. 20 and need to know more, this is only my second follow-up date and with time at a premium I don't take these events lightly! Like on our first date, I spend much of our breakfast studying her, trying to work out whether we'd fit, mentally and physically. She's a funny girl, very expressive, incredibly intelligent. She has a wide social circle, cares deeply about her friends and is very pretty, but I'm not sure and I can't explain it. Throughout this thing I've been waiting for a spark, a real spark, but I don't think Date No. 20 and I have had one. Saying that, our two dates have been over coffee and then breakfast, there's always a table between us. How much can I tell from that? I leave her at a bus stop and the chance to meet again is left open. There's a cunning twinkle in her eyes as I walk away but I don't have a clue what it means. My inability to read women is still worryingly acute despite having a date a day for four weeks, and I'm not sure whether drawing a blank after two dates is a bad sign, or a product of my current scattergun approach to dating. Or maybe it sometimes takes more than two dates for a spark between two people to really connect. I'm still searching for answers.

Of course, a second date doesn't count towards The Hundred, so I've organised another for the evening. Date No. 28 has an intriguing photo taken from above, she looks pretty, has a pile of dark curly hair, and let's face it, I like curly hair and am looking forward to meeting it tonight. Her messages have been short, slightly witty, yet abrupt and without too much information, so in conclusion I walk to the date having no idea who I'm about to meet. There she is, waving at me from outside Clapham South Station, looking slightly bigger than her photo suggested. Her hair isn't even that curly, either. I'm disgusted! The date doesn't go well. She moans about her job, how she doesn't know where she's going in life, how shit things are.

'I need some careers guidance,' she tells me, 'you seem sorted, what would you suggest?' Quite bluntly I suggested that she might stop talking about her problems, and actually do something about them. That may sound harsh, and please believe that I was firmly suggestive, not cruel, but a first date isn't the place to reveal that you don't know who you are. No. 28 tried to offer up a saving grace to show that she did have an ounce of enthusiasm about life, but it was merely a picture on her phone showing a fox asleep in a flower pot in her yard. Jesus.

I'm disgruntled, yet from another bad date I've learned more about what I'm looking for from a potential partner. I'm after someone who is comfortable in their own skin, someone who knows what they want and where they're going, a girl who is totally secure with themselves and their life. So, in conclusion, spending two hours with a 27-year-old lass who can't stop moaning and seeks constant guidance is slightly annoying. Thank you, and goodnight.

Friday: Day 28
Dates No. 29 & 30

I'm really looking forward to meeting this one. She has a great profile, a pretty smile and her email banter is second to none. I can't explain why, but I get the feeling that I'm going to meet somebody special tonight. And when she walks up to me outside Covent Garden tube station, 15 minutes late and breathing quite heavily, the anticipation falls; she just doesn't look as pretty in person as she did in her photo.

She's sharp though, this one. Clearly a professional, she works as an editor for an online financial publication and has had a long day talking to reporters about an issue that has been all over the news. We walk and talk, finally nuzzling into a crowded pub. It takes about half an hour for us to warm up conversationally; bad dating stories and her candid portrayal of living with a housemate who hates her guts slowly reveal that we have a similar, sarcastic humour. From then on, we take the piss out of each other. She goes to the toilet three times and I can't help asking her when the bladder replacement is scheduled for. Her smile, so pretty in her photos, appears more and more, and she really is quite radiant. We both have other engagements – her a party in Chiswick, me another date just around the corner (don't tell her that, obviously) and we wander closely until I point down a side street and announce 'that's me, I have to go down there.' I go for the one cheek and she goes for the two, and we are so close to accidentally touching lips I stand up and say, 'well that was almost quite embarrassing, so I'll give you a third cheek kiss to make up for the disappointment,' and I pecked her left cheek and hugged her, and rushed around the corner to meet Date No. 30, hoping to God that No. 29 didn't slouch on her way to Leicester Square. Had I continued walking with her, we would have passed right by Covent Garden station, which might have been very embarrassing because it was there that I was meeting another female, and not a male friend called Will, as had been my excuse.

No. 30 is waiting for me, probably because I'm 15 minutes late, and I rush her away from Covent Garden and any potential of being spotted should No. 29 have been a slow walker. Poor girl must have felt like she was being kidnapped. We sit in Navajo Joe's and she goes into the toilet for ten minutes, what is it with the girls and toilets tonight? I met No. 30 at the speed dating event a few weeks back, the one where Will kept talking about trains, and out of the blue she texted me yesterday asking if I fancied a drink. Our date is lacking fruit, and we chat very plainly for an hour about the very basics of our life. This is not a good sign. If two people hit it off immediately then they can talk about anything, and the boring, relatable facts don't seem so important because deep down you both know you'll have plenty of time later to find out where they're from, and how old they are, how many brothers they have, what brand of toothpaste lies by the sink. After an hour I know everything about No. 30's family, and age, and background, but we haven't veered off the introduction and I'm infected both by boredom, and also slight disappointment that the first date of the day hadn't quite lived up to expectations. Again, I'm glad to have had two dates in one day, but as I tube home I start to wonder whether I'll ever meet anyone who makes my heart beat faster.

Saturday: Day 29
Date No. 31

I have football today but have managed to squeeze in a breakfast date beforehand. She's 22 and plays rugby. It was one of those meetings when I looked around and saw one person standing there outside the tube station, and then started praying that she wasn't my date. She was, of course, and we had a pleasant breakfast, but No. 31 was very young, looked it and acted it and even had those little flushed cheeks that some young girls have before they've properly developed into a woman. I'm not sure I'm going to date any more girls under 23.

Sunday: Day 30
Date No. 32

'Rosie?' I ask, leaning in a little.
She looks at me, confused.
I try again.
'Are you Rosie?'

She shakes her head, furrows her brow, holds her bag tightly as though she was about to swing it at my face, 'No,' she growls.

'I'm so sorry,' I say grimacing, and shuffle away.

Two minutes later the real Rosie walks towards me, there is no doubt about this one. She has piercingly pretty, enormous brown eyes, and come to think of it, she actually looks a lot more like her profile picture than the other girl, who is looking over at us in mild amusement as we greet each other like strangers do.

Earlier, as I strolled through the leaves towards Clapham Common tube, Will called me:

'I'm meeting this girl in a minute,' he said.

'Where are you meeting?' I asked.

'Outside Clapham Common tube,' he said.

'See you in a minute then, mate!' I chuckled.

Rosie was a little late and by the time she arrived I had already had an impromptu meeting with Will and his date, who looked worryingly goofy. Will's a good-looking bloke, but he doesn't do himself justice sometimes.

'We're going to the Coach and Horses,' he told me, and I smiled.

'It seems that our dates are going to be rather similar today,' I said, 'I'll probably see you a bit later!'

On the way to the Coach and Horses Rosie tells me that she's just taken up football. 'I'm not very good,' she says, 'I just run up and down and crash into people, and there's this fat German lesbian who insists on marking me, so that doesn't help.' In the pub, Will winks at me before disappearing around the corner.

Rosie is 22, six years younger than me, but she's mature and funny and slowly her initial nerves disappear. So much for not dating anyone under 23 again. There are no tables in the pub so after our drink we venture into the rain and wander for a while. She has glorified slippers on and reveals that one of them has a hole in, and I mock tell her off for dressing inappropriately. She tells me to watch it, and suggests I should carry her.

We settle in The Windmill and hang around at the bar for a sofa to come free. It's cosy, we're getting on like a house on fire, and her eyelashes are so long there's a little gust when she flutters them. A roast dinner and two drinks later we finally get a sofa and start to move closer. She has a gorgeous face and every time she looks at me I melt a little bit, and for the first time since I started dating I know that I've met someone who I could fall for. We're side by side on the sofa, not quite shoulder to shoulder but close enough for hands and legs to brush occasionally; it felt right, good, comfortable. Well, almost comfortable.

She was comfortable. We were comfortable. But I wasn't, not totally. In the toilet I ask myself what's wrong, *what's wrong with you, Dave*? I shake my head at my reflection and then I see it in my eyes, I'm terrified. Here I am on Date 32 and finally after all this time I've met somebody who could be somebody. But still there's something wrong. No, there are potentially three things wrong. One, she's 22. If this is such a problem, you ask, then why are you even dating 22-year-olds in the first place? Good point, but I hadn't really thought about it until yesterday, had I? I dated a 21-year-old on Date 4 and 22 year-olds on Date 26 and Date 31, and they all seemed young, very young. But Rosie, although she looks 22, doesn't act 22. She acts 26, 27, maybe even 40, but she's still 22. My point, and it's probably not a good one, is that I'm terrified and I'm blatantly searching for excuses. If what I'm doing is actually looking for The One, then perhaps a 22-year-old shouldn't be right. Surely she's too young to be looking for a life partner? Surely she still has a bit of seed sowing left, or seed receiving, or whatever women do. When I go off on my journeys is she, still in her early twenties, going to be happy spending months on end attached to a bloke who isn't there? She's 22, and suddenly I realise it's a problem.

Am I attracted to this girl? Brilliant face but she doesn't look like she goes to the gym much. It's not something that's bothered me before but have my tastes and perceptions changed on this challenge? I'm enjoying myself, I fancy her, but does that mean she's relationship material? Looks have never dictated whether I've fallen in or out of love with a woman, but we all have our own thresholds of attractiveness. Subliminally, we all know where we fit on the ladder of attraction and therefore we also have a gauge for who we can be realistically attracted to. Like it or not, we live in a horribly shallow and visual world where we'll look in bewilderment at a pair when one of them is noticeably prettier than their partner. Of course, there are other factors at play here; personality, sense of humour, self-confidence, even wealth. But without physical attraction the ground for any blossoming relationship is shaky. There is a regular pattern once the honeymoon period is over and the initial spark and sexual appeal starts to diminish, negatives then begin to sharpen their edges. I've always become bored of things very easily, and I've come to the conclusion that part of my boredom lies in the truth that almost every relationship I've ever been in has gone stale sexually, and it's because the relationship itself was so comfortable that physically we let ourselves go a bit. As a consequence the sexual appetite slowly slipped down the drain and there we were, staring at each other, a pair of comfortable bloaters choosing to stay in and watch the telly. Maybe hindsight is playing tricks on me; maybe I'm using physical reasons for an argument where they don't belong. It's not as though I have a washboard stomach by which to judge all others, it's not as though I don't find Rosie attractive – I do! These feelings are coming from somewhere! But I can't control my mind, and as I walk back from the toilet and look at Rosie smiling up at me I realise that I am ever so attracted to her face, but I'm not necessarily attracted to the rest of her. Or, as part of me suspects, am I confusing my quest for The One for a quest for Perfection, and simply using anything I can as an excuse? Am I being fussy because I don't want to settle, or because I won't settle for less than what I deem to be the perfect partner, whoever she is? After all, would I be worrying about barely-important physical stuff if this was just a date, one date, not one in a hundred?

Problem Three is the challenge, The Hundred. Am I making a mountain out of a molehill when it comes to the attraction Rosie and I share, purely because I know that this could develop into a tough decision? I've just met somebody I really like and perhaps my fears are being compounded because in reality this girl is a challenge to my challenge. Am I just backing off because The Hundred is in jeopardy if I meet someone? Am I actually terrified of finding exactly what I claim to be searching for? Is the book more important than the girl? Is that why I'm finding negatives in such a positive situation?

But we're still getting along, and there is some very real chemistry between us, it's just that now with all my swirling questions, I feel uncomfortable. Not with her, not with us, but with myself and the thoughts I'm having. Am I honestly discounting this girl because I'm not attracted to everything below her neck? Am I really that shallow, or am I just being true to myself? I have no idea, is it shallow not being attracted to someone because of the way they look, or is it natural? Perhaps I'm being honest, maybe I'm a horrible person, maybe I'm a bit of both and I don't know how to deal with that because it's never nice realising you're an arsehole. So I start staring off into the distance because it just seems like the easy thing to do.

We walk in the rain and I put my arm around her because she's cold and her feet are wet due to the hole in her shoe. We stop for a minute and hug and get rained on, and I'm torn by the desire to kiss her, but I don't want to lead her on. I've already tried to tell myself that this isn't going to work, but genuinely I've just had the best date yet. We got on so well and at long last I've felt some chemistry with somebody, yet it's not right. What am I doing? Why am I feeling like this?

After what was probably too much deliberation we decide to go back to mine for a cup of tea to warm up before I walk her to the station, and because her stocking'd feet are wet I offer to rub them down with a towel, and then I end up giving her a foot massage. I'm doing all the wrong things if I want this to end easily. But we're still laughing, and she's still melting me with her eyes. And I'm totally, utterly confused.

Outside the tube station forty minutes later I bring the umbrella down. She's looking up at me and I kiss her ever so briefly. Her lips don't respond. She's still there, doe-eyed, standing close to me, blinking at me like a puppy dog would, and we hug, hold each other, but I don't move in again. She looks up at me for one final time and I can't tell whether we're standing too close for her to comfortably move away, or whether she wants me to try and kiss her again. But I don't, I peck her cheek and wink at her, and we go our separate ways. This has just moved into a whole different ballpark.

I can't stop thinking about Rosie all evening. I'm wired, head buzzing, grasping hold of the fact that finally I've met a girl who has made me stop and reconsider what I'm doing. I'm not even a third of the way through this challenge yet but should that matter? Is my unwillingness to believe that I could finish this challenge for this girl tied up in a self-indulgent need to prove that I can actually make it to the end? Or is the obvious smacking me in the head; Rosie was great company, beautiful, easy to talk to and like me doesn't place much importance in her footwear, but if she was really someone I wanted would The Hundred honestly get in the way? I'm not so sure.

Across Clapham my friends are clearly having a more simple time of it. Amanda tells me that after a date she had met a soldier on the tube and is considering going out with him despite his instant openness about the fact that he left the army through frustration, as he hadn't killed anyone in nine years. 'But he was hot!' remonstrates Amanda. Will also texts just before bed:

My date didn't go on for long because I was bored... fucking great food though!

Monday: Day 31
Dates No. 33 and 34

Piccadilly Circus is a scrum and I bustle through the melee, head down, a confused and baffled mess of a man. Yesterday, for the first time since The Hundred began, I met somebody who albeit briefly I could see myself being with, long-term. Ordinarily, had we met on a one-off date, I wouldn't have contemplated seeing anyone else, I would have met Rosie again and again until it was obvious that we should be together, or not. But here I am heading to another date, with another woman, my hand forced by the intensity of the challenge, and whilst I'm not doing anything wrong theoretically, emotionally I think I might be. At the risk of sounding like a complete drip, even without being convinced of any potential longevity with Rosie, I'm still doubting the ethics of going on another date when she's still in the back of my mind. What I'm doing may be making it easier for me to meet women, but is it holding me back from going further than just a first, cursory date?

Hannah, Date No. 33, only has one photo on her profile. It's taken from a side angle, blonde hair obscuring most of her face, but she seems very pretty. Her profile corroborates that:

> *Hannah is the girl that men point out when they see group photos and say 'wow, who's that?' Beautiful, petite, and with a legendary figure, she tends to stand out no matter what the crowd.*

However casual a guy is, that's quite a profile for a girl to live up to. I had no choice but to try my luck and see what all the fuss was about. She's a journalist, which for some reason excites me. We both write, and in some ways it feels like an automatic bond. She was brief in our initial message exchange and didn't give much away, but we slowly warmed up and when she suggested an afternoon coffee on Monday I jumped at the chance.

And there she is, in Leon at the bottom of Carnaby Street, standing at the counter with a red flight bag beside her; she's off to Slovakia straight after our date, she told me in her last message. She's beautiful, prettier in person than in her photo, and she smiles a lot as we decide on drinks. She recommends the house brownies. When they arrive I take the tray and she's off, walking in front, pulling her bag. I'm not sure if she did this on purpose, but the corridor is narrow and I'm two metres behind her, and she has an incredible figure. I swallow and collect my jaw off the floor. My God, I don't have a chance in hell with this woman.

For an hour and a half we sit, chatting, smiling, laughing. Her body language is good and positive, we're both slouching a bit but far legs are crossed over near and her toes are pointing right at me, wiggling a bit. It's mid afternoon on a Monday and it's not a romantic place, but we're on a rounded corner table and we're getting on well. I talk too much, overly carried away with my stories, saying 'it's a long story,' every bloody time I start telling another story. Oh God, don't blow this Dave. She's articulate, intelligent, funny and prettier every time I look at her. I can't help but compare her to Rosie and after all my doubts, the questioning, my fears about meeting Rosie and getting on so well then feeling guilty about meeting someone else so soon afterwards, well, those thoughts have instantly abated. I may have got on amazingly with Rosie, but Hannah and I are enjoying each others company and I realise that I wouldn't have turned down the chance to meet this girl for anything, or anyone.

Hannah tells me about the café's legendary brownies and sensing that she has a little too much knowledge about the biscuits, I ask if this is where she brings all her dates. She doubles up and somewhere under her blonde, cascading hair I can just about see her nodding! She's only had one before me, she says, a doctor who had an off-puttingly weird voice, and after admitting this she says, 'I can't believe I told you that this is where I came with him, I could have lied!' My heart is thrashing the inside of my chest when she excuses herself and makes for the toilet. I gulp down some hot chocolate and take a hold of myself; *Dave, calm down, she's just a girl, you're just a boy, just be cool. And if you can't be, just try a bit harder*. She emerges a minute later and stares at me. She isn't moving, she's just come out of the toilet door and is now paused in the middle of the café, some five metres away from our table. She's still there, eyes wide, but there's something in them now, I can't make out whether it's interest, or alarm. I glance at the other tables because it's not normal for someone in a small café to just stand still and not eat or drink. Especially when they're pointing, and that's exactly what Hannah is doing now. She has raised her arm, extended a finger and both are now in perfect alignment with my head. Or maybe, the bridge of my nose.

'You have brownie, there,' she says, emphasising the invisible line between her finger and my face. This isn't cool at all, I don't even want to know. Slowly, I turn and look in the mirror up on the wall to the side, and I have the biggest piece of chocolate stuck to my face, sitting there like an enormous brown Hindi spot. I turn back to Hannah with an expression so apologetic I probably look like I'm bearing bad news. She takes a seat beside me, a little further away than we'd become used to, and I thank her for being so officious in the food-on-face department. Inside, I'm screaming. What a rookie mistake, desperately sipping the dregs out of a hot chocolate, the rim of the cup leaving its mark on my head and making me look like a child at a birthday party. If I ever had a chance with No. 33, the hot chocolate and I just blew it, surely.

She needs to get to Luton so it's all over at half five, I hate that it's over. We walk to Oxford Circus and double cheek kiss before the gates. She's going North, I'm going South. She's going to Kings Cross, and then Luton, and then Slovakia for a four-day job. I'm going to Clapham, for another date. I don't care about the other date, I want to see Hannah again. Now, preferably. But I'm too scared to say that I'd like to see her again, and remember those awkward moments when others have said it to me and it was just, well, awkward. There's a chance (a good one, thinking about the chocolate forehead) that she has absolutely no desire to see me again, so I don't want to put her in a difficult position. But at the same time I'm hoping she's going to say 'hey let's hook up when I get back, and maybe we could get married next week,' but she doesn't. Instead, she spins away and then looks back over her shoulder.

'Take care,' she says, and then she's gone.

Exactly what does *take care* mean? That sounds like something I would say to a date I didn't want to see again. A sickly sensation rises as I step onto the escalator, and I stop and think about how I'm feeling. As the steps take me down into the earth I realise that if she had said, 'I really like you, let's spend some more time together, I think this could go somewhere,' then I would have stopped dating. Altogether. No more. I liked her *that* much. But in reality I have no idea whether she even wants to see me again, and my insecurities bulge within me and I tell myself I'm a fool for thinking I had a chance with her. All she said was 'take care,' it all seemed so final. For the second time in two days I'm terrified, but this time it's for a completely different reason.

Two hours later, having spent most of it dousing water on my face, I walk the twenty minutes to Clapham Old Town and spend it on the phone. First to Will, who has found a last minute date having been cancelled on by another, and is also heading to The Calf for the Monday quiz. Then I call Mette and tell her about the last two dates. When I talk about saying goodbye to Hannah and not telling her that I'd like to see her again, Mette tells me off. 'You should have told her,' she said matter-of-factly.

'But I didn't want her to feel awkward,' I said.

'Why would she feel awkward?'

'Well, if she didn't want to see me again, it would be very uncomfortable for her if I said there and then that I wanted to…'

'Well, if she didn't want to see you again then it wouldn't matter, would it.'

She has a point, and I know it, but I still think I abided by First Date Etiquette, and perhaps that involves a little bit of self-protection. By telling Hannah that I wanted to see her again I would have put her in a position to make it clear how she felt, and because that could have been negative, I wimped out. I could get hurt now, I think, and it scares the crap out of me. I tell Mette this, and she says that I could be putting other people in the same position.

'But that's dating,' I say. And thinking about it, it's true. I've already decided that nothing is going to happen with Rosie, and having had such a good time yesterday, will she be hurt by that? Maybe. I don't want to be putting people in that situation.

And it's my date with Nicola, which I was slightly apprehensive about considering the two dates preceding her, that highlighted the importance of a dating situation. Yesterday Rosie and I had hours together, on a Sunday. Plenty of time for drinks in one pub and then a meal in another. Time to recline on sofas. Time to bond. Hannah and I had barely an hour in a café, chatting over coffee. It wasn't intimate, and although we got on maybe it's impossible for a first spark to really jump during a date like that, where chemistry doesn't have the catalyst of alcohol, or food, or mood lighting. Or, even, time.

Speaking of time, Nicola is late, and she apologises several times for being so, but I don't mind. It starts off like a normal date, she's a friend of a friend and therefore knows about The Hundred, but the fact that she does barely comes up. Both of us laugh insanely about nothing at all and miss questions on the quiz because we're chatting so much and frankly, people only go to a pub quiz when they know each other and don't want to talk all the time. This is the first girl I've seen who I get through a whole date with having not talked about my little skating adventure purely because we're just enjoying each other's company. Perhaps it was because we were doing the quiz, maybe it was the fact that immediately I told her about the disaster with Date No. 18 and she instantly took a faux dislike to David the Quizmaster for 'stealing' her. Maybe it's because she already knew about my dating exploits and we had a commonality. Or maybe, against all odds, I'd just met another girl who made my pulse race, another girl who made me think about not dating anymore. 'What number am I?' Nicola asks me, and I look up at her,

'I'm not putting a number on you, Nic.'

She has dark hair and a twinkle in her eye and little freckles on her cheeks that almost seem to glow when she laughs. She looked very good in jeans, and had a kindness of spirit no more evident than when she talked about our mutual friend, 'I absolutely adore him,' she says, 'he's been like an angel to me.' Once the quiz had finished we pick up our drinks and settle into a vacated sofa, shoulder to shoulder, opposite legs crossed over near ones. At one point, just one, she puts her hand on my knee and then takes it off again, hovering for a moment before turning into a gesticulation. We talk about our childhoods and university and travelling and when she goes to the toilet I sit there warm and fuzzy, like a friendly pussy cat that's been stroked all day on a blanket next to an open fire. How is this happening?

Rosie aside, because although we had an amazing time I wasn't immediately ready to end what I was doing for her, I have just met two girls on the same day who I really want to get to know. Nicola and I leave, waving across the pub at Will and his date, who incidentally won the quiz while Nicola and I came somewhere towards the bottom – possibly because our team name was 'At Least The Quizmaster Didn't Steal My Date, This Time.' We leave the Calf and she quickly tucks her arm into mine. It fits. And we walk in the rain and talk about having wet jeans, and she tells me she has new sheets on her bed and about how skint she is because she's just had new windows put into her place, and when she asks me about how many dates I have for the rest of the week I want to turn to her and tell her I don't want to have any more dates. But I don't say that, because perhaps that would freak her out, or I'd just come across as being really bad at challenges. Or maybe because I feel some element of guilt for having been dating for over a month and then getting my favourite two dates both on the same day. I'm not sure, all I know is I feel like my instinct has kicked in and amongst the confusion I know that something has changed over the past two days. I went five weeks and met 32 different women, and then in one day I met two who have turned my head upside down.

Nicola and I pause on the south side of Acre Lane and I pass her umbrella back. We stand for what seems like minutes and don't do anything, but really it's just seconds and we're just there in each other's shadow, wondering what happens next. If she feels anything like me then it must be even more confusing. She leans in and kisses my cheek, so slowly, so close to my lips. I press my face into hers so we're cheek to cheek, then nose to cheek, and then I lower my head, I have no idea what to do.

'Good luck with the rest of your dates,' she says, as the rain drips off our noses. I don't want her thinking I want to go on any more dates and sigh, although it's more like a deep, heavy groan. I don't know what to do, I feel so lost and I just want to kiss her, but I don't. I should. But I don't.

And she kisses my other cheek before walking away.

'Be in touch,' she says, turning and smiling.

Lying in bed later a thought strikes me, something might be happening here, and there's a sentimental starting point that I want to save just in case anything happens with Nicola. So I send a text to David the Quizmaster:

> *Mate, I don't suppose you kept the quiz sheets from tonight?*

I fall asleep thinking how funny it would be if I could present a framed copy of our quiz sheet to Nicola on some special occasion a couple of years on.

Tuesday: Day 32
34 Dates so far

I'm floating around this morning, stuck between a perfect day yesterday and a long line of potential not-so-perfects to come. David texts me back, replying to my request about last night's sentimental quiz sheet:

> *Sorry mate, threw them away in the boozer. Sounds like it went well then!*

Great. At least it's the thought that counts.

Messages still arrive into my online dating inboxes and I shuffle through them, organising dates and continuing conversations, but it doesn't mean much anymore. My dates with Hannah and Nicola were so brief that I realise however well we got on I still don't know either of them. I don't know who they are, how they act in certain situations, I can't quite shape their faces in my mind. But as I write to more girls on My Single Friend I realise that I don't want to anymore, that I'm doing it half-heartedly because I honestly believe that yesterday I found someone, only I'm not sure which one it is that I've found. Physically I was closer to Nicola, but we had a more conducive evening date than the daytime coffee with Hannah. I want to get to know them both. But in the meantime, what do I do? The devil on my shoulder says that I felt something strong with Rosie, but then I met Hannah and Rosie faded a little, and then remarkably I met Nicola and Rosie was totally forgotten and maybe even Hannah faded a little, so what is there to say that I shouldn't continue, because perhaps there's still someone else out there who will make everyone else fade away? If the last couple of days have given me anything, it's the knowledge that the notion of just one person being out there waiting for you is romantic, but nonsense. How can we ever know that we've met the perfect partner? It's all a question of time and place. I wonder if my place was in The Calf at 8pm with No. 34, or slightly earlier in Leon on Carnaby St, with No. 33.

I sent Nicola a text late last night and there has been no reply, and I'm thinking about her so much I decide to email too.

> *Hello you, thought I'd send an email as well as a slightly sleepy text message. Had a really lovely time last night and would love to hook up again, if you'd like? I know you're a busy bunny but if you're at a loose end just let me know, wouldn't think twice about fobbing off a random date with a stranger to see you again! Challenge shmallenge. xx*

As the afternoon draws on I can do barely anything, all I'm hoping for is an email from Nicola saying *yes, I'd love to go out again.* But nothing comes and it begins to drive me mad. I had such a good time with her I just want to talk, to arrange another date. Instinct told me that she felt the same, so why isn't she getting in touch too?! I'm sat in my flat winding myself up and I need to start thinking about something else, this just isn't healthy. I have sent Hannah a message through MSF, too, but she's working in Slovakia and I'm not expecting her to be able to reply until the weekend at the earliest. And therefore my head returns to Nicola, who could be replying, but isn't.

A date with a lass from MySingleFriend falls through, but I couldn't give a hoot. And then almost at the same moment I get an email from Date No. 14. We've been messaging infrequently saying that we'll meet, and then making excuses, but I know heart of hearts that it's probably pointless us meeting in the sense of a prelude to romance, even though we had a very nice date and I ended up kissing her neck instead of her cheek. I liked her a lot, and ours was probably the best date I'd had up until then, except maybe the one with Jo. But I don't want things to become complicated, so we arrange a second date for tonight and I make up my mind to come clean and tell her about the book.

In the afternoon I'm half-tempted to text Date No. 14 and cancel our date, and after a bit of self-confessional I then decide to go on the date and do exactly what I was going to do in the first place, which was to be honest and open, and most of all, sensitive. I'm feeling vulnerable at the moment and more than ever I'm over-sensitive to the potential collateral damage of this dating challenge. Typically male, I'm only truly thinking about the concept of rejection because I am now at the mercy of two women who I'd stop dating for in a heartbeat. I have no idea how Date No. 14 feels about me, or any of the others for that matter, but now I have to be a grown-up and face the music. Either I shut off completely and ignore all future messages, or I man-up and tell No. 14 in person exactly what I'm up to.

So I did, almost. I told her I was writing a book about relationships and that it involved a whole lot of dating. It may have been down to nerves, but I didn't tell her about the 100 in 100 concept. I'm a coward. Still, I don't think it really matters because she seems fine about the idea of a book, and we chat about relationships and love and where we are in life when it comes to these enormous things. Date No. 14 is 3 years older than me and has a five year plan. She wants kids, and doesn't want to rush into a relationship with a father, and time is passing by. It puts our meeting into perspective and we both know it's clear that her five-year plan doesn't at all fit with my leanings towards adventurous freedom. But still we get on, and laugh, and be honest, and she tells me about the fact that she's practically the only one in her friendship group who isn't married. But I don't feel sorry for her, because she's beautiful and kind and intelligent, and sooner or later justice dictates that she's going to find her proverbial lobster.

Kate No. 27 forwards me a message sent to her by a man from the dating site, Stag and Dove, which may or may not be attracting a foreign audience: '*I want to have a nice freind and dove should be caring and know how to enjoy on weekend. Lets talk*

and find each other and meet if we like each other. Hope this beocmes
Christmas gift and I get a good light kiss. Waiting'

Walking home in the spitting rain, Jo calls me and we chat for an hour. She's reading my first book and asks me about my ex and why we split. I share the story and we realise that whatever physical attraction there is between us we'd much rather be friends for the long term than anything else. I tell her about the dates yesterday, and how stupidly wound up I've become about Nicola not replying, and Jo is perfectly right when she says that Nicola must be feeling odd (if she's feeling anything at all), because she knows about my dating and if she'd asked advice from a friend the friend would probably tell her to run a mile. If this is all confusing for me, then it must be awful for someone who likes me, you must they feel? I just hope she writes tomorrow, it's time for me to lay my heart on the line, and hope it doesn't scare the girl away.

Wednesday: Day 33
Dates No. 35 & 36

Nicola writes just after lunch:

> *I'm so sorry for taking ages to reply again!*
> *Thank you for the other night, I had a really nice time. Absolutely on for doing it again, but the next few weeks are really hectic for me with work. Let's do something in December once the nightmare is over and I get some time off. Sound ok to you?*
> *Hope you've had a good week since I saw you! Nicola x*

Now, I don't know how to feel. Having occasionally been a busy man myself, I know that however busy work is it's practically impossible to go two or three weeks without any spare time. Work is never so busy that you can't make time for someone you like, it's a cardinal rule of dating and 'I'm busy' is usually a metaphor for 'I don't want to see you'. But I can't accept that Nicola didn't feel something that night. She put her arm in mine. She even touched my knee, once! So maybe she's playing hard to get, or is enacting a bit of self-protection, which would be completely understandable. Or there is the chance that she doesn't actually want to see me and is just being nice in the hope that I'll have forgotten her name by December. Yes, we've only had one date, but for some reason this one date has me breathing a little heavier and thinking about nothing else. My main concern is that Nicola might like me, but is afraid to do anything about it and get involved with a guy who has another 60-odd dates to go on. If she doesn't then so be it, but if that is a possibility then I have to quash it right now. I think I have to tell her how I feel.

I stare at the screen, panicking slightly, this has to be done right:

> *Hello you,*
>
> *Thanks for writing back, I know you're busy!*
>
> *Without meaning to sound totally dotty (and also in the spirit of honesty!) I walked home in the rain on Monday having had the best night since...well, since this dating thing began. I'm not sure whether you've given it any thought, but I know the whole concept of the 100 in 100 is potentially a bit confusing and I just want to say that there's no doubt in my mind that if I meet the right somebody then I'm not going to carry on dating for the sake of a book. Honestly, Monday was the first time that I felt like packing it all in.*

> *I needed to get that off my chest, but don't worry,*
> *I'm not here to boil your bunnies! If you're not free*
> *'til December then of course I'll happily wait. If in*
> *the meantime a free night/ lunch slot comes up then*
> *let me know and I'll skate to Camden with bells on!*
> *Hope the nightmare calms down soon,*
> *Dave xx*

Send.

Oh God. Should I have put two kisses at the end? She only put one. Does it really matter? I know some friends who have had major dilemmas over the amount or lack of kisses they receive after a message, but I have a simple rule. I never kiss boys (unless they're very, very special), and I give all girls two kisses. There is one exception, when I'm with a girl, when she's my one, I only put one kiss. But I'm very aware that some people might read a little bit more into two kisses than they should. The strange and wonderful world of digital dating rears its ugly head again.

Last Sunday evening, after my date with Rosie, I was originally going to the pub quiz in the Windmill with Kate, Date No. 27. Instead, we decided not to do the quiz and to sit on the sofa and watch Top Gear and the Long Way Down. Before she left Kate laid a challenge on the table, 'this week you have to get a date with a complete stranger by approaching her in public.'

Sure thing, Kate, I'm not so sure that's going to happen, I don't have the balls to chat up a bird in a bar, let alone pick up a girl on the tube. Still, the challenge forgotten I continued with the week, and this evening found myself walking towards Starbucks in Clapham Common, the suggested meeting place with Date No. 35. In her picture she looks great, and her profile echoes this

My friend is a stunning, 5'7'', long haired brunette with blue eyes. She has a slim build and great legs! But best of all she has an amazing personality.

Outside Starbucks there is a girl waiting, brunette, slim, kind of like the photo. She looks at me then looks away, 'ah right, not her then.' We stand there for about three minutes at opposite sides of the café frontage, tapping feet, looking around, and eventually I sidle over and ask her name. She's not my date, but she laughs. After a moment of silence, I turn my head and say, 'So, waiting for a date?'

She nods.

'First date?'

She nods again, but this time she looks at me as though I've been stalking her.

'My Single Friend?'

'Yes!'

Brilliant! I have this strange sensation that for the first time in my life I've just found something in common with a complete stranger who I ordinarily wouldn't have spoken to. A wave of cheekiness comes over me,

'Well, if our dates don't turn up fancy going on one together?!' She laughs, maybe a little nervously, and then it's all silent for a while. Something in me snaps and the cheek comes out again, 'hey, I'd ask for your number but if your date comes it could be a bit embarrassing! My name's Dave, by the way.'

She tells me hers, but it goes straight in my left ear and out the right. 'Lovely to meet you,' I say, slowly sidling back over to my waiting point. This is hilarious! Two people, both having agreed to meet first dates from the same website outside the same café. What are the chances? I'm starting to get nervous, gearing myself up to take a chance. I think I should ask for this girl's number, but realise I've already forgotten her name, and it wouldn't go down at all well if I asked again, so I dig into my pocket and pry a business card from my wallet. Crab-like, I move sideways towards her. 'Hey, I know this is a bit odd, but if you ever fancy a drink...' I pause, 'or just if you want to let me know how your date goes!'

Someone clears a throat nearby. It's a male throat, and they've got quite a lot of clearing to do considering the noise they're making. How rude, I think, people should really do clearing like that in their own homes. But then it becomes clear, there's a man standing right next to the girl whose name I've forgotten, and he's awkwardly waiting for her to notice him, because her attention has briefly been taken by a business card.

Seconds later they've gone, and although that was a mighty embarrassing situation I can't help but feel like my balls have just grown a little.

By ten past eight I get the feeling I'm going to be stood up, but at quarter past I spy a woman walking along the pavement on the opposite side of the road, and I instantly recognise the cheekbones. Date No. 35 is indeed, gorgeous. But as she crosses the road and gets a bit closer it seems like something's wrong, I just can't place it. We stand face to face on a traffic island, do some kind of weird air-kiss down the side of each other's heads, and then she speaks. It's awful to say it, but she sounds like a deaf person. 'Excuse me,' I say, leaning in, 'Mwah wah wah,' she says, and I feel my heart sinking into my trouser legs.

You can tell within 10 seconds whether a date is going to be fun or not and this date is going to be bloody awful. No. 35 walks a little bit like Bambi with a limp and my ears are straining to make any kind of sense when she says something. This is hideous. She seems so discernibly self-conscious and socially wonky it makes me just a little bit mad. Just for a moment there I wonder whether I've been set up by Will, or Jeremy Beadle, and then I realise that Jeremy Beadle's dead and Will can't have had anything to do with it because I was the one who contacted No. 35 in the first place. When she speaks she holds a hand in front of her mouth, which just isn't funny when lip-reading would be the only way I could possibly understand her. Meanwhile, my pocket is buzzing every ten minutes as Jo sends me football updates of the

England vs Croatia qualifying game, which just reminds me of what I'm missing. Date No. 35 and I have nothing in common whatsoever, and I'm a little bit cross at whoever wrote her MySingleFriend profile because it was all a blatant lie. There is no possible way that this girl has a wide social circle, or is a high-flyer in the city – you need communication skills for that! She might play the oboe, and I'm sure it's conceivable that she's capable of keeping fit even if her circuit training might be limited by her limp, but I feel as though I've been duped. The only obvious truth is that she's very good-looking, but you can't get to know someone by sitting back and staring at their bone structure.

I have no idea how Date No. 35 feels about me, because if she has made anything clear it just sounded like 'mwahh war war muhuew,' so when she goes to the toilet everything goes slow-mo, I see my coat at my feet, then realise the door is just inches away. I see the street! The outside! Freedom! Even on the worst dates so far I haven't actively considered dashing though the back door, and as I begin to reach down towards my stuff I stop, because even though I desperately want to leave it's just not fair on anyone to come back to an empty table. Not even this one.

'Hah mwarny dartes harve yar bern ern?' she asks, and I pause, disseminating the information. How. Many. Dates. Have. You. Been. On? What the fuck is wrong with her voice?! Right. I have a little think and realise she is the 35th, so I say,

'oh, not many, three...four,' not adding an *or* in between the figures but knowing she'll never think that by three...four I actually mean thirty-four. It was temping to add, 'and you're the worst by a long shot, and definitely the only one who sounds like Chunk from The Goonies,' but she looked quite pretty sat there on a stool and I decided to tell a long story so she wouldn't open her mouth for a while. The service in the bar is exemplary but it's totally impractical for a situation like this. When our glasses have a full inch of fluid remaining a lady approaches and asks with a smile;

'would you like another one?' Date No. 35 looks a bit scared, but I have to be blunt,

'Shall we call it a night...' I say, without a question mark. No. 35 nods.

'No thank you, may we have the bill,' I say to the waitress, who spins and struts away. Sometimes there's just no point in making life more difficult for yourself.

I'm actually quite angry at all of this. I'm not exaggerating about her speech impediment, not one bit. Fair enough, we all try to sell ourselves on these websites, but at some stage the creative licence has to be reigned in, because when you meet somebody in person it's no holds barred. No. 35's voice didn't affect me like a strange, grating accent, it literally didn't make any sense and it wasn't fair. Again, MySingleFriend, voice file, please.

After we say goodbye I check my phone. England have lost and there's no Euro 2008 for them, or the country. But there is a text from an unknown number, and it reads:

> So... how's your date going? Mine's not so good so might have to make some excuse to leave soon! Poppy.

The girl from Starbucks! Poppy! That's her name! I text back, saying I'd just finished mine and that it was worse than a bag of spanners falling on my head. Fancy a quick drink? I ask. She replies a minute later:

> I've just left and was going to head home, but could have another one!

Bullseye! We beam at each other as I walk into the bar. She's sitting there legs crossed with olive skin and big brown eyes and I realise I know even less about this girl than the other strangers I've dated, this one was literally found on the

163

street. 'I feel very naughty doing this,' I say, failing miserably to hide my grin, and she smiles right back, 'I know!' I slump onto the bench beside her and we discuss the dates we've just shared. 'He was just so boring,' said Poppy, 'it's so true what they say about accountants, he just went on and on and on about what he had on his desk at work.'

'At least you could understand him,' I said.

'True, I'm not sure who got the worst end of the stick'

'This is quite weird,' I say, 'turning to her, 'I have absolutely no idea who you are. I know we're always meeting strangers through this website but we do at least get to find out a little bit about them before committing ourselves.'

'Yeah,' she says, 'not that that helps, if it did we'd be able to avoid all the bad ones.'

'So true! Ok, so in this instance we haven't had a chance to lie to each other on MySingleFriend in the hope that our untruths will be attractive enough to date, so we have a totally clean slate. All I know is that you like hanging around Starbucks, you don't like accountants, and you're not too timid to text a stranger who you met on a street corner.' She giggles and says,

'Well all I know about you is that you don't like spanners falling on your head, and that you've got rubbish timing when it comes to giving a girl your business card.'

'At least I gave it to you! You don't know how hard that was for me.'

'Well, I'm glad you did, at least we'll have a funny story to tell our friends when we get home tonight.'

It hadn't seemed possible a couple of hours ago, but the evening actually worked out quite well. Not only had I unknowingly managed to succeed in the challenge Kate had set me the other night, I'd also managed to get two dates for the price of one, and thankfully all of the action had briefly stopped me thinking about Nicola. Poppy and I had chatted away, discovered that we both went to Swansea University, she even read my column in the newspaper, and we share a mutual friend or two. Laughing at the oddity of it all, we updated each other on the stats that we would have known had we met online, and we reassured each other that meeting outside a coffee shop was probably a good way to avoid having a totally awful first date. We had a good laugh, but only stayed for one drink and didn't really have much of a spark. She did invite me to a party at hers this weekend, but I had a feeling that it was more out of politeness than a desire to ignite a relationship, and anyway, I'll probably have a date or three. There was no fairytale ending, but I might just have gained some confidence to ask a total stranger out on a date in future.

Thursday: Day 34
36 Dates so far

I wake up feeling exhausted and unhappy, and not quite sure where to go from here. I'm really looking forward to seeing Nicola again but it feels all very up in the air – 'sometime in December' is a long way away and not very specific. Maybe I shouldn't feel as cooped up as I do, but I think I'm suffering from a well-known feeling, the symptoms of love-sickness are showing. Now, hold your horses. I'm not tearing my eyes out, crying in the shower, ripping up letters and setting fire to the pieces with a lighter. I'm just a bit empty; thoughts like these are parasitical. In a very small way I fell for not one but two people on Monday and not knowing that either situation is mutual eats away at my gut. I know I'm being irrational and that I shouldn't read too much into anything, but I've worked myself up into a stupor and feel a little lost. It's having a real impact on me. I now feel more lonely than ever.

The power of things unsaid (my goodbye with Hannah) and the risky unknown dangers of expressing your feelings (second email to Nicola) are just two new pitfalls I'm facing during this challenge. Everything is different: I'm following the path of a bastard, but I'm essentially a good and honest guy, trying to deal with it all in the best way possible. I'm a nice guy in wolf's clothing, and I'm not sure how I feel about that. I'm not quite within touching distance of halfway and I'm already worn out. I feel like I'm not quite on my toes and have become so focused on finding and going on dates that I've actually left a little bit of myself behind, and if that's true then surely I'm not able to be myself when I meet girls. Monday enabled me to sniff an end to all this, yet the end still couldn't seem further away.

Friday: Day 35
Date No. 37

I feel so low today, almost like my heart is broken. It's utterly ridiculous; I've just got emotional man-flu. Didn't see this coming, I've dated thirty-six girls and suddenly I'm coming apart at the seams. Females are dangerous. They know it. The rest of them probably sent Hannah and Nicola along to mess with my head. I try to make sense of the muddle with the tiny parts of my brain that are still functioning. Undoubtedly, I have too much time on my hands. Work, sport, friends; they've all taken a hit since I started dating. I quit my football team, don't have time to meet my mates, all I do is date and then think about it. If adults have to adopt their new partner's lives when they get together how the hell am I going to sell my life to anyone? I just sit on a sofa and arrange dates then obsess about body language. Yes, I'm low because of Nicola, who I want to have an about turn and invite me out tonight, and the next, and the next. And yes, I want to hear from Hannah, who is now back from Slovakia and has just sent a short message, but didn't mention going out again. Where Nicola is concerned, a lack of contact is never a good sign, whatever anyone says you never play hard to get if you really like someone, there's no three-days-before-you-call rule if instinct tells you that a long-termer is on the cards. I almost feel as though it's over when it hasn't even started, and although I suppose there's still every chance it could still go somewhere with either Nicola or Hannah, I'm just being impatient and over-emotional and I'm really not dealing with it very well.

I have to be realistic with myself, perhaps part of my current predicament is down to my wanting to speed everything up. Dating a different woman every day isn't fun, it's exhausting! For a whole month I was dating dating dating and had barely a sniff of relationship potential. Even if mutual attraction did poke its lovely head around the almost-as-important biological connection now and then, it was barely worthy of a reaction. Then two sparks came along all at once and I got excited. As the days go by the intensity of my feelings for Nicola, and to a lesser extent, Hannah, decrease. The simple fact: I don't know either of them. I haven't heard back from Nicola since I told her how I felt and in truth I should really look at the cold bare facts. We spent just a couple of hours together, hit it off, then said goodbye. I don't know her, I'm not sure how busy she is, how many social engagements she has, even whether she is actually looking for somebody. All I know is I liked her a lot, she's a wonderful, honest, kind person, and I want to see her again. I felt lucky to meet her, but pepped myself up so much about our chemistry the reality that she won't see me until December didn't initially seem to be anything but confusing. But actually, perhaps it's obvious; if she did really like me she probably wouldn't be happy to wait a few weeks before seeing me again, busy or not.

Ultimately, I can't try and get inside Nicola's head, I just have to get on with things and do what I feel is right. I have a 4pm coffee date with a girl called Anna, who lives in East Dulwich and runs her own make-up/ hairstyling business.

Our online conversation didn't dandy around the boring stuff, in her first message she sent this list of questions, always a brilliant way to circumvent any formal nonsense and judge a person's sense of humour:

Anna - Do you have any brothers and sisters?
Dave - I have one brother, he's 24 and a jet pilot!

Anna - *Do you wear pink?*

Dave - *I once wore a pink tie for a breast cancer awareness party. But it's not a habit.*

Anna - *Do you use an electric or normal toothbrush?*

Dave - *I used to be electric, but now I'm all normal.*

Anna - *Do you like tomatoes?*

Dave - *Love tomatoes! I eat them on their own, like an*   *apple.*

Anna - *Do you dance (in front of bedroom mirror/on pubs tables/ballroom)?*

Dave - *I am probably the worst dancer in the world and try not to impose it on anyone. But now and then I do a quick two-step when nobody's looking.*

Anna - *Do you like dogs/cats/jellyfish/jelly sweets?*

Dave - *I'm a cat person, try to avoid jellyfish, and have an unhealthy fondness for jelly sweets.*

Anna - *Is there any point in these questions? Probably not, but I thought I should make an effort to know a little more!*

It took maybe two days for her to send the following:

Good news, my accountant tells me that I have enough money to have coffee with nearly, but not total strangers, who hold a minimum of three world records and have a taste for red fruit beginning with t. Do you know anyone who fits those requirements?

My reply:

Hmmm, hold on, I'll just ask my mate...He's not picking up. Will I do?

Although the conversation had been marvellous I wasn't sure what to expect from her photos but when she walks in I'm a little taken aback. She has a coy smile and sparkly eyes, amazing curly hair (I know I'm in trouble now!) and there's a bit of style about her, which I guess you'd expect from a stylist. It takes us almost an hour to finish our lattés and it feels like we've barely started. A bottle of rosé hits the table and I study her as she talks. She's sorted, knows herself, loves her family and talks intelligently. She's very open about personal stories and details; whether that's because we've hit it off and she trusts me, or because of the liberty of talking to a total stranger, I'm not sure. Crazily, I can see myself fitting into her life – her three year old nephew sounds brilliant, and her enthusiasm for him rubs off and I want to meet him. This is one of those dates where I believe there is chemistry in the air, I'm just not sure where it's coming from. I can't work out whether I'm attracted to her. There are times when I'm not, and others when she looks positively gorgeous. Her profile photos don't do her justice; they don't show her eyes, the cheekbones, the lust for life! She talks and talks and I get the feeling she's interested in my story but not really in me, I'm talking for 15%, maybe 20% of the time and she fills in the rest, but she tells a good story and I'm happy to listen without really knowing where the date is going. She takes a call from her mum and starts chatting to her and I wonder about it, is it rude or a hint to me, maybe a pre-planned call designed to lead the date towards a conclusion? I visit the toilet and return to find her chatting to the people on the next table, she's certainly not shy about striking up a conversation.

We move on to a pub and start getting into the drinks. She's still on rosé and I'm now doing the gin and tonics, always mindful of Saturday afternoon football, clearly! We chat away but her body language isn't quite right, her shoulders are turned away from me and there's a wide space between us, and I'm quite sure that she just likes the company. The thing is, even though I've spoken about ten words in the last two hours, I like the company too. She's an enigma, this one, and I want to get to the bottom of it.

'Do you dance?' she asks me, and I look at her sideways. Basically, no, I can't dance, and I know it. I tell her this, and she tells me everyone can dance, and I tell her to hold on as I get my book out of my bag and show her the paragraph about my not being able to dance. Yes, I dance so badly I've written about it.

'Oooh get you with your book,' she says, but laughs at the chapter and accepts that we're not going dancing tonight. It's important to note here that I don't take a copy of my book to every date!

We play table football and she's hilarious, swearing like a trooper. I double up in laughter and somehow manage to head butt the table. It's like tripping in the street, I looked up at her and then around the bar and no one seemed to have noticed, so we carried on and finished the game, then sat down, and then I wandered to the toilet. And there in the mirror was me, a little drunk, blood spilling out of a cut on my forehead, running down my nose, dripping in the sink. I can't quite believe this. A few days ago Hannah came out of the toilet to find my forehead handsomely littered with chocolate, and now I've just made myself bleed by banging my head against a table and there's a little bit too much blood for Anna not to have seen, which raises a question, why the hell didn't she say anything?! I dab away at the cut until the blood seems to have abated, wash my face, then go back out to find Anna happily chatting with a couple of strangers. I ask her whether she saw me bleeding, thanking the dim lights for putting my blushing cheeks in shadow, but she denies all knowledge. She's now stripped off to a white vest and perhaps it's the alcohol talking, but suddenly there's no question whether I'm attracted to her or not. I'm busying myself by trying to work out how this incredibly stylish girl is now showing a completely different side to her dress sense when, just as I'm starting to melt a little she turns to me and says, 'look, this might seem a bit weird but in the spirit of honesty, you're a nice guy, but what I really notice about you is how similar you look to my ex. Your colouring, your height, your blue eyes…'

Well, after that, I didn't know where to look. Whether it had been said or not, I felt like that was just a confirmation that we weren't going anywhere. It wasn't as if I'd fallen for this girl, she just had something and I couldn't work out what. By now midnight had passed and I was ready to go, but Anna and I found ourselves side by side again and I realised I'd slightly misread her comments about my appearance. She still had more, though,

'Your jumper is horrible,' she told me. Now, I'd worn this green jumper for a lot of my dates, it was old and bobbled but very me, very casual. And here was this girl telling me it was horrible. She felt so strongly about the subject that she physically took it off me and threw it across the floor! I couldn't quite believe her chutzpah, but kind of admired it. She's a feisty one, and with the clock dragging on and the alcohol taking effect we found ourselves kissing, laughing.

'Whatever happens between us,' she says, 'can we please be friends. I think you're an amazing person and I'd really like to show you off to my friends.' I kissed her some more, after that.

At half past two in the morning, more than ten hours since we embarked on our date, I find myself outside her front door. We pause; this could go two ways now. She's lovely, has amazing curly hair, a great body, kisses like a dream, I really shouldn't be thinking twice about this but I'm already questioning whether I was doing the right thing by kissing this girl when the matters with Hannah and Nicola remained unresolved.

'You want some toast?' Anna asks.

I actually do, I'm starving, but I have football tomorrow and two other girls sitting on my shoulder, so I shake my head. And besides, when someone asks if you want some toast, there's a chance that there's some butter on offer, too.

'I have toast back at my place,' I say, reluctantly, 'and a couple of hours to sober up for a football match.'

'Oh,' she says.

'Keep me entertained at the bus stop?' I ask. So she does. And twenty-five minutes later when the bus rounds the corner,

Anna picks up my longboard and runs away. The bus drives straight past and I look at the girl in disbelief. It could be so easy to stay now, go up to her room, have some toast, get a bus in the morning. I walk over to her, never losing eye contact. She looks up at me with puppy dog eyes, smiling at her own deviousness. I reach out with my left hand and take the board, then kiss her cheek.

'Thanks for a lovely night,' I whisper, then step onto my board and skate off down the road.

Maybe I'd just spurned an opportunity; there were certainly times in my past when toast with Anna would have been a foregone conclusion. I knew though, that I couldn't stay, however tempting it was. I'm not sleeping with anyone else until I'm ready, things are already complicated enough as they are. Plus, I think that if anything is going to happen with Anna and I, then not sleeping with her on the first night really isn't going to do us any harm.

Saturday: Day 36
Date No. 38

At half past seven I find myself in a bar on Northcote Rd waiting for Date No. 38. I've been chatting to her online for a couple of weeks and have been looking forward to meeting her. She's a freelance writer, seems very funny and intelligent, and good looking to boot. She's fifteen minutes late but I don't mind, I'm in a nonchalant mood now and after last Monday feel I have nothing to lose and everything to gain. Yes, Hannah and Nicola are still on my mind, but for all I know those dates may turn out to be pie in the sky and there might be someone else waiting right around the corner.

Date No. 38 and I have a couple of drinks and chat away, laugh and tell stories, connect on a professional level but without any chemistry showing its hand. The bar is dark and candlelit but romance couldn't seem further away, and as the clock ticks on I start to stare at Date No. 38's head (which, by the way, is covered with some wonderful curly hair) and realise it bounces around as she talks. It makes me dizzy, so goodness knows how she feels, and I start to drift away, thinking about Nicola, about Hannah, about how quickly you can feel the chemistry when it's there, and how stark a date is without it I can't help feeling a little bit of sadness when I meet a girl like Date No. 38 who was so sharp and witty on email, but in person isn't right for me. It's another date down, but I'd much rather it offered promise rather than two hours of small talk and then a black hole. When our second drinks are finished I suggest we make a move and Date No. 38 appears a little taken aback.

A singe of guilt lines my throat but although she has shown signs of being interested we have no chemistry and I don't feel like dragging it on for the sake of it. There's a quick goodbye and we go our separate ways, and as I skate across the common I wish I wasn't doing what I'm doing.

Sunday Day 37
38 Dates so far

Another weekend where the days grow and the dates don't. I try in vain to secure a last minute rendezvous with a strange woman, *any* strange woman, and although I already have three meetings settled for next week the weekend remains bare. Anna, Date No. 37 texts me:

> *Friends: absolutely. You are wonderful. Lovers, I don't know, but just to be in your life would be a rare treat. I'm so pleased we met. Thank you for a special evening x*

Tonight Kate (No. 27) comes over. Most of Top Gear and the Long Way Down goes by without us watching any TV, and instead I fill her in on the week of dating and we discuss questions about the challenge that Kate has thought up. She sets me new ways to organise dates – falling off my board as I pass someone, dropping my book at their feet, helping a lost tourist out. And she stresses that I really need to place a Lonely Hearts ad in The London Paper. I tell her about Hannah and Nicola and most recently, Anna and how I skated away at the end of Friday's date rather than stay and play,

'Staying with Anna would have just added to the complications,' I shared, 'I surprised myself, usually I wouldn't have thought twice, but now I'm learning more about myself I realise it's ok not to drop your pants on the first date.' Kate understands, but she seems to think that sleeping with one in thirty-eight dates is a pretty poor hit rate. Lucky I'm not playing baseball. I ask her what she thinks about Rosie and I not being in touch. We had such a good date but since then there's been no contact. For me, it's because I met two girls I liked more just a day later, and I didn't think it was right of me to get in touch and say,

'Hey, had a great time but I met someone else.' It's probably best left unsaid, right? On the other hand, is Rosie not writing because she's waiting for me to do so, or because she too has been on another date and found someone she liked better, too? It is the twenty first century now and I'm on the fence when it comes to the expectations of men and women on dates. There's nothing wrong with expecting some traditional chivalry from a bloke, but at the same time we didn't have mobile phones in the forties. If nobody gets in touch after a date, can either have any complaints that nothing has happened?

I canvas Kate's opinion on Nicola, who still hasn't written, and neither of us can reach a conclusion on why she hasn't been in touch. I've been worried that perhaps my reply on Wednesday has scared her away, but Kate makes a point, 'even if she is busy, I can't see why she can't take the time to reply to such a lovely message.' At least she thinks it's lovely, not scary. I've been concerned all week that maybe I was a bit full-on by telling Nicola how I felt, but with four more days passing without hearing from her I'm starting to draw conclusions. Either she simply doesn't want to see me again, or she does, but is put off by the dating challenge. Right now, there's not much more I can do about that.

Monday: Day 38
Dates No. 39 & 40

It's been a week since I met Hannah, a week since I met Nicola, and I still no sign of a second date from either. How depressing. I need to start dating again though and after an empty weekend have a bit more life in me, and I've racked up a lunch date for today. I meet Date No. 39 in London Bridge and have a very pleasant meal with mulled wine. She's quite a straight girl but I sense there's a dry sense of humour lying in wait somewhere, plus a couple more surprises. She has a laugh like Marge Simpson and hails from Boston in Lincolnshire. I look wistfully into the distance while saying,

'Boston it has a catchphrase, a tagline….it's coming to me. Oh, yes! Boston, Lincolnshire, the Home of Incest…' Luckily she laughs. It's an odd date, not least because in a month she's going travelling, for a year.

'Has My Single Friend been so bad that you need to go away for that long?' I ask cheekily, but in all honesty it's nice not to have any pressure. Basically, she wanted to meet me so she could pick my brains about her travel destinations, and I thank my lucky stars that there's no attraction there otherwise I probably would have felt quite cheated. We have a little hug before she heads to an early afternoon meeting, and she apologises a little too much for having to leave so soon. She reminded me an awful lot of my primary school beau Sophie Smith, on who I had an almost indecent crush on despite a savage bout of pneumonia. Thank goodness I've grown up, clearly beyond the crush stage now!

I find a pub in London Bridge and work all afternoon on the laptop, I have another date in the area at 6pm and there's no use going home and then coming back. Date No. 40 cancelled on me last week and I'm not at all sure about her from her picture, but she seems cheeky and sparky and she might be worth another go.

When she walks in I instantly know it's not going to work. Call me petty but I can't get past her nose. Literally. It's like an eclipse has just walked in. She's a bright girl who lives south of the city, an hour-long commute away, and she has a funny habit of sucking in a long, hard sniff and wiping her nose. Tell tale sign of a cocaine addict, but because her nose is abnormally large in the first place I can't tell whether her nostrils are naturally the size they are, or inflated by a hobby. She has a great laugh, though, one she supplements by banging the table simultaneously with her hands from above, and knees from below. She catches me off guard by asking if I want another drink and as we'd only been there for twenty-five minutes I had to say yes.

'What would you like?' she asks,

'I'll have a…coke!' I say. She looks at me sternly, flared her nostrils and stood up.

'A coke it is, excellent choice.'

You have to be kidding me.

There is absolutely no chemistry with No. 40 and I know a date is going nowhere when the only saving grace is that I'm one date closer to finishing, but I'm sick of them now. Besides, this afternoon Hannah suggested we meet up again in a couple of days, and I just can't concentrate on anything else. From deep within, I'm feeling butterflies starting to stir.

Tuesday: Day 39
Date No. 41

I'm flipping exhausted this morning, but am cheered up by an email from yesnomayb.com, and they've decided to use my photo on their newsletter. In return for my facial generosity they've given me a free elite membership, which basically means I can talk to everyone on the site for free, even those tight girls who haven't signed up. Jo calls and I tell her the good news. She pipes up about how good my photo is, and then seamlessly starts to talk about how people never look like their profile photos.

With no dates on the cards I decide not to stay indoors. I'm not getting any satisfaction from online dating at the moment, even though hundreds of new people sign up every week I've sent messages to every woman who appears to be pleasant and frankly, I'm not learning anything new from the experience. There's only so long a man can spend staring at his computer screen waiting for a potential date to ping into his inbox, it's time to hit the streets and try to find Date No. 41.

I've never done this before, has anyone? I bought a Day Travelcard and jumped on the first bus I came across. I started in Clapham and went north to Trafalgar Square. I wasn't really sure what to do with myself, any woman who caught my eye seemed to be walking somewhere and I hadn't prepared myself to talk a potential date, so I opted for buses because talking on public transport is such a taboo in London, and I fancied a chance to break it. I moved towards the back of a bus heading east, and sat where there are seats facing each other. They were empty until two young lads with hoodies sat down for a few minutes, both nodding simultaneously to the offerings of a shared iPod. For half an hour I watched the doors, waiting for someone interesting to step on board, and then, finally, there she was.

In all honesty, I hadn't expected to meet someone today. It's not unheard of for attractive women to ride buses in London, but it is unheard of for me to try and talk to them in the vain hope of getting a date, least of all succeeding. The girl was short, maybe 5'3", and wore a long black leather coat. In fact, apart from her pale white skin and bright red lips, she was all black; hair, tight neckband, fingernails, and the shoes. And what shoes! It was mid afternoon and this woman was dressed for some kind of sexy vampire party. Being male I've always struggled to accurately define the true length of an inch, but the heels on her shoes were so slim I'm surprised they could support even a small human, and they were at least six inches long. She took a seat two rows in front of me on the other side of the bus, and started playing with her phone.

There comes a time in everyone's life when they have to face a fear and do something that scares them. This was my time. I was terrified of what I was about to do, mainly because rejection is never nice, but rejection from a girl with high heels that big just drives home the fact that you're a total loser. But hey, I'm not sure my pride or dignity has survived the last 39 days, so what have I got to lose? I figured it would look strange if I appeared from the back of the bus so stood up, shuffled to the front just as we were approaching a stop, waited for people to get on and then walked confidently back to the girl's row, and sat down beside her. She didn't even glance up from her phone. Here I am, all confident (a bit), the epitome of a Dating Cowboy.

Of course, I had no idea how long My Little Vampire would be on the bus, so time was of the essence. Naturally, this contradicted the urge to sit there and not say anything, which would have been much easier. Instead, I waited until she appeared bored of her phone and said the first thing that jumped into my head,

'Nice shoes.'

It was like her head was on a revolving platter. A gothic owl! It spun slowly towards me, big eyes with heavy mascara'd lashes, but hold on, *blue* eyes! Her face was beautifully round and hair just fell around her face, bunching on the shoulders.

'You like them?' she asked with a smirk.

Having expected nothing more than a grunt I was quite taken aback, partly because she'd actually looked at me, and also because she was remarkably well-spoken and didn't hiss at all. I've always relied on a bloody awful attempt at humour to save my skin in an embarrassing situation.

'Well, they look lovely, but I'd imagine they're quite impractical for an average day's work.' I said. She smiled with those blood red lips, and said,

'I guess that depends on the work.'

Who is this strange flirty woman wearing bondage gear? She's brilliant! I should talk to girls on buses more often! I opened my eyes wide in mock surprise,

'I guess you're right, how silly of me.' And then I decided to be cheeky. 'So, have you finished work for the day?'

In reality, these conversations shouldn't really ever take place, not between strangers. Not on a bus. Not ever. But life recently hasn't been normal for me and it seemed that things were set to continue, because her next line surprised the hell out of me, mainly because I'd been sat next to her for less than two minutes.

'Would you like a drink?'

Excuse me. Did you just ask me out on a date, Miss Vampire? I think you did!

'I was just about to ask the same, where are you headed?'

'Home, ages away,' she said, 'let's get off now.'

So we did. Me and the girl with the six-inch heels that just about made her my height walked into the nearest pub, and she ordered a Guinness.

'You don't look like the typical guy who chats me up,' she said as we sat down, 'are you a good listener?'

'I can be,' I said. And I wish I hadn't, because for the next fifty minutes I barely said anything apart from 'hmmm' and 'ahhh', and they weren't exactly heartfelt. I'd chosen to talk to a depressed part-time dominatrix part-time burlesque dancer, who hated her jobs and wanted nothing more than to break away and get a desk job.

'It's just so demeaning,' she moaned, 'these little white bald men about eighty years old asking for a whipping.'

'Why do you do it, if it's so bad?'

She grunted. 'The money is fucking brilliant. I love the dancing, it's liberating and none of the cash-in-the-knickers stuff, it's just the prancing around for sad old men that I hate. I've never been able to find a boyfriend that would accept me for who I am, it's too hard. If you were in my situation, what would you do?'

I wanted to say, *I'd get freaked out pretty quickly if I were walking around wearing that,* but instead went for the age-old, 'I think I'd try and do something that makes me happy.'

'Oh, don't think I haven't tried, but without the money I'm just miserable, so I go back. I'd rather be paid well to be miserable than not at all.'

As she talked she played with her hair constantly, twisting it around her finger, becoming more and more vacant as she convinced herself before me into how happy she was doing what she was doing compared to other options, like getting a proper job. Even after an hour she'd drunk barely half of her pint, always a fine measure of ones ability to talk the hind legs off a part-time prostitute. It had been an experience, I'd picked up a woman on a bus and at the same time realised that a theoretical male fantasy involves absolutely no talking whatsoever, which should have been predictable. Not at one point did she tell me her name, or ask mine, and I left feeling pretty sorry for her. I rode the tube home, casting my mind back to every face I'd seen and story I'd heard in the past few weeks. Is it healthy to expose yourself to so many people in such a short space of time, with so many of the meetings ending abruptly, often so final? Is it too much to ask for something to last, just for a change? On the other hand, what exactly was I hoping for, one hundred simultaneous relationships?

Wednesday: Day 40
Dates No. 42 & 43

I get the feeling Date No. 42 is a bit different even before I meet her. One of her pictures shows her inline skating in Hyde Park, and she recognised me as the Guy who Skated Britain from one of my photos, but still decided to make a point of not giving me her number before we met:

> *If you don't mind, I'm not going to give you my number, and I won't save yours... I'll just take it in case I get held up. If you're running late, don't worry. I'll wait - just not forever :)*

Ok then.

It's not a big deal, but it's always nice to have a point of contact in case of delay or emergency. Add that to the fact that Date No. 42 has been on my website and clearly knows I'm not going to stalk her, she seems very cagey and protective. In person, once I've navigated a rather busy lunchtime Embankment Station, I find that she's very small and well formed, but with a blustery blunt air to her. I actually quite like the girl and we laugh a fair bit, but it doesn't take long for her to come out with the following:

'My friends and I were on your website, and they looked at me and said, 'this guy seems quite driven. And you're not driven at all. It's not a good start.'

'Shall we just leave now?' I said, flicking my thumb towards the door. She decides against that and tells me she was born in Sidcup,

'which isn't in Essex,' she adds, pointedly. She went straight from college into work and now she's in her fifth year as a PA in the city. She has a flat and a cat, and can't see herself ever giving them up. Not ever. 'I just don't have any ambition,' she says, again, 'I have what I have and I'm happy with that.' She tells me she went to Australia once, because she thought she might want to move there. 'I came home after ten days,' she says, 'I was really lonely.'

Despite how it may seem, we actually got on quite well. She was wearing boots (I love boots, especially with heels) and when she showed me I purred. Yes, I purred. Out loud! Opposites attract might be going too far (although she quite openly suggested that I had my camp moments – great!), but we had a bit of banter and although I can see where she's coming from I just don't think she's going anywhere that I'm going. She crowns herself in glory (and highlights a distinct lack of taste) by telling me stories about her ex boyfriends, who, she stated, 'were all psychos.' One of them was clinically recommended not to be released into the general public after he stabbed someone through the hand, another was very jealous, and there was another weird one too, but she couldn't remember anything about him, apart from the fact that he was very bland and vaguely troublesome. I found myself looking over my shoulder, after that.

Our date ends after the girls sat behind us are obviously pissing themselves at what we're talking about, and anyway, it was half four and Date No. 42 was supposed to be at work. As we cheek kiss goodbye she starts to say that she'll keep in touch, and I cut her off with best wishes for her upcoming weekend of mince-pie making. She's perfectly pleasant, but it's not going to work.

I've been chatting to Date No. 43 on MSF for a few days. Articulate, funny and well travelled, she should be good company. I take a bus from London Bridge after leaving Date No. 42 and twenty-five minutes later have my Camberwell Virginity taken from me, which is just a perverted way to say I went to Camberwell for the first time. No. 43 is going to be late, my mobile phone informs me. As I wait in the Dark Horse Pub my table is waited by a brunette girl with a face like an angel. There's something about a nicely fitting white vest top, and this girl wears hers well. She looks like Micha Barton, just smaller. Beautiful. She wanders over a couple of times to ask if I need anything, she calls me Sir. I want her to call me Sir in a far more intimate situation, but maintain some decorum and keep myself to myself.

Date No. 43, like Date No. 42, is perfectly pleasant, but she has 70's hair with a badly cut fringe that hangs tantalisingly over her eyes to only show the bottom half of them, and she's all...well, gangly. We chat for a while but when I'm not looking over at the waitress I'm trying to keep my eyes open. Boredom may well have been part of the problem, but generally I'm tired, worn out. I've tried, but I can't for the life of me think of anything that happened during our date. When we leave and walk towards the bus stop I have to blink twice a second to keep my contact lenses in they're so dry. Two more dates, fairly dull dates, another day down, but I'm totally unsatisfied. In these moments of need men lose their desperate yearnings for what they can't have (Hannah, Nicola, the waitress in the Dark Horse) and start wondering what's more attainable. For me, at that time, I thought of Anna, Date No. 37. Our stretched-out Friday night date was riddled with general confusion, but ended with a fair bit of passion. It may have even ended up with the ultimate passion had I not bitten my tongue and skated off down the road towards Herne Hill, but I must admit I've been thinking about her for a little while, half because she intrigues me, and half because she's shown more interest in me than any of the others. I text her, asking what she's up to, but she comes back to me saying she's just got in from work and has a night in watching Heroes to look forward to.

No passion for me, then. Which, let's face it, is probably a very good thing at this stage. If I need anything, it's sleep.

Thursday: Day 41
Date No. 44

Date No. 44 is looking at clothes in Oasis when I turn up. She appears from between two piles of winter sweaters and walks towards me beaming. She has an hour-glass figure, perfect skin, a small beauty spot beneath the left curve of her lower lip, and she looks bloody friendly. She's also Australian, as is revealed when she opens her mouth. I've dated a couple of Aussies already, but this one is the only one that didn't tell me her nationality before the date. She introduced herself on MySingleFriend with what is now a familiar line:

Hi, are you an axe murderer?'

I was ever so tempted to write a simple:

Yes, I hate you.

But instead supplied something more promising:

You'll be glad to know that I've never even owned an axe, and murder isn't on my bucket list, although for some reason the soundtrack for Psycho continually plays in my vicinity.

She still wanted a date, though, which was brave of her.

In the pub we fight the noise. Date No. 44 is very softly spoken, as apparently am I because she keeps leaning in with a cocked ear so close that at one point I could have licked it if I wanted to, and we go through the motions, talking about our lives, where we are, where we're from, why we're on My Single Friend. Her body language is good, she's attentive and very smiley, but again, there's no spark. After our second drink we reach that stagnant stage where another drink might be on the cards, but neither of us would mind if it wasn't...and then she says,

'I'm going to have to go.' Since I started The Hundred this is the first girl to cut the date having not made a prior excuse, quite refreshing! Her housemate is home alone cleaning the house in preparation for a cheese and wine party the following night, and No. 44 tells me she feels guilty and needs to do her bit to help. I'm impressed. As excuses to end dates go, fetching cheese is a pretty good one. We wander close to Charing Cross and say goodbye, two-cheek kiss, 'enjoy your cheese and wine party,' 'take care', anything but say 'let's do this again sometime'. But actually, I'd quite like to see her again; she has a very nice smile.

On the tube home I watch people. An announcement that the train will terminate at Tooting Broadway causes one woman to exhale so loudly everyone looks at her. She puts her head in her hands, and shakes it. Total exasperation, it's no big deal, just a couple more minutes to wait, but her sadness is evident and tragic. City life tears some people apart. A man is in the corner hugging a girl, who is sleeping with her head in his neck. As women walk past him he stares after them, eyeing them up until they leave the train. I can't help wonder how many relationships are in the process of ending in this city, on this train, in this carriage. And how many are starting, or going strong? And whether there are any which will stand the test of time, or the test of the fit bird's arse which is currently wiggling its way past your very nose, even when you're hugging your girlfriend.

I call Will as I walk home. He tells me he asked his brother what he was supposed to do with a date that keeps texting even though he's not interested.

'What you do is sleep with her and make it an awful experience,' said Will's brother.

'To be honest, I'd probably do that anyway,' answered Will.

Friday: Day 42
44 Dates so far

I spent the day feeling very nervous, mainly because I'm finally going on a second date with Hannah tonight, and partly because as the day goes on I realise I was so spun out by meeting her that I can't remember a thing she told me about herself on our first date. Oh god.

In reality, my lack of knowledge about Hannah didn't turn out to be an issue. We chatted easily, catching up on recent exploits. She tells me she's been offered a short-term placement in Mumbai, it starts in late December. Great, even if this does work out, she's in India for four weeks and then I'm in Australia for six more. That doesn't bode terrifically well, but it's not exactly insurmountable.

This girl is sorted. The more we talk the more I like her, and as this happens I feel myself splitting. I want to get to know her more but I can't help but close off a little, I'm being protective of myself because I don't want to get hurt, or muddled, or be anything other than content. The rain pours down and she walks close beneath my umbrella. I take her to a magic little Moroccan restaurant, cosy and intimate with low tables and lamps glowing deeply in the corners. There's a little tea candle burning ferociously in front of me and it's giving out enough heat to melt my nose. I reach out to move it away and Hannah says quickly, 'oh don't blow it out!' She's clearly misread my romantic intentions; I'd rather burn than spoil the mood tonight.

We talk fluidly, sharing stories and building easily on our 4pm coffee date eleven days earlier. Considering how dire many of my dates have been, I slowly become uncomfortable with the realisation that I can't be picky about this girl and if I tried then it just wouldn't work. There are no awkward silences, she's intelligent and makes me laugh so much my cheeks are beginning to hurt. She's actually so together that she starts to make me sweat a little. 'Do you have a ten year plan?' she asks, and quite honestly I say,

'No!' The thing is, she does;

'Get settled, buy a house, become an editor of a decent publication, have kids and retire to write novels in the country.' It's a fair plan, seemingly realistic too, but for the first time in my life someone else's ambition shrinks me a little bit and puts me in my place. I realise that I actually don't have any ambitions, not because I'm devoid of a need to be successful and live a life of achievement, but because I have been living my current life for all of two months and I have no idea where it's going to take me. We're both successful but in very different ways, and I don't know her well enough to have any inkling whether we could work together.

I feel the need to own up to her,

'I must admit, I feel a little flaky when trying to justify my ten year plan...' but although she waves it away I feel, perhaps irrationally, like my lack of focus prizes us apart, as though perhaps she's going to look down on me from now on. The journalist in her teases me when I refer to my brother as 'bro' and a t-shirt as a 'tee' so I start to abbreviate everything, just to show her that she can't change me. And there's another thing, earlier on in the night she mentions a friend of a friend, an explorer called Dan, who in Hannah's words was 'a bit of a wanker.' Towards the end of the night I'm talking about travelling, about journeys and adventures, and she looks at me and says,

'oh god, you're just like Dan.'

I ask for the bill, as she needs to go and catch a train. 'Do you want any money towards this?' she asks, and I shake my head,

'Not at all, I was the one tempting you with this meal...'

'Damn, I'll have to take you for chips next time,' she says, clenching her teeth and staring me down with a pair of deliciously piercing eyes. Chips sounds just fine, if you ask me.

So here we are again saying goodbye in a tube station ending in Circus, beside a supporting column just inside the gates. I've really enjoyed myself, again, and still think she's an absolute star, but certain things – mainly the ten year plan and the fact that she thinks I'm just like that bloke who's a wanker – have combined with a general need for self protection and even as I say, 'hey, if you fancy the pub quiz on Monday...?' I've convinced myself that this is it; that nothing is going to happen, that I'm about to say goodbye to Hannah in Piccadilly Circus expecting never to see her again. She responds, 'this week is really busy...' and I shrug, my thoughts seemingly confirmed, and then I wink at her.

'Did you just wink at me?' she asks rhetorically.

'Ummm, yes,' I say, thinking I'm about to be told off for being cocky, or something.

'That's so unfair,' says she, 'because I can't wink.' And she stands there with her arms by her side and both her eyes squeezed shut and then she points to her face and says, 'this is me trying to wink.' I can't help but laugh.

'Oh come on, you can do it, wink properly!' But sincerely, she can't. She stands there a little longer looking like a very attractive South Park character, opening and closing both of her eyes at the same time, and then we move away from each other and just as she turns I wink at her with my right eye this time, just to rub it in. We both spin and head for our respective escalators. I turn to my right and look at her just as the wall appears between us, and she's laughing and looking over at me, and then she's gone. And it's only then that it strikes me; I really should have kissed her when she was standing there with both eyes shut trying to wink.

Saturday: Day 43
Dates No. 45 & No. 46

I wake up to a message from Date No. 42, the one who refused to save my number from a couple of days ago. Most dates come and go and I've neither written nor received a message from the girl, but when it happens all it takes is a little bit of honesty.

> *No. 42* – *Hi. You've gone very quiet or are you following the 'three day rule'? Anyway, hope you had a good week... I've got to go back to my mince pies...*

I'll save you a few if you're interested.

Me - There's a three day rule?! I got the text, thanks for that! Hmmm, so you didn't think our differences in ambition clashed then, hey?

No. 42 - According to my girlfriends there is a rule that you don't make contact for at least three days after a date. But to be honest, I've never been a fan of mind games. Which leads me to ask, after your 'differences in ambition' comment, if I hadn't emailed would you have bothered? Be honest!!

Me - I'll remember that... No mind games here either, honestly it's not about being bothered. Call it overly romantic but I'm a big believer in instant chemistry and I'm not sure we had that - did you think differently? That said, I enjoyed meeting you despite being called camp!

No. 42 - Fair enough. Thank you for being honest...I agree the clap of thunder wasn't there...but you did make me laugh till I nearly cried. I'll never forget that you purred at my boots... :)

Me – *Hehe, I forgot I purred at your boots! You did give me a good giggle though! You know, claps of thunder aside, there's nothing stopping us being friends...although clearly I'm just saying that whilst sidling towards your mince pies (that's not intended to sound rude)... ;)*

Two dates today. The first is a midday coffee in Clapham Junction with Date No. 45, 30 years old, wearing red. I'm tired today, feeling the weight of the final push towards halfway, but this girl is actually a breath of fresh air. She's had a serious illness recently and looks slightly gaunt with drying skin around her nose, but her lust for life straightens me up in my seat. She has a tinkling laugh and has travelled far and wide, one of those people who values life to the full; it's an infectious trait and I open up a little more than I usually do. We laugh and crack jokes and I sincerely enjoy her company, but after a couple of hours it's time to go. A lovely, honest person, but nothing more.

The afternoon date is a real strain. Date No. 46 doesn't look like her photo and I'm not in the least attracted to her. The plan was to give her a skate lesson in Hyde Park but I'd completely overlooked the Christmas Fayre, which takes up half of Serpentine Rd. We stand for a while, getting acquainted and watching small children fall all over the ice rink, then circumnavigate the lake and have a quick coffee in the Lido café. I can't get out of there fast enough, so make out I have a cheese party to organise, and we're done.

It's one of those evenings where everything feels wrong. I'm utterly miserable, the rain drives horizontally outside, I'm alone and don't want to be. At these times you reach out, wishing for company, remembering those times where you were close to someone, the warmth of love flickering so far away it actually hurts. I think about my ex and the almighty mess that forced us apart. I think about Anna from eight days ago and feel the temptations of that night. Jo's going out with a guy she met speed-dating and invites me to join them, but I don't fancy that, it's a potentially ugly situation.

Will calls. 'Mate! I'm heading out tonight with a girl called Martha, second date!'

'Get you!'

'Mate, seriously, I've had my guilty phase about dating too many women but I'm over it now.'

'That's good buddy, what are you going to do with Martha tonight?'

'I'll do whatever she wants, she's really very pretty...'

The night wears on, I sink into my seat as Match of the Day begins, and even an invite from Kate No. 27 to head out to Clapham's weekend meat market, Infernos, doesn't appeal, I have worn out Saturday night sofa fatigue.

Sunday Day 44
Date No. 47

Pissing it down. I have an 11am coffee in Clapham Junction and my jeans are sodden, umbrella rendered useless and broken by the wind. Date No. 47 is small and elfin but from five seconds in I knew it was going to be a short coffee. We're both hungover, her from a night on the tiles, me from a month and a half of dating. I'm almost halfway through now, and I'm looking forward to pushing over 50 dates, it might give me a new wind. Date No. 47 hasn't touched her coffee, she tells me she doesn't like it when the taste of alcohol is still in her mouth, and when I offer to get her some water she shrugs and says she doesn't like that, either.

'How have you managed to survive this long without water?' I ask, tongue in cheek, and she looks at me like I'm mad.

'You don't need water to survive,' she says, definitively.

'Ah yes, silly me,' I agree, 'water is very overrated.'

Naturally, our date ended very soon after that. With a tailwind across the Common I jump on my board, unleash the umbrella and use it as a sail, drawing delighted grins from everyone I pass. A man and a familiar-looking woman walk hand in hand and the girl looks at me, her eyes widening and mouth smiling as I whiz past.

'Hello!' I mouth, totally taken aback by seeing Date No. 1. We dated forty-four days ago and here she is, walking across the Common with a guy, and I can't help but feel happy for her. However good our date was we were never made to be together, mainly because I don't have a driver's licence, yet it's comforting to know that she's found someone. In that flashing, blinking moment of surprise she looked happy. I suppose I did, too, though.

This time yesterday it seemed possible that there'd be four dates on the cards – a record Sunday! But one by one the others have fallen by the wayside. One says she's working. Another writes late and apologises for giving me the wrong number as she rushed out of work on Friday. A third messaged at 8pm and said she had only just got in and was too tired for a date. I'm slowly getting there but wanting to finish, wanting to find someone. But now that feeling is slightly different. A few days ago I was excited by the potential of Hannah and with the chemistry Nicola and I shared, with the feeling that I had found that someone, whichever one it might be. Nicola occupied many of my thoughts and because of that my instinct kicked in and convinced me that something was going to happen, but since we walked apart in the rain on that wet Monday night she's been in touch only once, saying she was too busy to meet until December. Well now it's December, albeit early in the month, and still I haven't heard from her. We spent just a couple of hours together, but now, with ten days of non-communication filling the darkness, I'm quite sure now that's all we'll ever have, and it hurts. I opened myself up, put my heart on the line and the ball in her court, and it wasn't returned. Yes, that hurts. It niggles. It bothers me. What could have happened?

I don't know Nicola, if she's been hurt badly before then perhaps she is trying to protect herself, however honest my message to her was maybe she just doesn't want to put herself in the line of fire. I have no idea, because I don't know her. If we ever do meet again, will I just be mindful of the fact that she could so easily disappear after our second date, just as she did the first? I do wonder how long I'll think about Nicola, and whether I'll always wonder what could have happened. What if I meet another girl, how will she react to this little episode of my dating saga? A silly question perhaps, the right girl will accept that what happened is in the past.

The lack of a line drawn under with Nicola, though, means it's not resolved yet, not physically, not theoretically, not realistically. And definitely not in my head. But I know we had something it was too good a night for it to have stumbled straight to a halt, yet it has. And this is why I'm protecting myself with Hannah, the other knockout from Magic Monday, who I've een twice and would love to see again, but am forcing myself to doubt whether we have any potential. Is this challenge which is centred around love actually counter productive to just that? Is what I'm doing too intense to allow love to blossom? We've had two dates, Hannah and I, a coffee then evolved into a romantic dinner, but we haven't yet kissed, still haven t been in much of a position to gauge physical chemistry. And when we said goodbye on Friday evening it was in another tube station, and when I walked away I wasn't as dizzy a I had been the first time. Not because I liked her any less, but because I had convinced myself nothing was going to happen.

So when she writes on this dark Sunday evening, I'm quite surprised. She tells me how her weekend was, how she wandered hrough fields with friends in the rain and now has a bag of wet clothes and drove home wearing her friend's boyfriend' tracksuit. She says how much she enjoyed Friday, and asks ii I want to meet again, and I find myself wanting to see her in he tracksuit, of course I want to see her again! I jot something back, along the lines of how much I enjoyed Friday as well and that I'd love to meet up after she's finished her week of interviews, and I tell her I've been thinking about my ten year plan and that I'll update her over chips. She doesn't take long to respond:

> *oh my god, I'm such a ten year plan dweeb, I'd completely forgotten about that, I'm so sorry…*

I felt like it had been such a big deal, but she'd forgotten all about it. Maybe I am trying to find holes where I shouldn't. A Sunday that had been fairly miserable suddenly becomes much less so. Hannah, 27, blonde, journalist, Date No. 33. Is something happening with you?

Monday: Day 45
Date No. 48

It's Monday night again, and for the first time since Nicola I take a date to The Calf pub quiz. It had looked like an empty evening until Date No. 48 wrote to me this afternoon, but I chanced my arm and asked her out, and she went for it. We had only exchanged two short messages so knew nothing about each other, and I certainly wasn't prepared to be dating an Estonian beauty in Clapham Old Town! Her English was good, but slow and forthright. She'd studied business languages in Tallinn and that, coupled with a typical Eastern European directness, made her appear quite blunt. She also had a little cold, and for most of the quiz she was sat back with folded arms looking into the middle distance, occasionally reaching into her bag for a tissue.

'You really don't want to be here, do you?' I asked, only half seriously.

'Oh no, sorry, I really am having fun, I'm just thinking about the question...' she would say. I looked across at her and studied her face. She's 24 with sleek, thick black hair. David the Quizmaster said hello and as he walked away turned his head and mouthed,

'Fit!'

During some paper-swapping with another table David, who tonight is for the first time equipped with a microphone, mumbled to the whole pub, 'hold on, that guy up there, is that Dave Cornthwaite, the famous writer...?!'

Cheeky bugger

No. 48 didn't react and popped out to make a phone call during the halftime break, so David wandered over.

'How's the dating going?' he asked.

'Tonight is Number 48, mate,' I said, 'I'm quite tired.'

'Please tell me they haven't all been this pretty.'

'I don't judge them on their looks.'

'You are going to write the most boring book in history.'

I laughed, 'You're not dragging me down to your level like that, I'm not here to date for the sake of it, I've got my standards and I'm sticking to them.'

'Sure you are. Mate, Uggos always slip through the net somehow. If I were an ugly bird I'd probably become a recluse. Definitely wouldn't advertise it online. They should have a different site, My-Single-Because-Shes-Rougher-Than-Your-Average-Friend-Dot-Com. Only fair, you wouldn't get caught out then.'

Needless to say Date No. 48 and I came last in the quiz, but that was fine because it meant David had to read out our team name... *Never bring a first date to the Calf quiz, because the quizmaster a bastard.* He went on to tell the laughing crowd how one of my dates had fancied him more.

'Suck on that,' he said in my direction, no doubt with his tongue out

I couldn't read this girl. She was clearly under the weather but I liked her. Confident, intelligent, sexy, said things like:

'I have no idea why some men don't like to talk about sex, everybody does it, so what's the problem?'

At the tube station she suggests we meet again, and I agree with total sincerity and then completely blow it when we have a very quick, slightly drunken kiss and I somehow lift my arms way too high and end up clamping the sides of her head between my biceps, which would have only been an excuse if I were seven foot tall. Despite my inability to function like a normal human any more, I think this one's a real dark horse; I like her.

Tuesday: Day 46
Date No. 49

This is the first date I've had through Stag & Dove, a fairly new dating website designed to target London's creative population. There's only 100 or so people on there, total, so not the greatest pickings. Date No. 49, though, had a fresh face and a nice turn of phrase, and after a little banter initiated we're now meeting outside Clapham Junction station. I'm not totally sure what she looks like, so when I turn up and see an enormous woman hanging around outside Sainsburys I feel my willy shrivel up like a nut. Please god, not her, I'm not a fan of elephantiasis. I've told No. 49 that I'll have my board with me, so when the larger lady looks at me then looks away again with a bored expression, I breathe a sigh of relief and then walk outside, just in case.

Date No. 49, wonderfully slimmer than the creature indoors, appears at about twenty-five past seven with dark hair and a wide smile. The five-second judgement suggests that this is going to be a fun date, if nothing else. I've been in a silly mood for a couple of days and can't help but attempt to crack a dry joke every sentence. She laughs at about half of them, which I think is quite generous. I have a TV interview in Cardiff in the morning so get that in early and say I'm going to have to leave by half nine to get some kip, and then we chat. She works in advertising for a shoe company and as one of five daughters is somewhat bizarrely a self-confessed tomboy;

'I love football,' she says, 'playing, not watching. I get too emotional.'

We talk about some dodgy date experiences and she tells me she went on a date with a guy when she was in a cast after breaking her leg. They ended up going to a club and once in there her date started to respond to a blonde who was blithely chatting him up, so poor No. 49 decided to make an exit. Only she was in a cast, so it wasn't a proud, confident escape, but an ungainly, hobbling one! I share a few dating exploits of my own but neglect to provide details of numbers. Date No. 49 hasn't travelled much but loves the idea of Dave Gorman and Danny Wallace's books,

'I think it's really cool when people cook up these real life challenges, they're hilarious,' she says. Even after that, I can't bring myself to tell her what I'm up to.

Wednesday: Day 47
Date No. 50

Now, considering I usually have a five second commute from bed to sofa, I was sweating a bit at 08:29 when standing on the Clapham South northbound platform in a swelling crowd. I'll get to the station by 8am. I told myself, which should give me plenty of time to make the 9.15 to Cardiff from Paddington. So I did. I was at Clapham South three minutes to eight, and there I was, 32 minutes later, stood with arms pinned to my side in exactly the same place. There's something almost funny about hovering there in a clutch of suited people watching tube by tube pull up, stop and move off, bodies squashed against the windows, no one getting off and therefore no one getting on. Finally I take a chance and squeeze aboard, my poor hood trapped in the sliding door for the four minutes between South and Common. And yes, luckily I made my train, but only just and with a very real comprehension of why people hate the London commute. Dear God, that was horrible! A couple of hours later I'm in Cardiff, where I'm asked to sit on a sofa between two lovely presenters with whom I chat about my skateboarding journeys and other projects. It was an interview ridden with giggles and I'm really starting to like this TV lark, but the most heartwarming moment was when the producer gave me a big hug and said, 'Dave, you're my hero. Thanks for coming down, that was awesome.'

I was back on the train slightly later than planned, mainly thanks to a Welsh bloke who drove his car into a railway bridge somewhere in eastern Cardiff thus delaying the day's timetable, but eventually we got going, hit rush hour on the way back into London, and had just enough time to get home, shower and venture out again. It's date time.

'She's blatantly a pill popper,' said Jo a few days earlier, reading No. 50's online profile which refers to her being 'a trooper on a night out and a lover of festivals.'

'Oh come on,' I say, raising an eyebrow, 'you don't know that.'

So there I am, sat in a bar with Date No. 50, who does seem a little bit nervous. Maybe it's first date syndrome, but I've been on dates with other nervous women who don't jerk their heads at right angles now and then. And, it's fair to say, she has a real issue with concentration, she asks me a question and then as I start to answer she bends double and sticks her head under the table, inserting a folded beer mat under a leg. The table wasn't all that wobbly, but I suppose I couldn't see it for what it was, being sober and all.

On many levels, she's lovely. She's dressed well, has a good job, and like many early thirty-somethings she has a sense of vulnerability about her shrinking world; she's single while all around her are coupling off, falling pregnant, leaving London. And this, I sense, is much harder for No. 50 to deal with because, to put it kindly, she has a love for socialising. Or, in simpler terms, she likes partying and getting off her tits. Jo, you hit the nail on the head, the somewhat emaciated, drug-addled head. In the toilet I realise a troublesome contact lens has made my right eye very bloodshot, which might explain why No. 50 is flirting with me so much.

It's a real shame, because despite her slightly slow manner of speech (dope) and incessant chatter about pubs in the Brixton-Clapham-Balham area (alcohol) Date No. 50 is a friendly, kind person, but her face is slightly gaunt and her tongue stud has chipped away at her teeth over the years, meaning the head doesn't do justice to the body. We have a few drinks and then both start to wilt (in my case I was feigning it because I was ready to leave, in her case she may have gone two hours without injecting and it was clearly taking its toll), so we leave. Outside I say, 'it was lovely to meet you,' and move in to kiss her right cheek, and as I do I blink and miss the fact that she's made a move for my left cheek, and there I am, lip to lip with this girl I really don't fancy. The first kiss with anyone is usually a tentative affair, a quick peck then perhaps a more passionate lunge. The thing is, I hadn't even intended the first peck, so as I tried to rectify my positioning and moved round to her cheek she was going in for the follow-up and her tongue came out and made worryingly slimy contact with my ear. I quickly pulled away, in shock, basically, and then gave her a quick hug because she looked a bit hurt (it might have been the sunken eyes, though). And then, before it could get any more awkward, I said 'see you later,' and walked away, panicking and giggling nervously because this girl had clearly wanted a bit of a pash, and I'd just gone and given her a good dose of false hope. Saying that, she probably appreciate a good dose of anything. How horribly embarrassing.

Thursday: Day 48
Date No. 51

I tell Kate No. 27 about last night's date and she emails back:

Body from Baywatch, face off Crimewatch.

By mid afternoon it's looking like I'm dateless tonight, not good news with the Christmas period rushing up.. Then Kate No. 27 steps up with some pimp-like genius. Two emails in quick succession contain details of friends who want a date with me, so I text one of them, an Irish lass named Kath, and organise a little drink for later.

As I wander down Abbeville Rd I realise that this is it, I've made it over halfway. My fifty-first date in forty-eight days, a quite ridiculous statistic. And here's another one, Kath is my first real Blind Date. I've never met her, never chatted to her and have no idea what she looks like. I do know that she has a fairly thick Irish accent though ('you're going to have to concentrate pretty hard,' Kate told me), and thus I wasn't expecting for Kath, who arrived ten minutes late, to spend an hour saying 'pardun?' at everything I was saying. She seemed a bit bemused at the whole thing. Being a friend of a friend she knew about the dating challenge, but in the hour we spent together she didn't really seem like she wanted to be there. There's always more worry when dating someone that a friend knows, you don't want to cause any friction, but that was never a worry with Kath, we just didn't really click and after an hour we left, had a hug and walked separate ways down Acre Lane. Ah well, apparently it's all downhill from here, if that's at all possible.

Friday: Day 49
Dates No. 52 & 53

'Downhill from here' sounds more negative than I'd like it to. Another forty-nine dates loom like a dark, growling cloud, and I wonder what they'll bring. If I had lined fifty women up before the project I would have expected a good handful of them to be potential partners. As it is, I've only met two women who blew my socks off. Hannah, with whom I'm still chatting online and have just organised a third date with next Wednesday, and Nicola, who has disappeared off the face of the earth. With the latter I'm starting to realise that no contact equals no interest. The frustration is slowly but surely dying though, and that leaves Hannah as the only woman from fifty who I still have a chance with. But here's the thing, she's just accepted her four week job in India so even if something did start to happen between us it would be put on hold for at least two months. Here's my point; I've dated over fifty women, and chances are bugger all is going to happen with any of them. What the hell is wrong with me?

I try and cast these thoughts away as I venture to London Bridge to meet Date No. 52. She works in publishing and as we chat it transpires that she used to work for the only people who know about my dating challenge, my publishers. We run through some names and I realise there is practically no way that I can get away without Date No. 52 finding out about the challenge at some point, not least when she tells me she's meeting up with some of the old crowd next week. I stare into the middle distance and whisper,

'Oh God.' She laughs, because she thinks I'm 'Oh Godding' about it being such a small world, but I'm clearly not. There's no connection between Date No. 52 and I and it's another one of those dates where we won't meet up again as potential suitors, but usually there's a finish point, a goodbye, and then that's it. When I come to write about these dates I know that the girl will have a pseudonym and that I'll likely change the place we meet in order to protect their identity, but this time around I have a dilemma. I decide to tell her what I'm doing but just as I'm about to blurt it out No. 52 says something that is really very nice. She says,

'You're an amazing person to have done what you've done, and it's admirable that you haven't put your achievements on your dating profile.' It stops me dead and I'm not sure what to say, and suddenly I don't feel like I can tell her about my challenge because although I'm not exactly doing anything wrong I have no idea how each girl I tell is going to react, and frankly I don't want this girl who thinks I'm very nice to turn sharply and empty her gin and tonic over my head. I just feel uncomfortable and am speechless for pretty much the rest of the date. Which was about ten minutes, for I have to go across town to meet another girl.

Date No. 53 is a few minutes late, but I don't mind. I lean up against the railings in Piccadilly Circus with my back to the bright lights and watch people. Couples mill around, tourists take pictures, and occasionally a person on their own walks around the statue of Eros once, twice, perhaps a third time, looking around. Looking for *someone*. How many people out there are looking for someone, for a partner they can call their own? However independent we are is there ever a time when we don't long to be loved, to hold another. For me, on this cold night in London, I feel as lonely as I ever have. I'm content to a degree, but I'm also tense in the thought that perhaps I'm looking *too* hard. I've now had 52 dates and I'm still alone, so what is it exactly that I'm searching for? At times like this I text friends, just to remind myself that I have some, and one of them gets back to me almost immediately responding to my *I've passed 50 dates!* with the predictable, *Oh boy. You need to go be with some men for a while!*

No. 53 is lovely, bubbly and talkative, but at 33 years old I get the feeling that our current aims in life are different. Did I mention she was talkative? This was another date when I spoke for far less than twenty per cent of the time, and I found that I could drift off into my own thoughts and tune back in a minute later just in time to tag onto the back end of a spiel. She's successful, happy and worldly, but she's not my type, and we say goodbye after two drinks.

Saturday: Day 50
Date No. 54

The email banter with Date No. 54 has been good. Her picture shows her from the neck up, a cute face, black hair. She looks like she could be curvaceous, as her profile says, but you never know. So let's see. We both share a similar humour and hit it off straight away. Hungover from last night, I was in another funny mood when everything was an off-the-cuff remark or a dry comment. We supped on lemonade and giggled for a while, and for some reason I told my skateboarding story in the third person, just because I could. It was a good date, one that I hope will result in a friendship, but nothing more. I started to wilt after the second drink and with another big night on the cards needed to head home for some shut-eye.

A dateless night it was, but I shared it with two former dates, Jo and Kate No. 27. That I can go out with two of the girls from my gloomy 50 day-old past and have a ball does show me that even if that special someone doesn't emerge from this thing then at least I've made some good friends. And then, in the middle of a crowded Clapham bar, there's another twist: 'Dave?!' There's a girl cocking her head at me through the crowd and I recognise her as Natalie, my ex from Wales.

'What the hell are you doing here?' I ask, giving her a hug. It's been almost three years since we split after spending a similar amount of time together beneath the same roof in Swansea, and whatever emotions that lurked following our break-up are well and truly abated. She's the same girl, fun, party-loving, music obsessed. But she seems smaller than I remember, maybe I've just grown up a bit?

How strange, to spend so long with a person and have it all disappear into the ether. Here we were in a bar years and hundreds of miles from the ones we frequented when we were in a relationship; absolutely nothing tying us together now, nothing in common except a long-extinguished love. Not in a million years would we have thought it when we lay together at night, that one day in the future we would meet again as total strangers. It was great to see her, however briefly, before we both moved on into the separate directions of the night.

Sunday Day 51
Dates No. 55 & 56

Hungover to buggery, I wake at noon. I have two dates today and the first is at 2pm, it's time to get a wriggle on but I feel like a day of sleep should be on the cards. Two dates couldn't be less welcome, but it's my own pesky fault for being so greedy.

Date No. 55 is a little pixie with a wonderful face and, I realise when we meet for the first time outside Covent Garden tube, she's American. We were due to meet up last weekend but she typed her mobile number wrong so my texts disappeared into cyberspace, and I teased her for being the type to let things slip her mind right up until I offered to pay for coffee and realised I didn't have any cash on me.

'I promise I don't usually do that!' I said, blushing,

'The way you say that it sounds like you're always going on dates,' she replied,

'Well, don't get me wrong, I love it when women pay,' I gulped, avoiding the insinuation, 'it's just that I promised myself when I signed up to My Single Friend that I'd pay for dates on Sundays, and I absolutely hate breaking promises.'

'You'll have to take me on a date next Sunday, then,' she said, and that was it, we were off like a house on fire.

However tired I am, whatever mood I'm in, and whether I'm dating one, two or three girls in a day, meeting someone I get on with is always such a pleasure. Even a beguiling chin which seems to cast its own formidable shadow when her head is tilted at certain angles doesn't make me like No. 55 any less, and over the course of our one and a half hour date the foreboding I felt when I woke up this morning dissipates, and I begin to see some light at the end of the tunnel. You see, there is an unmistakable energy abound when two people meet and are genuinely compatible, and it's practically impossible to feel sleepy or disgruntled when there's a good looking girl across the table eyeing you up and licking her lips after every sip of coffee. Even when I say goodbye to Date No. 55 and watch her slink off the tube en route to a posh do in some Kensington hotel, it makes me happy to be alive, because I know that even if the other dates today aren't all that inspiring then at least the day won't be a failure. I don't even know if I'll see No. 55 again or not, but at the very least she's been a hangover cure.

En route to the next date in Putney, I decide to throw caution to the wind and send Nicola a text. I don't expect anything back, but it's now December after all, so one more attempt at contact is worth a shot:

> *Hello stranger. Hope all is well and that the busyness is…well, less busy. If you fancy another catch-up I'd love to see you xx*

One of the first things Date No. 56 tells me is that she lied about her age on YesNoMayB. 'I'm not 30,' she tells me, rabbit eyes wide and concerned, 'I'm actually 33.' She pauses, looking at me and working out very quickly that I know she's still being economical with the truth. 'Ok, ok, I'm 36,' she says, and I raise my Gin and Tonic in salute to eventual honesty.

'36 is better than 56,' I grin, and although she has no way of understanding my joke she smiles back, more out of relief than anything. We chat for an hour and then walk down the road to the station. She's a lovely, enterprising girl but she's not my type.

Monday: Day 52
Date No. 57

An email from Kate No. 27 awaits when I turn my computer on.

> So, here is a selection of messages I got from Stag &
> Dove over the weekend:
> 1. hi how are you its a strange angle you got in for
>   the photo.
> 2. do you think you will ever go too india
> 3. Hi Honey I love to see it fully and give it
>   hard...lets get together and do it...please reply as
>   fast as u want.

Men are funny creatures.

I have a date tonight, but have decided against going to The Calf. I text David the Quizmaster

> *Me - Dude, I'm not coming in tonight, but Will has a date, you could steal his…*
> *David – I could, I'm much more Alpha than him*
> *Me – By Alpha, do you mean Christian, or fat?*
> *David – It's cool, mate. You could say I have a thick skin when it comes to those gags. But thanks for dragging up years of mental abuse and bullying. I'm not going to the quiz now, I can't face it, I'm going to stay at home and eat and cry and eat and vomit and eat.*

Total prima donnas, these quizmasters.

It seems the number of people signing up to online dating sites have declined in the approach to the holidays, and I was facing a potentially barren spell over Christmas. That said, with the halfway mark now falling into the distance behind me I've got a spring in my step, one possibly buoyed by progress with Hannah. Still, the dates must go on, and a few days ago I came across a profile on MySingleFriend, that suggested the lady in question *had a gym pass, and she's not afraid to use it.* Apparently, she could massage as well.

> *Me - Hey Kara, Even a brisk mention of a massage is enough to make men come running, so here I am…! If only it was that easy, eh. How's the weird and wonderful world of online dating treating you?*
> *Kara – Hi. How is this for adding to the weird and wonderful world of online dating. I have a funny feeling that we went to the same school years ago, a friend was talking about your skateboarding exploits a while back. Small world eh?*
> *Me - I'm guessing you were in the year above? Now*

we're all growed up can I tempt you with a little drink sometime before Christmas?

Kara - You know you'll never impress a girl offering anything 'little'... but sure, a drink would be good.

Me - Really over analysing why I used the word 'little' now, usually I lay the cards on the line and offer an enormous drink straight away... Up to anything on Monday?

So there we were, on a Monday, in a small backstreet pub in Clapham. Despite having shared a school almost two decades ago we hadn't known each other at all so this was much less a reunion than a recollection of mutual friends and places. She was a sparky lass, quick-witted and just about as relaxed as anyone I'd met since The Hundred began. I liked her, we laughed in bouts and began a strange unwitting game of speaking in dry, sarcastic tones in an effort to outwit each other. I told her quickly about The Hundred and she shot off some questions with one eyebrow raised. It seemed to all intents and purposes like we'd settled into a comfortable friendship almost instantly, so much so that we decided to finish off the date by meeting a mutual friend just down the road.

Alex had also attended the same school as Kara and I, and the three of us sat around a table next to a burning log fire with Alex's friend Johnny, and typically the conversation quickly turned to dating. Johnny had been single for a while so I suggested I'd write him a profile on MySingleFriend, after all, if I couldn't put a good one together by now there'd be no hope at all.

On the way home, I call Will and ask about his date.

'Ah mate, I went on a bit of a rant again, mainly about hating German people. I realise that I kill the potential in some of my dates by doing that. Apparently I started ranting about

Irish people at one point, and then she said she was half-Irish. I won't be seeing her again.'

Tuesday: Day 53
Dates No. 58 & 59

Date No. 58 is slim and brunette, and in her hand is a lead, and at the end of the lead is a dog that is possibly a rat in disguise.

'Oh, look at that, I didn't realise we'd have company today,' I say to No. 58 before leaning in for a hug that ends with both of us wrapped up by the lead.

'This is Bernie,' she says brightly, 'he's very well behaved and won't get in the way.'

Three minutes later, after we've untangled ourselves, we start to walk towards the park and I trip over Bernie, who seems determined to get in the way.

'So, is Bernie your dog, or do you just happen to make a living from pet care?'

'He's mine, I love him sooo much.' And then No. 58 launched into an overwhelming array of Bernie-related statistics all of which I couldn't possibly recall. It went something like this. 'We found him in a kennel in southeast Devon, he was blonde when we bought him and turned brown in the first year. He's three years and three months old, seven inches tall, loves chasing sticks but will never return balls. At night he sleeps on the pillow beside my head, it's so cute! When he's sleeping he sounds like a whistle. He comes on all of my dates because it's important that he likes the men in my life, and it's important that they like him. He never bites, except once, when he nipped the first guy I met off MySingleFriend, he was a 36 year-old accountant, I know Bernie thought he was too old. Such a clever dog...' No. 58 continued for several minutes with her wave of information, often bending down and pushing a biscuit into Bernie with a short but emphatic 'Good Boy!' So a typical sentence actually sounded more like '…and then the accountant was bleeding from the arm Good Boy! and it's a shame because I liked him a lot but Bernie comes first Good Boy! He's always had such intuition with my friends but we've yet to find a suitable man to join the family Good Boy!…'

'It's amazing Bernie isn't fatter,' I suggested, but No. 58 appeared not to hear me.

'Do you like dogs?' she asked.

'Well, I'll be honest, I'm more of a cat person, but dogs can be quite cool.'

She stopped walking and for the first time showed some firmness with Bernie. He strained on the lead; his little head quickly becoming purple, and his Mother stared at me with cold eyes. 'They can be…cool?'

Oh God. She's crazy.

'Definitely!' I rejoice, trying to save the situation. 'Dogs are great company, and *some* are so clever! I bet Bernie's clever, I bet he can bring me a stick.'

No. 58 warmed instantly, predictably desperate to show how incredible her Biscuit On A Lead was.

'Good Boy!' she shrieked, giving him some food and releasing the lead. Then, turning to me she said, 'throw him a stick, go on…'

'Shouldn't you reward him *after* he's returned the stick?' I asked quietly, choosing a medium-sized branch and lobbing it as far away from us as possible. Bernie watched its trajectory and then ran off in the opposite direction towards some pigeons.

'Good Boy!' shouted No. 58, her hand outstretched and filled with biscuit. 'Come here Bernie, come!' Bernie didn't come, Bernie did a crap by a tree and ran further away.

'How long have you had him?' I asked.

'Three years and three months, seven days,' she answered robotically.

'Is he always this naughty?' I chuckled.

'Why, do you think he's naughty?'

'He…just…doesn't seem to be listening to you.'

'Oh, he is, he's just happy to be outdoors.'

I've always thought that women with disobedient dogs might make lax mothers, but this morning I realised that they also make disastrous dates. I learned nothing about No. 58, which was a shame because behind the Bernie-façade she actually seemed very nice, and cute, and together. It just goes to show, that when a young life is overly complicated by a pet, a human loses some of its glow. Pets should be for families, not individuals. Not until they're seventy, that is.

'Can you guess where I'm from?' asks Date No. 59 in a thick Essex accent, and thus began a date that showed the other side of my accent-phobic coin. Ordinarily, Essex girls aren't my type. Not even close. I'd run a mile. But if they're pretty, blonde, have an acerbic sense of humour and seem happy to laugh at even my most unfunny jokes, then I'll contentedly make an exception. Luckily, I was in a position to make an exception for Date No. 59, who told me she hadn't had much luck at Internet dating because all the blokes she had dated were retards who she couldn't bear to have more than one drink with. Then, our first drinks hastily supped, she dragged me across Covent Garden, stopping outside an Extreme Sports clothing store and shaking her head at the front-of-house display. 'They have no idea,' she tutted, pointing at the plastic men and women within, 'that should be there, he should be there, she shouldn't be there.'

I'm curious, either a display of in-depth window dressing expertise is underway, or she's just really fussy about mannequins. She turns from the window, glumness spread from ear to ear, and then catches my raised eyebrow and smiles, 'Does my head in when they fuck it up like that,' she says, and even that articulate summation of the situation doesn't make me like her any less, and neither do the next two sentences, which she delivers in a faux-cowering position. 'I have a confession to make,' she says, looking at me sideways and pulling out a cigarette, 'you know when I told you I didn't smoke...?'

She jumped on a bus at Piccadilly Circus with a wave and a toothy grin. It is bitterly cold and I hunch my shoulders up, pulling my scarf tight as I tread the streets towards Trafalgar Square. For two months and almost sixty dates my life has been utterly bizarre and it's starting to take its toll. I long for a day when I don't have to think about women, or me, or dating, or what any of it means. There is no disillusionment though, fifty-nine dates and still single may seem like a total failure, but Hannah has been writing more and we're now set for a third date tomorrow. My first third date: maybe this is going somewhere, finally.

Wednesday: *Day 54*
Date No. *60*

I am in two minds about dating today, because tonight I am meeting Hannah for the third time and I don't want to sully it. But that said, the sooner I can get all of this dating nonsense out the way the sooner I can become a normal person again. So I don't cancel my date with No. 60, I meet her at half past ten for a coffee.

No. 60 started her reply to my initial message on MySingleFriend with:

> Hi, I'm Ana.

She was making a point, mainly because I'd called her Hannah. What was more embarrassing was her reply to my apology, which said:

> Well it's ok as long as you weren't thinking about a Hannah.

I so was.

We sit in the downstairs of a musty yet cool independent café and chat a little bit, but not too fluidly, about anything and everything. She makes bags, I skate, she's German, I'm English. She's tiny, I'm not. It's just not going to work, especially when she tells me that all of her housemates recently had a meeting because she marked an egg in the fridge. She's not repentant;

'I thought I should mark it, it was mine' she shrugged. We left, soon after that.

The day ploughs on and I potter on my emails, on dating sites, on my phone. I'm nervous. Here comes a date with Hannah again.

Everything in Bayswater is new to me except the ubiquitous Underground sign and entrance. I don't stray far from its familiar gaping mouth, which spews people and more people. She'll be coming out of there soon, but I'm ten minutes early. A quick walk to a nearby Starbucks, I need to pee, nerves are rising. This is Date Three, I am venturing into new territory. Back outside the station I lean up against a lamppost and think about when I met Hannah, when she walked ahead with her flight bag down the narrow corridor in Leon, blowing me away, adding a new conundrum to this silly thing I'm doing. Potential. And it's still there, this potential, after all, we're on Date Three, but what does that mean? Like a long lost lover I try to picture her face, but instead of it being faded with time it hasn't even formed in my mind. I don't know her yet; I haven't kissed this girl, held her close to protect her from the cold, walked arm in arm. But this is our third date and I am spiralling towards a T-junction, do we go one way and move this along, or the other, and wave goodbye?

And there she is with a chirpy hello, cute as always in a long coat with a collar that wraps around her neck and fondles her jaw. She's smiling and guides me down these new streets, shoulder to shoulder but not hand in hand, chatting easily, as per, joking and laughing, as per.

'When do you go to Australia?' she asks.

'27th January,' I say, knowing she leaves for Mumbai exactly one month earlier. Which is, in fact, in two weeks and two days time. 'When do you get back from India?' I ask,

'30th January,' she says, looking at me sideways, and I force out a little ironic groan.

'Why are we on a third date, again?' She chuckles at that, and we walk on. She promised me chips but she's giving me a posh burger as well, which I am quite happy to accept, and we sit down again across a table that now feels like a salt plain, the distance between us screaming and highlighting the lack of physical contact we've had so far. This is Date Three, what does it mean?

In our emails Hannah doesn't rise to anything. Early on she was short, blunt, and articulate without giving much away. As we dated and talked more she opened up, exclamation marks began to appear, just one per message after our first date, then more after the second. But still she doesn't play to me, she plays away, and it reels me into the chase. My confidence rises and I flirt with her, but she doesn't reciprocate. I'm absolutely sure she's capable of it, there's a cheeky glint in her eye that screams 'flirt!' but I'm all clenched fists surrounded by walls of non-physicality and my usual instincts are being thwarted by this lack of closeness. She hasn't even given me her mobile number yet, but we message online all the time and we're on our third date. So why am I questioning this? Why am I feeling like maybe this isn't meant to lead anywhere? Maybe she thinks we're just here as friends?

Why the questions? Because, probably, I've never been on a third date before and I have absolutely no idea what I'm going to do when we say goodbye at the end of this night.

But God, this new ground, the looming geographical distance that threatens to descend, it makes no difference. We chat fast, learn about each other, interrupting because we want to know sidelines and ask new questions. I go and order the burgers and a side bowl of chips. My phone rings but I don't answer it, and I only realise that it was Hannah when I return to the table sheepishly saying that they want us to pay now, and she springs to her feet and tells me she called me to say we

213

should have chips, and I tell her it's covered, everything except the money. And when she trots to the counter I check my phone and see Missed Call, and there it is. Finally, Hannah's number. Nice to know she has a phone.

On the first bite of my burger I cover half my right cheek with mayonnaise and she immediately points it out, making a reference to my chocolate forehead incident on our first date. By this time, I'm so used to making a clot of myself there's no use being embarrassed, but I feign it anyway, holding my napkin up like a clean air mask, dabbing at the white smears to the side of my mouth. Help me Lord, save me from myself.

There's no silence. Laugh a minute. Questions answers jokes stories effortless piss-taking sip some wine ask an inappropriate question bite burger. We talk about dates we've been on recently; still open about the encounters we've had since seeing each other last. There's no awkwardness, we don't owe each other anything yet, we haven't kissed, but we're honest. Well, as much as can be. There are points when we come dangerously close to crisis, like when she told me I didn't look anything like my profile picture and I said, 'well what? You expected me to turn up in black and white?' And then I open my big mouth and lead her down the path, 'Just a couple of my dates have said I don't look like the pic, the rest all say there's a likeness,' and she holds out a hand and says,

'Ok, so two are right, but *all the rest*? Exactly how many are we talking here?' She counts out her fingers, 'more than ten?'

I nod grimly, and change the subject rapidly, and now all I can think about is whether I should tell her about The Hundred or not and I realise that we're getting to know each other and I like her and hopefully she likes me, and I can't just lay this bombshell down. It will spoil things and make the process unnatural, won't it? She's going away, I'm going away, but most of all what we're feeling is real, it's not affected by a book, by a challenge, I'm not doing anything wrong, but maybe she'll be affected by it if she knows. I want to kiss her first, to show her that I like her, to show her it doesn't matter that there's a book, but if I tell her about the 100 maybe she won't want to kiss me. She'll think it's too weird, knowing she's part of an ongoing story. I don't want the challenge to upset the balance, so I keep trying to avoid the issue because in fact, for the first time in two months, it is now the girl who is making me reconsider the challenge, rather than the challenge making me reconsider the girl. She asks, 'so what is your next book about?' and I pause, again contemplating the ramifications of telling the truth, and I play for time and shrug, then change the subject. Again. Each time she lets it go, not suspecting anything, and honestly I'm not at all sure what to do. With the truth. With the date. With anything. All I know is I like her. A lot. This is genuine. I can see us walking in parks together, I want to teach her how to skate so she understands how it feels, I want to wake up with her and read papers on a Sunday. I'd like to make her tea in the morning. But, before all of that, I'd quite like to get my head around the fact that as the minutes tick by the end of our third date approaches, and then it's crunch time. Because after three dates, well…stuff should probably be starting to happen.

She constantly makes jokes about me, tells me she hates three-quarter-length trousers and that I talk a lot, two of my favourite hobbies. I feign offence and sigh happily when she reveals she's a cat person. I need a woman who can take me down a peg or two and Hannah is capable of doing this every time she opens her mouth, yet she apologises and tells me she just doesn't have an inner monologue. We cover a lot of ground and I don't shy away from the difficult questions about past relationships and childhood bullying of redheads and just what you do when you're on a date that is just plain awful. We're both there, different people in different lives, but both on top of who we are and what we want. She's honest, and I am as much as can be without blurting out the whole bloody dating story, but I make do with telling her about the girl with the deaf voice and handing my card to the other girl outside Starbucks, and then I tell her how I felt when we said goodbye in Oxford Circus after our first date and all she said was 'take care', and she holds her head in her hands and says 'oh no' and it's all so evident, that we can read so much into incidents that have an impact on our emotions but at the same time both feel so differently that our worries are totally pointless. Why, when something monumental threatens to approach, do we hide our feelings behind false concerns?

We move on to a pub and finally sit close without a table between us, and she asks about my ex and how that relationship ended, and I tell her with complete honesty what happened, and then I go to the toilet and when I walk back into the room I see Hannah staring at one of the big TV screens, looking absolutely beautiful in rays of light, and I slow my pace so I can watch her more, then she turns and smiles a wide, gorgeous smile. And we start to layer up, because it's time for her to catch a train. This is it. This is it.

What do you do at the end of a third date? I want to kiss her, I need to kiss her. If I don't, she's going to walk away thinking *this dude is frigid, we've had three dates and still no action*! But my issue is this; *if* I instigate a kiss, will she just be kissing me back because it's the third date or because she really wants to? And how do I initiate it when I know so little about this girl on a physical level. It's not like I've never been close to a woman but here I am back at square one, confidence barely hanging above zero. Somehow, all of a sudden, I feel like I have something to lose. The station draws up like we're walking through a zoom lens and we enter, pass through the gates and then stand side by side in front of the tube map. There are stairs to the left and stairs to the right. Right is north to Paddington, her route. Left is south to Victoria, mine. This is it.

We stand side by side, looking at the tube map and commenting about red splotches on it.

'Is it wine or blood?' I ponder.

'Ewww, it has to be wine.' She says.

But we can only talk about red splotches on the tube map for so long before it gets awkward, so I take a deep breath and turn to face her, wringing my hands, which I suppose is a sign of preparation. We're a metre or so apart and I can tell she's beading her left eye at me, seeing me level up, yet she remains side on, facing the map. *Oh shit*, I think, *she's either going to avoid it or is going to kiss and run*. Please turn. Please turn. And then she does something amazing.

'Hey, i was good to see ya,' she drawls in a mock accent that may have been an attempt at American, but just turns out Strange and Cute. She's rocking from right foot to left foot, slowly turning her far shoulder towards me and faux punching my arm in slow motion, pressing her fist so gently into my bicep, which of course I tense to make it feel bigger, and as she follows through she continues to rotate and moves closer and then she's there, finally facing me, and I realise what she's done and I start to think *you cunning bugger* as I take one step in and she does the same. Our heads move closer and I'm still marveling at the genius of her icebreaker as our lips meet and people rush around down the steps to the left and right and we're still kissing, my hands tight on her waist, hers on my arms and back.

And we're still kissing and it's been about two minutes now but it feels like five and I want more and now I'm quite sure she's not kissing me just because we're on a third date. But I pull back to take a look at her face and she's still got her eyes shut, so I kiss her some more and raise my hands and run my fingers through her hair. And then there's the ugly rumble of a train. We pull apart, kiss again and then duck to look through the railings below the map, waiting for the train. 'It's mine,' she says triumphantly, because she's the competitive type, and kisses me one final time before looping round and making for the stairs.

'Hold on!' I shout, and dig into my bag. I hand her a copy of my book and she takes it coyly;

'I'll sign it for you next time,' I say. She smiles, and descends.

I am grinning like a little boy. Across the empty rail there is a train containing a blonde woman who is craning her neck towards me, holding up my book and mouthing the words *look at this*, and then she points at the cover of the book and then at me, and I do the same, and we're playing charades in Bayswater tube station. Yes, I am grinning like a little boy.

Thursday : Day 55
Date No. 61

I'm not sure that I should be doing this, walking through the crowded evening streets south of Oxford Circus, dodging people and bags and piles of refuse sacks, past Leon where I first met Hannah the first time and down Carnaby St, late for a date. I'm thinking about Hannah but I'm meeting someone else, who is sitting outside the Alphabet Bar on Beak St with a smile on her face. We walk and squeeze into a crowded bar and move on and have a bite to eat in a Thai restaurant with enormous bowls of soup. She's an absolutely lovely girl and she's setting up her own business and I quite like her. But it's not enough. We laugh and talk like friends, about dating, about life, about silly things like which would we choose to keep if we had to lose either our hands or our legs.

'I'd keep my hands, for writing, to feel with. I'm not sure I could enjoy sex without my hands,' I say.

'You're probably going to struggle getting sex if you have no legs,' she says, and I hide my hands down my sleeves and pretend to chat up an invisible lady, then bring up my handless arms and say,

'Oh no, I've blown it. You're not coming home with stumpy.' She laughs but we're both starting to wilt. We walk to her bike then say goodbye outside Oxford Circus, she's a fun girl but I'm relieved to get away, only because my head isn't in this. It was fine dating everyday when I was looking, but now I'm not so sure I'm looking anymore.

Back in Clapham Kate No. 27 meets me and I pour my heart out over a G&T. Poor Kate. I talk about the dilemma I face with Hannah, who with the first kiss out the way I'm now meeting again tomorrow.

'This is the date when we should walk along the river, hold hands, hug a bit, kiss some more, become more tactile, see our feet find some rhythm,' I say as Kate nods, 'but Date Four is serious stuff, it's the beginning of something new, a beginning which is going to be cut short in a couple of weeks when she flies to India. I'm sure something is happening between us, but when do I tell her about The Hundred? Now, or in March, when it's all over, when I'm done with the dating and I'm still stood there in front of her saying 'Hey, this is what I was doing when I met you, but it's over and I want you, please.'' Kate agrees that maybe waiting is the best way as I hold my head in my hands and mutter 'I just don't want to fuck this up' again and again. And then she says,

'Whenever you tell her, don't start by saying *I've got something to tell you*, it's awful.'

'Oh god! Did I say that to you?'

'Yes! I thought, oh god, is he married? Is he gay? Just start in a different way…'

'But how?'

'Oh, I don't know, you'll work it out.'

I hope so, I really do.

Friday: Day 56
61 dates so far

I'm pathetic this morning. It's one of those where I pour hot water on my cereal and milk over my toast before I realised what I was doing. I stopped just in time before butter went into the teapot.

The whole bloody day goes incredibly slowly, I struggle to get on with anything and slump around watching the clock, which kindly pretends not to move, for hours. I'm meeting Hannah at half past seven outside Earls Court station so I walk, Counting Crows on the iPod, my feet taking me through narrow pathways and to the left of forked roads until I emerge opposite Earls Court tube, again ten minutes early for a date with Hannah. Fourth Date. Unlike Date Three, though, I'm suffering from a different state of nervousness. I don't really have any doubts that this girl and I have potential; I'm just feeling like the secret I'm keeping is weighing heavier every time I meet her. I want to cast it off, to be honest and open, but I don't want to risk losing her. So as those final ten minutes tick down I wait, tap my feet, puff out my cheeks, and when she appears through the crowd I kiss her. And she doesn't exactly kiss me back.

Maybe she doesn't like kissing in public?
But what about Bayswater train station?
She'd had a couple of drinks by then...
Maybe she's nervous, too?
Maybe. Maybe she's writing a book about dating lots of men and has exactly the same dilemmas that I have.
Or maybe she doesn't have any dilemmas, and in her book follow-up dates do count.
I'm just a number to her! Four numbers!
Probably best not to worry about this though, eh, as you're just talking to yourself, Dave.
You're right, let's get back to it.

We walk along, meandering towards the river and talking about A-Level art projects and other people's weddings. Our hands are firmly in our own pockets and I guess I jumped the gun when it came to assuming we'd be strolling along like a married couple, but I can cope with that, she's here, I'm here, we talk and laugh but every time we pause and I give her a little peck on the lips she seems a little startled. Bloody hell, this one's a tough cookie, but she's reeling me in and I can't help but adore her. Had I stopped to think about why she wasn't being so tactile I might have realised that in two weeks she flies to India and maybe, just maybe, she's got that on her mind and doesn't want to push things with me. But I don't think, I just walk and walk and we cross a bridge and walk some more and chat and chat but don't find a pub until we've done about five miles having wandered from Earls Court to Battersea, where she says, 'isn't Clapham pretty close to here?' and I realise she might think I have naughty intentions,

'Umm not far, but don't worry, I'm not taking you home!' I say, sounding half serious. 'Oh god, I'm so sorry, we've almost done a marathon. We definitely deserve that drink.'

We find an old man's pub back across the river near Sloane Square and put our feet up. Side by side, arms touching, the occasional hand on leg, I'm still finding my way with her. She tells me she once had a little book that detailed information about every boy she kissed before she was 16, at least 60 of them, apparently. Jesus! Then, totally unrelated to her kissing information, I accidentally get a bit too close when I point at something across the pub and gulp apologetically, 'umm, I think I just touched your boob.'

'Yes you did,' she said, and in response I shuffled away just a little bit to show I'm not a pervert.

'Shit!' she growls, 'look at the time! I have to go and get my train, I'm so sorry.'

We're halfway through our drinks yet in seconds she's up, pulling on her coat, taking me completely by surprise. I don't know how to feel, this wasn't exactly the intimate date that perhaps I was expecting, we haven't even had a snog! Yet here we are making our way out the door, hurrying down the road, almost sprinting towards the end of another date. On the positive side, we haven't been quite as close as we were last date so I haven't had a chance to ruin everything with a revelation of my silly dating game, but still, I'm disgruntled. Kissing or no kissing, flirting or no flirting, I just like being with her, and very soon I won't be. I don't know what to make of the rapid exit and ask, 'what time's your train?'

'Around eleven,' she pants.

'You're going to struggle to make it,' say I, as we continue to jog.

'I know, but I could go to Maidenhead and get a taxi,' she suggests, and she sounds serious.

'Well look,' I offer, 'it's only Date Four and there's absolutely no pressure, but I have a spare room at my place, you're welcome to stay over if you need to.'

She looks at me and grins, 'Thanks, but I'll try and get the train, maybe I'll give you a call if I miss it.' She pauses for a moment, then adds, 'and if that happens then it'll be Date Five, because then we will have spent a little time apart.'

And you know what happens on Date Five.

Her plan is slightly flawed, though. If she misses her train and does indeed try to call me then I'll be hidden away in a tube somewhere, out of reach. 'I'll come with you to Paddington then, just in case,' I say,

'Are you sure?'

'Of course, it's silly you getting a train then a taxi.' She nods, thankful.

Secretly, I don't know what to hope for. A hastily departing train and safety from Impending Revelation of the Dating Challenge Story That Might Just Make Her Run A Mile. Or, if she misses the train, Hannah then joins me on the way back to Clapham, where undoubtedly I'm going to struggle to avoid a situation where I tell her about what I'm up to. I am terrific at putting myself in sticky situations. Why am I doing this? Oh please, god, give me a sign, what do I do next?

Hannah is on the phone to her Mum and I am offered a sign. The next tube to Paddington leaves in six minutes. It'll get to Paddington precisely when Hannah's westbound train leaves the station, which obviously is a little too late. She hangs up the phone and walks over to me,

'Are you sure it's ok if I stay at yours? I've told Mum I'm staying at a friend's in Brixton.' I nod, and start to panic as we climb onto the escalator and head across the bridge to the southbound track. 'Are you smirking at me?' she asks, and I shake my head, although I suppose I am in a way. I mean, of course I'm smirking, it was all looking so bad, our fourth date ending with her practically running away from me, yet now she's here, with me, coming back to my place. Brilliant, right? Well yes, but at the same time no. My hand has been forced and my head is swimming with reasons and things to say and the fact that my bedroom's a tip. Come on, I know what you're thinking; I said I had a spare room. Yeah yeah, but you make your own luck, right?

We hang about on the platform and I stand next to her, still smirking.

'So,' I say, 'do you do this on all your fourth dates? Pretend to miss the train so you...OW!'

She's given me a smart kick to the shin with a little, 'oh fuck off!' into the bargain. Well, I don't know what she expects, I'm going to dine out on that one for a while. On the tube I stand across the aisle, making it clear that I'm positioned away from her because *there's no pressure*, palms up, staring over at her in her coat with her cute face and big eyes looking at me and hair around her shoulders and yep, she's coming back to mine. I am in so much trouble.

'You can come over here if you like,' she suggests, and I'm a bit taken aback, because it's actually the first time all night that she's been forward with me. So I jump over like an eager dog and we kiss all the way to Clapham Common.

We have a drink in a pub just around the corner from the flat. It leads to more kissing and slowly I build up my courage. I feel like I need to tell her before we get home, because if I tell her at home then we're not on neutral ground. I don't want to trap her or make her feel uncomfortable, so I start talking about dates.

'I've never been on a fourth date before,' I say, 'but this is the definitely the best one I've had. Have you been on any others?' She shakes her head, then suggests that I'm fishing, so I say, 'I hadn't even been on a third date before Wednesday, had you? I'm not used to all this dating, it almost formalises getting to know someone, and because I'm unused to it I'm still struggling to read you,' and she looks at me with slightly closed eyes like a cat would before it tears the head off a mouse, and says,

'Dave, I'm not here for shits and giggles, if that's the information you're after.'

I don't shit, or giggle, but at the same time I feel quite smug, because despite all the hours of talking and clinking glasses and the kiss at Bayswater and the other kisses all the way home on the Circle, Victoria and Northern lines, this is the first tangible line that confirms that she likes me. It's nice to hear, and I figure she should hear it too, so say, 'I like you quite a lot,' and kiss her. And it's one of those kisses where we just drown in each other, not because of saliva, we're just deep in passion, and her hands are around my head and my right hand is on her thigh and then I shift position and our lips break when I almost lose my balance and suddenly my right hand is cupping her breast, again, in the middle of a bar.

'Ummm,' I say, 'probably not the time for that, was it,' but she giggles and kisses me some more. And then, finally, I make the decision to tell her that she's Number Thirty Three out of One Hundred, because our drinks are running dry and it's almost home time. I open my mouth to speak and suddenly I'm interrupted by a large creature to my right, a man, a strange man declaring that it's his 29th birthday, and I can't help but think to myself that he looks at least 32, and I shake his hand and say Congratulations and he says 'Wow you've got a handshake on you, let's arm wrestle.' So we're hand in hand, elbows on the arm of the couch and I'm preparing to do battle in front of my lady and end up looking like a right idiot because when he says 'go' his arm goes purposefully limp and I drive it into the sofa looking like I was trying far too hard.

Seconds later, Hannah and I are putting our coats on. We're leaving. We're going back to my place. And I haven't bloody told her yet.

Outside my front door we slip past four girls who are waiting for a party next door – this is the first time any girls have been waiting outside my flat! – and as I fumble with the key I use the delay to warn Hannah,

'I wasn't quite expecting anyone to come back tonight, so you're going to have to close your eyes and count to a thousand while I rush around with my duster.' I pop her on the sofa, fetch her a drink, put the TV on and start to clean and tidy and panic all at the same time, because here I am changing sheets and throwing clothes in cupboards while there's a gorgeous woman in my front room who has no idea that she's in the front room of some bloke who's 61% of the way through a dating marathon. Oh shit. Oh shit. Oh shit!

About twenty minutes later I'm done and half expect to find her curled up asleep on the sofa. Luckily she's not and I settle in, we kiss for a bit and I feel my blood pressure rising. Eventually I sit up straight, I just have to get this out of the way and if I don't do it now I'll never do it, my mouth is so dry I feel my lips cracking, so I take a sip of water and look at her,

'I'm writing a book,' I say.

'What about?' She looks at me with an eyebrow raised.

'About dating.'

'You're kidding me.'

'I'm not.' I take one more sip of water and move closer to her. 'Look I'm really nervous telling you this so please bear with me.' I reach for her hand and hold it gently. Then I tell her, how I've wanted to write a book about relationships for years and about how I felt ready to meet someone again when I moved to Clapham. I told her how looking at online dating sites gave me the idea for dating 100 women in 100 days and I told her that is exactly what I've been doing for the last 56 days. She's quiet throughout this and looks straight at me as I finish the story, and then I say, 'and the thing is, now I've met you I don't think I want to date anymore.' I stop, and add, 'At the same time, I know that sounds really pressured, but I just wanted to be honest with you. You're going away and then I'm going away, and I had no idea when to tell you about this, I really didn't know what to do.'

'It's ok' she says, 'two things come to mind. One, I'm still not actually sure if you are writing a book, but either way it's a really good line.' She leant forward and kissed me gently, just to confirm this. 'And two, it's a really good idea and I wish that I'd thought of it first.'

Oh thank God for that.

'Well, I am writing a book and I can prove it to you, want me to read you something?' I say,

'Ok,' she answers, clearly still not sure whether I have anything to read to her.

I shuffle over to my computer and look back at her, 'what do you want to hear, Date One, Date Two or Date Three? I'm fast, but haven't quite finished Date Four yet...'

She makes a faint noise of disgust, then smiles, 'Date One.'

So I read it out loud as she lies down on the sofa and buries herself in cushions, protecting herself from the words. A groan comes from her direction when I talk about her leaving me in Oxford Circus with a non-committal 'take care' and when I finish I sit down all nervously beside her and she tells me it's all ok again. Then she looks up at me with big eyes and a smile and says, 'you're going to be really busy for the next month, aren't you.'

'What do you mean?' I ask, perplexed.

'Well, I think you should finish this, you've started it and it's research, right? So you should finish it.' I can't quite believe what I'm hearing, this girl is almost too perfect and I start to wonder whether I've been kissing a robot all night. She continues, 'look, you never know, you might meet someone in Australia and come back married with three kids.'

'Well, considering the average gestation period, that's unlikely,' I say, 'but thank you for being so cool about all this. I know the India-Australia thing isn't exactly perfect, but I'd still like to see you more before you leave.'

'I'd like that too,' she says, and slowly my heart returns to its natural beating pace.

Saturday: *Day 57*
Date No. 62

'You've given me love bites!' she shouts from the bathroom, and when she returns to the bedroom she sits on my legs and I take a look. I'm quite sure I wasn't overly nibbly but Hannah tells me that her skin is 'sensitive and wussy' and she's right, there are faint patches of red on her shoulders.

'Well,' I say, 'let's not be too hasty and refer to them as *love bites*...' and I turn her and lay her on the mattress and she laughs. It takes such an effort for me to be nonchalant around her, but she responds to dryness and I'll oblige when I can…

Outside the flat Hannah notices that the builder's portaloo has *DavLar* written on the side.

'Are you two related?' she asks. We wander to Clapham South and I can't help but notice that our feet are in sync, left feet, right feet, perfectly in time. A few metres before we reach the station she slips her hand into mine and gives it a squeeze. 'You're nice,' she says 'well done.' And then she kisses me quickly and walks away, almost floating into yet another train station. I feel quite dizzy, but with lighter shoulders than I've had for a while.

I know now, I don't want to date anymore. *Why am I doing this?* I thought as I wandered into town to meet No. 62. A sly, sarcastic Northerner, she called me last week and peppered her sentences with humour as though we'd known each other forever. She texted one morning asking if I liked meat, and I replied in the positive, suggesting that only a veggie would ask that question. She replied:

> *Me no am northern meat, meat, meat! Jus wondered*
> *© thought came as I was about to say u sit on the*
> *couch n I'l arrange a nice breakfast n then I thought*
> *eggs n bacon may not float ur southern fairy couch*
> *sittin socialite boat* ☺

I texted back; *Don't they have full stops or commas up North?*

> *No just steak n chips n eggs n women wit short skirts*
> *©*

We met in town and walked to a bar. When we entered there was Jo in a corner, on a date. 'What are you doing here?!' she screeched, striding across the floor, hair a' flicking.

'I'm on a date,' I say, and Jo's eyes widen and mouth opens in a perfect circle, the words *of course* slowly tattooing themselves onto her forehead. I introduce the girls without getting into specifics, wave at Jo's date who seemed a little befuddled but was almost certainly about to get a full and graphic rundown from a talkative giant, and then for two hours the Northerner and I sit and drink and chat and laugh at Jo, whose conversation is still very much within earshot despite us being on opposite sides of the room. In person Date No. 62 does pause during sentences, she's friendly and good looking without much make-up, but I still find myself drifting off and silences pepper our conversation as a consequence. A text comes through from Hannah that is completely distracting:

> *I have just got the last knots out of my hair. Thank you for...er...having me! X*

Date No. 62 is talking to me, asking me what I think about something. I stare back at her, obviously caught out like a naughty child at the back of the class, my eyes full of apology. *Just what am I doing here?* She's got balls, No. 62, and she likes smiling, I'll give her that. But I sat through our date barely moving, barely thinking, just staring at a pretty girl thinking how I couldn't imagine doing anything worse. But I'm not being fair. She's lovely, a teacher, very articulate and funny, but I feel embedded in an awkward limbo. Almost like I'm getting over somebody I'd been seeing for a while and I've just realised that it's way too soon to start dating again. And when you're in that position there's only one thing for it if you're going to be true to yourself and to the girls you're seeing, you just stop dating and get yourself sorted.

Sunday: *Day 58*
Date No. 63

This is my second date since Hannah and I spent our first night together and my heart is no longer in this challenge. I set out to find someone and I have found her, so why continue? At present I'm not sure I have a good reason, after all I'm halfway through a paragraph before even mentioning the girl I'm dating at the moment. She can wait a little bit longer. I've come so far and met so many that throwing the challenge away so quickly would be silly, wouldn't it? So I'm now testing this new ground. Meeting girls now is making me assess how I feel, right? Whether or not I can get anything out of continuing yes? Is it fair on the girls I'm seeing? Well, perhaps not, but on a first date nothing is set in stone, and at the same time I might meet a friend or discover something new. I'm just not sure that I'm any longer in a position where I could feel strongly for a girl, because frankly it's hard enough for me to boil an egg without thinking about Hannah.

'Are you ok, Dave' asks No. 63.

'I'm so sorry, I was miles away.'

'No seriously, are you ok? You look like death!'

'I'll be honest with you, that wasn't the look I was going for.'

She laughed at that, but I'd been caught out, again. I felt something rising inside; a tumbling, bubbling, fluttering mass, spiralling from the base of my stomach upwards, through intestines, tickling the inside of my skin in a warming cloud. I felt like an upside-down cough syrup commercial, slowly filling up with a new colour, a new substance. It was getting close to my head now, filling my throat and then, then...

'Dave, is that a butterfly coming out of your mouth?'

She didn't actually say that, but if she had I wouldn't have been at all surprised. Instead, she was still looking at me, wondering why I looked like I looked, waiting for an explanation. So I smiled with mostly a straight mouth, and said,

'I'd quite like it if you didn't punch me, but you are the 63rd woman I've dated in the past 58 days, and in different circumstances I think I'd be much better company, but as it happens I'm not sure I should have even met you tonight.'

One of Date No. 63's eyebrows was so high I couldn't see it anymore, but the next thing she said came as a very pleasant surprise.

'Fancy another drink?'

'Yes please,' I said, 'I think I need one.'

'Trust me, you're not the only one,' she said.

Even though she'd suggested it I thought it appropriate to buy this round. She joined me at the bar and looked at me after she'd pulled her eyebrow down to the middle of her forehead.

'I should explain,' I said. And I did. I told her everything; why it had all started, how No. 1 had been lovely but she was fond of cars so it would never have worked, how No. 4 had been illiterate and terrified of everything, how I'd slipped up on Date No. 12 and slept with Jo, how No. 18 had basically decided to date David the Quizmaster, and how utterly disheartening it had felt to date thirty one women and still not meet anyone special. And then I told her that actually life has a way of treating you just how you treat it, because just as I was feeling so low that the only answer was that I'd committed a bad act somewhere along the line, along came No. 33 and No. 34 to give me hope again.

'So,' said Date No. 63 quietly, 'you've met someone already?'

'Yes,' I said, 'I'm pretty sure I have.'

'I'm really happy for you,' she said, 'and even though this is one of the strangest dates I've ever been on I'm still glad I met you.'

'Thanks for being so understanding,' I said, 'I couldn't have had a nicer last date.' And with that we downed our drinks, hugged each other and headed for the door.

'Let me know when the book comes out,' she said, outside.

'I will, good luck with your dating.' I winked at her, turned around and then walked away. When I was sure she wasn't looking anymore I stopped walking, raised my arms above my head and looked up at the night sky and spoke two words that made me feel very happy indeed. 'It's over!'

NINE

And it Ends

This is the first morning of the rest of my life. Obligation is tiring, and with no pressure to date anymore I have a little lie-in. Do I feel guilty? Not one bit. It was confusing for a while there, and who's to say that I wasn't wrestling with the varying factors at hand: for the best part of two months I was looking for a girl, counting off items from a list, dating dating dating, and hoping to write a book based on all of it. What was the most important bit? I didn't know for quite a while, but now I do. The girl, that's what. Frankly I'm delighted not to have to meet Nos. 64 to 100, because somehow, out of the blue, No. 33 arrived. And, I'll be honest, I'm glad she came along not just because she's quite brilliant, but also because I'm absolutely knackered!

I spend the day looking forward to seeing Hannah later. She's joining Will and I at The Calf but will turn up a little late. I haven't seen Will for a couple of weeks and he's taken aback by everything that's happened.

'Told you that you wouldn't finish it,' he said, gloating.

'Thanks for your friendship, mate,' I said with a grin, 'but actually you said I wouldn't get past fifty-seven, so you're a loser.'

'Ah, well, you barely made that,' he accepted his wrongness in mock defeat.

He got wasted at his work Christmas party on Friday, lost his dinner jacket and keys and got dragged away from popstar Sarah Harding in Mahiki.

'What happened?'

'Oh, apparently I was dancing with her and her bouncers took me away.'

'Mate you're a drunken idiot!'

'I know. But luckily everyone else seems to have heaps of shame on their shoulders too, so it's all ok.'

'How're your dates going?'

'Ahh, they're ok, had lunch with a girl yesterday, great tits, vacant though.'

'You're not still talking about the Northern line with these girls, are you?'

He pauses and looks at me sideways.

'Well, sometimes there's just nothing else to talk about.'

Later, I collect Hannah from Clapham Common and proudly sit her down at our table. We fiddle through the quiz and I can't quite believe my ears when David the Quizmaster – who has recently bagged himself a job starring in the new Video Piracy advert in the cinemas – reads out the following question:

'Which famous writer recently travelled across Australia, on a skateboard?' I bury my head in my hands, utterly embarrassed. Later David texts me:

Did she cotton on?

I replied:

I think her words were, 'you bleedin' idiot!'

Tuesday
63 Dates so far

I am falling apart at the seams, what is wrong with me? One girl, one totally gorgeous girl, and I'm done for. We wake this morning after our second night together, Hannah's blonde hair gushes around and she makes a quaint half-spitting half-blowing noise as she tries to blow it out of her face. We fit together; our bodies, our faces, our mouths. Our legs intertwine and we tumble. She lies on me, kissing me, then we're side by side talking about something serious, and then I'm on top of her, kissing again. We have a little giggle at the lack of stillness. I haven't felt like this for so long and I feel myself falling; so quickly, so dangerously. I know that in just a few days I'm going to hit the floor. She's going to fly away and I'm going to miss her like crazy, this girl that I barely know. I've been talking for months about finding this chemistry but haven't been able to explain how it feels, and now it's here, consuming me, tying knots in my belly even when we're apart for just a few hours. I can't explain how it works or how it has taken over my life. It just has. Nothing else is important to me anymore.

But does she feel the same? I have no way of knowing. She's not giving much away and I don't know her well enough to read her, but there are mixed signals. She tells me she left on Saturday morning feeling very happy, but this morning she buries her head in the pillows when I make a cheeky suggestion that may or may not have involved some physical stuff. 'I can't lie,' she says, and bumbles into a confusing explanation which involved sex in the stark light of day being different to sex at night, and at one point she mentioned sex with other people but quickly it was wiped over. Hannah raises a point that I hadn't considered before; she thinks that people in regular, highly stressful jobs have a lower sex drive. She tells me she knew from early on that I had a high sex drive, 'like an eighteen year-old,' was how she put it.

'God I hope not,' I said, staring at the ceiling, 'I didn't have sex until I was nineteen.'

But it's an interesting point, if my lifestyle lends itself to a higher drive, what if my future partner has a more regular routine and therefore a lesser need or desire for sex? Will that place pressure on a relationship, eventually? Maybe it already has, in my past?

Through these conversations it seems like Hannah is trying to highlight the obvious differences between us, and I get an unannounced but distinct feeling that she's telling me not to get my hopes up. But I tell myself I'm being irrational, because she kisses my arms and hands and lips and neck as we talk, and later when we walk to the station we do so hand in hand having spent a fair bit of time on the sofa in deep embrace. Despite the closeness there's still a distance, though, and I don't know whether it is purely because we don't yet know each other, or whether she's protecting herself, or something else entirely.

Before another train station farewell, I want to try and make things clearer. Up until now I hadn't found the right moment to tell her that I couldn't stand the thought of going on a date with anyone other than her, so I go for it. 'I've ended the challenge. I just don't see the point anymore,' I told her, holding both of her hands. 'Hey, we're hardly married here, but I want you to know how I feel out of honesty, not an intention to pressure anything.'

She blushed a bit, then released a bombshell.

'Umm, I think you should carry on, I think you should finish it. And, anyway…I…er…I'm going on a date on Thursday with another guy, he's bought theatre tickets already.'

'You're kidding me!' I blurted out. But I didn't have a right to do that because I'm dating 100 bloody women, at least I was, but it still bugs me, because I would fob off any date to spend more time with her, and that she's not willing to do that for me just, simply, hurts like hell. Or maybe, just maybe, it's time for me to take her to the theatre. She didn't react to my reaction; she looked away like nothing had happened.

I am twisting myself into knots, sprinting into brick walls, making myself sick. I am not in control of my feelings; they are now hers to drag along like a dog on a lead. I perk up in the afternoon when we text each other at exactly the same time, but deep down I'm a lost soul. This should be fun, meeting someone, and instead I'm doing my head in. I need to think about something else, maybe I need to do as Hannah suggested and date some more.

Will texts in the early evening, referring to Hannah:

> *She seemed pretty awesome actually – bright and very pretty.*

At least I'm not fooling myself. Tonight's sounding board is Kate and obviously I can't stop talking Hannah. Kate did nothing but take the piss out of me, which I probably deserved for being soft as a kitten's underbelly. Afterwards I walked home and called Jo, and she said 'ahhh' a lot, despite having her own dating problems. And then I get a text from Hannah saying she can't meet tomorrow now because she has an interview, and I feel like my heart has been ripped out, because although she can meet me on Friday that's three days away. I'm a total mess, what the hell is wrong with me?

Before I go to bed Hannah writes on MSF, finally giving me her email address, our tool of communication while she's in India. I reply through the dating site, for the last time:

> *Gosh, an email address. You're very modern! Well why not one last message for old times sake? Foolish of me I know, but I want to grab every minute with you I can before you swoop off, I just want you to know you're absolutely fabulous and you make my head spin. I'm so glad we met. If you change your mind about tomorrow or Thursday I couldn't give a hoot if you called at 10:55 to ask if you can come over, I may well eat my own arm if I have to wait until Friday, and a free house is a free house...*

She texts half an hour later, eluding to a pen of mine that she accidentally took earlier:

> *Of course, should you need your pen back sooner, I could always drop it round after the theatre.*

I check MySingleFriend before bed, and realise that she texted me without even reading my message. I felt calmer, after that. She was going to visit me after her date. Which meant she was basically going to the theatre with a friend, and then coming home to me afterwards. And more importantly, I only had two days to kill before seeing her, rather than three.

Wednesday
63 Dates so far

I'm a bundle of nerves and butterflies, but I wake with an uncertain feeling deep within my gut that I know by now is attributable to one woman, rather than one hundred. Although I'm still a bit confused by the fact that she's going on a date with another chap tomorrow night I feel okay about it, because she's promised to come and see me afterwards.

'I feel bad,' she told me yesterday, 'because I don't particularly want to go on this date but we arranged it ages ago and he went out and spent lots of money on tickets, so I feel like I should.'

'That's extremely nice of you,' I said, glancing at her sideways with my eyes a bit squinty, 'just make sure you don't accidentally make him like you a lot.'

'You think I'd do that?' she asked, in mock surprise.

'I think you're capable of it,' I said, 'besides, just to keep you on your toes I've organised two dates for tomorrow.' I widened my eyes and stuck my tongue out, which almost certainly made me look like someone who wasn't worth dating. I hoped she'd be all, 'Really?! Well, if I don't go on my date will you cancel yours?' and I would have said 'Yes!' And in reality it would have been very easy, because I hadn't organised any dates at all.

But Hannah didn't so much as grunt at me, which was slightly disappointing, because now I had to try and organise two dates, and pronto.

Luckily MySingleFriend saved my bacon, and for reasons I couldn't comprehend the only two girls who were willing to date me today were both called Amy. After lunch I headed to Clapham Junction to meet Amy No. 1, aka Date No. 64. Through our messages she has described herself as a former tap dancer, currently unemployed. When I pushed her for more details she explained that she spent much of her time under a duvet and liked taking vitamins, but that she felt flustered after moving house recently so was now doubling her daily dosage of Vitamin C. Thankfully I wasn't being too picky, so Amy made it through my updated and stringent pre-date tests (she was a woman) and I kicked a can around outside the station hoping she'd at least be pretty. At quarter past two I walked right into the station but couldn't see anyone who looked remotely Amy-like, and although I was tempted to check under a grubby looking duvet at the service entrance I restrained myself. At twenty past two I checked my phone for the umpteenth time and then began to contemplate something I hadn't yet had to deal with, exactly how long should you wait for a first date to turn up?

Clapham Junction is an overground station, so there are no *I was on the tube and the train was delayed* excuses. So this girl is just late or maybe, she's not coming. How long should I stand around for? I try to call her number but there's no answer, so I wait until half-past two, call her again, and then begin the long walk home. I'm not sure if there's an unwritten rule for this kind of thing, but half an hour seems more than enough time to wait for a stranger who hasn't suggested any likely tardiness. She's probably at home popping Vitamin C pills and dreaming about tap-dancing, in bed.

I've got a few hours to kill before my second Amy of the day, and spend it wondering whether I'm allowed to include dates that have stood me up. I decide, reluctantly, that I'm not, even though I did wait thirty minutes. I briefly wonder whether I've made the right decision to stop dating but a text message from Hannah that reads *I like gingers* reminds me that there's only one person I want to be dating right now, and therefore I'm sure that my instinct is on cue.

At 6pm and with not inconsiderable strain I chucked on some clothes and ventured out into the evening darkness, heading for my second Date No. 64 of the day. I was intrigued by this girl for the very shallow reason that she'd promised to wear stiletto heels on the date, and while I was quite sure I'd be able to resist the temptations that high heels deliver, I still very much looked forward to seeing them. I'm not sure why, but I've always had a thing for the rear ankle on a girl, and when it's all lifted up and stretched out by heels I find it handy for everyone involved if I just tie myself up for a few minutes until she's had sufficient time to escape.

I got to London Bridge just on time and set about scouting for sexy shoes. Five minutes passed, and then ten, and then a strangely familiar feeling began to develop, am I seriously going to be stood up twice in one day? Then, across the road, I spot someone who I think is Amy. I dash across just as the little green man lights up and then I find myself flying through the air and landing smack on the sharp edge of the curb. A little dazed, I turn to see a cyclist lying in the middle of the road, his front wheel all misshapen. In fact, if I look closer, I can see the dent is in the shape of *my* leg, which is starting to hurt a bit, by the way. Luckily nothing is broken, on me or the cyclist, although I'm tempted to change that when he blames me for all the commotion. I point at the pedestrian lights, still showing the green man, and then limp grumpily away from the compulsory small crowd that always gathers around accidents in London with not one of them thinking to lend a hand.

Of course, I can't see the girl now, so I return to our agreed meeting spot via another zebra crossing and continue to wait. After twenty-five minutes I get excited as a pair of heels clip clop up the tube station stairs, but the woman in them isn't called Amy, which is embarrassing as I walked right up to her and brightly said 'Nice shoes!' She walked away very quickly, and still I waited. I know what to do in this situation, being well versed at it, and I watch as my iPhone clock ticks up to 7pm. Half an hour, time's up, I'm going home. Then, just as

I'm walking to the bus stop my phone beeps: *Fancy some company?*

It was Hannah.

Ordinarily, at any other point in this crazy last two months of mine, I would have been well and truly pissed off by being stood up twice in one day, but the double-Amy-farce had just served to vindicate my decision to finish the challenge early. After all, No. 64 just didn't seem to want to happen and the only woman who wanted to spend time with me was the only woman I wanted to spend time with, No. 33. So, with a special surprise heading from town to my house, I jumped on the No. 133 and began my journey home, thanking the heavens that I didn't end up on a date tonight. I send Kate No. 27 a text:

> *Stood up twice today, is someone telling me something?!*

She seemed sympathetic:

> *Do you think they both saw you and left?! I think being stood up should count as a date...After all it's not your fault!*

In reality, I may have waited longer for both of them had Hannah not been on the scene, but now I could afford to cut my losses.

Thursday

We wake and roll around and eventually leave the house in almost perfect light, hand in hand along Clapham Common Southside. Hannah buys papers and we sip smoothies in the Glow Lounge with the Guardian and Express and Mail, and she tears pages out when a feature catches her eye and I pretend to read a paper she's not destroying when in actual fact I'm just thinking about her, and us, and all of this. There's a man in Yorkshire somewhere who has so many Christmas decorations around his house and garden that he can't make a cup of tea because there's no power left, but if he plugged Hannah and me in he'd be pouring Tetleys for the whole bloody county.

This girl, who does she think she is? She has walked into my life and turned my head upside down, then shaken it a little bit to see if anything's left. I am a man made of jelly; desperately trying to fake a backbone in order to prove to her I'm worth keeping. When we're in bed together my left arm goes numb. This has never happened before, I feel the blood ebbing and flowing above my left elbow, I have no explanation. I still try to explain to her, though.

'You know how your stomach feels when you're in a car and drive fast over a small bump or hill?'

'Yes,' she nods.

'Well, it feels like that, but in my arm, over and over again.'

'I'm not sure Byron or Keats would have put it quite so eloquently,' she says with a straight face, and there she is, blonde hair about her shoulders, making my arm numb and taking the piss out of me for it.

In the mid afternoon we walk across the Common and drink hot chocolate (me) and peppermint tea (her) in The Pavement Café. I've been grappling with myself, imploring my inner beast to relax and not be too full-on, too impetuous, too hasty. Yet I find myself unable to avoid inviting her to meet my family two days before Christmas. As soon as I do I stare into the middle-distance, wondering whether I've made a mistake. As she did at the end of our second date she answered immediately in the negative, and I swell with embarrassment. You see, I am out of control. My head is swilling with chemicals. Hannah is a drug, an addiction. My actions and words are now uncontrollable, I have no idea whether she feels what I feel but I am programmed to chase my heart and make her a part of my life. I want to take her home to meet the family, I want to show her off to my friends, I want to make her mine, yet I'm not sure yet if this is how it is going to end. I haven't felt this way for years; I'm overwhelmed with a horrendous cocktail of joy and fear. Yet I shouldn't be feeling fear, I should be falling through air with arms outstretched and a sense of blissful dizziness, and I'm not because I'm absolutely terrified of losing her. I am over the moon, yet we have so long apart from each other so soon after meeting I have no idea where it's going to end. So I'm trying, sometimes too hard perhaps, and each time I say something that perhaps should have been said a couple of weeks further into a relationship I check myself and look doleful. We plan to meet tomorrow afternoon after her work and discuss what to do, and me, being immensely cool and trying not to make a prat out of myself, said;

'We'll be spontaneous and see where the wind takes us.'

'What if there's no wind?' She asked,

'Then we'll make our own…'

My head is bowed in my hands, and a howling emanates from the rooftops. *Swallow me, retract my own words, please! Just stop talking, Dave, you'll only get yourself into trouble if you continue.* At 4pm Hannah and I say goodbye at Clapham Common tube and she tells me she needs to go home tonight after her date to see her mum. I wander home looking at my feet. This girl is a virus in my brain; I am high, I am low, I am a total bloody mess.

My thoughts about Hannah are temporarily suspended by a message from the second potential No. 64 from yesterday. She tells me she eventually made it to London Bridge, and didn't seem at all happy that I wasn't there. This might be an understatement, prepare yourself:

> *Where were you? I got to London Bridge and tried calling you but I got someone called Andrew. The way you behaved last night probably tells me a lot more than I would have learned by actually meeting*

you. Unfortunately I have concluded that you are impatient (is 30 mins some magic number? - all my friends said "Everyone would wait at least 45 minutes because you know what London Transport is like"). You don't think (did you even consider that perhaps something bad had happened to me - hit by a car/mugged and phone stolen). You have no common sense (you don't seem to have taken any practical actions like checking with station staff if there were any engineering works on my line, or any trains cancelled/delayed, or asking around for an internet cafe/booth and trying to contact me). You don't give people the benefit of the doubt (my first thought when I couldn't find you was not "he's stood me up" but "I must have taken down his number wrong" so the first thing I did after walking several times between the two exits was to find an internet point and contact you). Oh, and you were a wimp (obviously got cold and went home).

The whole thing was a massive role reversal - I am supposed to be the irrational strop-throwing female, yet it was me who, despite being completely impractically dressed, was running around taking all the practical steps to try to find you while you were sat at home drowning in self-pity in the warmth.

In addition, plenty of men tell me that I am very punctual and they practically "expect" girls to be "at least" 10-15 mins late for a date because something goes wrong with their hair/nails/makeup/clothing/tights/shoes when getting ready - I don't think you're quite appreciating the amount of time/effort us girls take to get ready or you would have certainly waited longer than half an hour. I only regret not arranging to meet one of the other men queuing up to meet me from this site (one was willing to drive from Bristol to meet me!) or spending the evening with my friend who just got dumped after 9 years, or my Granddad who is recovering from an operation, and that I wasted my time on you.

Blimey when you put it like that! Although it was slightly full-on and overcooked, it was one of those emails that got my heart beating. I'm not sure that my lack of thought on the matter had anything to do with her getting mugged or hit by a car, but she was clearly quite angry and I suppose I would have been after a troublesome journey that proved to be fruitless. I took a few lessons from her message; maybe I didn't wait long enough. Maybe I should have double-checked my phone number for errors before giving it to her. And yes, I probably should have found an Internet café – I didn't because I knew she had my number (didn't know I'd given her the wrong one though!). All of that said, in my defence she had been unwilling to give me her number and checking for train delays would have been difficult, because I had no idea where she was coming from. Also, and I don't think this is out of place, but if women do have a lot to do to prepare for a date, surely they should start preparing earlier? Owning lipstick doesn't give a carte blanche for tardiness and mentioning her ill Granddad or just-dumped friend was just a low blow. And jeez, she should have been on time - I got struck by a commuter bicycle because she was late! I didn't expect it to change her opinion of me, but I wrote her a little reply:

I'm really sorry about last night. I had no idea that I'd given you the wrong number and assumed that you'd text if you were going to be late, (you couldn't and that was my fault, I know). I understand you're annoyed but my reasons for leaving after 30 minutes weren't down to me being cold or impatient or the fact that I'm a no-hoper, I just didn't think you were coming. You didn't give me your number either, and if you had I honestly would have called it to see if you were ok. I had no idea where you were coming from, either, so couldn't have gained much by checking for delays. I should have waited longer and I'm sorry I didn't. Hope you have better luck with other dates.

Her reply zipped back straight after I pressed Send.

I didn't give you my number because I don't know you from Adam, there are plenty of nutcases out there and us girls have to look after ourselves. You must have a bit more faith in women and yourself! You are a Muppet!

Dating is definitely one of those things that can make you want to kill yourself. Thank goodness the other Amy didn't write, otherwise I may have struggled to make it through the night. Despite the drama, I'd be lying if I said I didn't spend the evening thinking about the fact that Hannah was on a date with another bloke. I didn't like it. As the clock crept past 11pm I received a text:

Play was ace, boy not a patch on you. Now getting v cold ears on way home. Sleep well, hasta manana x

Friday

I mulle l around before a midday interview on BBC Radio's new chan el, 6 Music, with George Lamb and Johnny Saunders. Ialfway through we're talking about skating across the Austra lian desert when George asks out of the blue, 'Dave, do you have a girlfriend?'

Talk at but a loaded question. The possibility that somehow he knows bout the dating challenge flashes through my mind and by the time it has I've answered him, 'no...' Flustered, I continue, ...but I did have one out there...' I pause again, because I've said far too much, I am out of interview practice and am tal king about my ex on national radio! '...but I'm not going to ta k about that, it's a bit...erm...emotional,' I say with a nervous augh, and George eventually leads me back onto his original point, which was, in fact, whether or not I had any skateboarc ng moves to impress the ladies. I round off a distinctly wkward section of the interview by telling him that no, I didn t, unless you count skating very fast, in a straight line, for a s upidly long time. I am such a loser.

In the afternoon I wait for Hannah in our place, at the corner tab e in Leon where we first met. She brightens up my day with her smile and she looks gorgeous, always impeccably turned ou, today in sheepskin coat and similarly coloured boots. She curls up in the corner and I fetch two teas, Peppermir and Earl Grey, before settling down next to her, lightly kne iding her neck, her legs draped over mine.

'How v as the interview?' she asks,

'Slightl / funny, slightly embarrassing, it really depends on how you l ook at it,' I grin. Everything and nothing, we talk about. 'Ha e you got baby names picked out?' I ask, and she instantly s ays 'Jack.' We've spent so much time together in such a sho t period of time that we're like married strangers, talking tor gue in cheek about the future, never establishing commitme it but still hinting at general plans which we could both happi y fit into should the chance arise.

Afterw rds we walk through Covent Garden to the National P ortrait Gallery and see the oiled faces of the people who shape l our country, and then we wander across Trafalgar

Square and over the river with Big Ben shrouded in mist and our fingers firmly entwined. Along the South Bank dark figures shuffle on the beach below, 'what are these sneaky characters up to?' Hannah whispers, instantly regretting her suspicion when we peer down upon a wonderful sand sculpture of an elderly couple and their dog watching TV. I drop some coins into the bed below, and they tinkle together to a muffled "thank you" chorus from the two men guarding their work.

Saturday

'I've had a wonderful week,' I say, looking down at her face as she nuzzles into my neck, her arm tight on my waist, mine around her shoulders drawing her in.

'So have I,' she says, and if it was possible she moved even nearer.

The crowds swill as we close in on Clapham Junction and we sidestep through them and into the station. She flies to India on Thursday and although we might see each other later this week Christmas plans may well get in the way. So as the clock shutters past 11:50am I know that she's about to go, and this could be it.

'Let's assume that we'll see each other before I go, it'll be easier that way,' she says, holding me, kissing me.

'Have a great day,' I tell her,

'Thank you,' says she, polite to the end. And then she goes, tiny and perfect in a grey top, her coat draped over her arm, blonde hair still slightly wet from this morning's shower. There's one glance back at me as she passes through the gate.

I am empty inside. Her impending departure is sucking a vacuum in my belly, replacing gushing joy with sheer sadness. We engineered this together, seeing each other intensely before the short-term shelf life kicked in was asking for pain, but last night has sealed us together. She told me she worried about my age, even that I had just moved to London. She's concerned about the fact that as we have no mutual friends and that as we met in fairly unusual circumstances I'm effectively a stranger to her. Her difficult childhood, she told me, makes her yearn for security. So I tell her more, prove to her that I'm not as flighty as the last two years might suggest. I lay to rest her fears that for all she knows I could be spending as much time with other girls as I am with her. I tell her to ask me anything, that I want her to meet my family and show her off to my friends because I've totally and utterly fallen for her. I tell her that three weeks ago I wouldn't have considered going on a second date with a girl I even half-liked, yet now I'd happily fly to India for her, if that's what she wanted. I held her hands and we left the pub and walked to Waterloo, and then on the other end of the train ride we walked closer than ever on the way back to Clapham where we drank in a crowded Belle Vue pub and perched opposite each other, her on a chair arm and me on a wet table. She opened up and shared her past, her fears. She confided in me, telling me things that bind us together, things that she wouldn't tell a stranger.

If I wasn't in trouble before, then I definitely am now. Hannah fills my thoughts as I take the bus home for Christmas. I haven't felt this way about anyone before, except perhaps the first time I fell in love, but we all know those initial feelings are slightly swayed by virginal tendencies towards thirst; for experience for sex, for love itself. Here, nine years and ten months on from my first taste of love, I try and discern just what it is that is going on with Hannah, but all I do is reach the conclusion that whilst I suspected I might meet a potential partner during these 100 dates, I hadn't for one moment considered the possibility that I might find a girl that I could spend the rest of my life with. My instinct has wavered occasionally during the last two months, but I'm not fooling myself now. My only doubts are what the next two months will bring, I am sick with the fear of losing her to distance and time. Before I get home my phone beeps, and makes me feel much better:

Bus action bearable? Am Training home now. When I get there could you have magic-d yourself into my bed please? Thanks. X

Sunday to Tuesday

It is now starkly obvious that I hadn't taken the holidays into consideration when I began The Hundred, and were I still on the challenge I'd have found it remarkably difficult to date when everyone dispersed into *Christmas Family Mode*. Instead, I find myself in familiar surroundings with handfuls of decorations and a pile of presents upstairs that at some point today will be very badly wrapped. Across the country the other half of our family is going through the same rigmarole, and it transpires that my cousin's young son, Toby, is learning the traditional family vernacular, crawling around saying 'Mummy is pished!' He'll fit in just fine, that one.

With the days counting down Hannah and I have been bashing messages back and forth, trying to find a way to see each other one more time. And then she invited me to join her and her friends for a get-together on Christmas Eve.

'This is a bit weird, isn't it?' says Hannah as she and I are sat knee to knee on a train to a little village near High Wycombe, and she's right, it is a bit weird. But if this is weird, then give me more of it. We spend the early afternoon rambling in the countryside and then baking a horribly misshapen cake at her Mum's house. I met the Mum very briefly before Hannah ushered me out of the door.

'I hope to see you again soon,' I said with a wave. She didn't say anything in return. Then to a neighbouring village where several of Hannah's friends had laid on a colourful platter of nibbles, and although I was a last-minute addition and exempt from the communal sharing of presents I didn't feel at all out of place, even when I walked to the toilet and overheard whispering in the kitchen that went something like; 'he seems nice, not her normal type…'

All too quickly, it was over. I said my goodbyes and Hannah drove me to the station and there we stood smugly, knowing we were now old hats at goodbyes on the platform.

'See ya then,' she said, rubbing her nose against mine.

'Don't eat too much curry, it'll do all kinds of things to your insides,' I warned.

'I'll bring some back for you.'

'Ooh lovely, can't wait 'til March.'

We said everything apart from the obvious, which was that we now had more than two months apart until seeing each other, it was a large hole in time, one we had no idea how to deal with. Instead, I found a clementine in my pocket and surreptitiously slipped it into her coat as we had one last little kiss goodbye. It just seemed like a nice thing to do, to leave a present behind. Later she texted,

I've just found a squashed baby orange in my coat, wonder where that came from…

On Christmas morning I took Grandad a cup of tea and found him staring out of the window. He jumped.

'Don't look so startled, Grandad,' I said.

'Well, I didn't hear you come in!' He said, taking a sip.

'Did you sleep well?' I asked.

'I woke up at five, which wasn't bad considering I went to bed at ten, and then I resumed normal activity for a couple of hours.'

He was always the centre of attention, was Grandad. As the day drew on and his consumption of beer and sherry increased, his dry one-liners dominated conversation. 'Well, if I'm not able to converse after the Christmas pud I'll be seeing you later in the evening,' he addressed us all with a smirk.

'Aren't you enjoying the TV, Grandad', I asked slyly. No answer.

'Dad, it's Dickens!' said Mum. Grandad looked at a scruffy lad running about on the screen.

'What he needs is a haircut and a good hammering,' he said.

'Dickens, it's priceless, isn't it,' said Mum, trying to find some enthusiasm.

'Long-winded…' said Grandad, before promptly beginning to snore.

Later I walked into the kitchen to find Dad talking to Mum, who had obviously been eating some alcoholic pudding.

'I've got this great book about how to avoid memory loss,' said Mum.

'Oooh, let's have a look.'

'I've forgotten where it is.'

Sometimes I wonder where I came from.

Wednesday

'I'm miserable, and it's bloody annoying,' I say to my Mum on Boxing Day. Mum looks at me and smiles.

'Don't be miserable darling, it'll be alright in the end.'

'It's not the end I'm thinking about, it's the now.'

I have no idea what to do with myself. What is it about human beings that makes us go decidedly mental when we don't hear from the person we fancy? She is still in the country but I can't see her, the space has begun to widen, unfathomable and heart-wrenching. It has been less than two weeks since we first kissed, possibly the most emotionally intense fortnight of my life. This is the sweet, tender time when two people begin to entwine and seed, creating emotional roots so strong you know there is nowhere from here but onwards into the future. We clumsily explore each other's bodies buoyed by the rich excitement that there is so much more to come, but even then sexual passion currently takes second place to an altogether different urge; that is to just spend time with this other person, growing as friends, learning each other, walking hand in hand, stopping to embrace and hold and feel. We are becoming partners, so much more than the product of a meaningless fling, surely? The next few weeks should be so uncompromisingly full of new love that when I am apart from her, even for a few hours, I have a deep surge of discomfort within.

I miss her. In the midst of this incredible beginning I feel as though I have been torn from side to side, emptiness now approaches from all angles in a place where love should be fostered. Two weeks, we had, and now over two months separates me from her. So cruel, so difficult. I feel like exploding in tears with the unknowing. Perhaps, if I knew it was destined to end well it would be easier, but I don't know a thing. I speak to my parents and tell them that I've never felt this way. I've never met a girl like this, not someone I could look at so early on and know with absolute certainty that I want children with her.

'Does she feel the same?' they ask, and honestly I can't tell them. I shrug and try to literalise it all. 'We just spent Christmas Eve together, I met her mother and her friends.' Whatever she feels, she has to feel something, but it is this not knowing that drives me crazy, and the India-Australia gap will stretch the unknown on and on into the Spring. I'm impatient, because I have fallen head over heels and back over my head again and I want to know what I've fallen for. I have committed more in my head to this girl than I ever did in reality to the others, it is quite unlike me and I'm starting to remember conversations with friends truly in love, engaged, married, together. 'I worry that I'll never be able to stay with one woman for longer than a couple of years, that it'll go stale, that I'm unable to stick in one place for long enough. How do you know that it's right?' I begged of them.

'You just know,' they said.

I have been so frivolous in recent years. I always felt too young to fully commit, too immature and scared to consider marriage, the creation of little ones, a life with One. Not even in jest would I dare to speak about a house we might share together or about plans for our future, even if we shared the same roof. Love always happened fast but was never treated with dignity, or patience. Yet there we were on Christmas Eve, Hannah and I, walking through fields beside the Thames with my arm over her shoulder and hers around my waist, just days into this relationship, joking about living besides people who have dogs so we could walk them, rather than have to deal with them in our own home. We could be Uncle and Aunt to the pets of others! I have been trying to hold myself back, knowing that this amazing time we are having is going to be halted prematurely, yet I'm incapable of resisting. We fit incomprehensibly well, our hands and fingers interlink, our bodies whether we're naked or fully clothed, our humours, our persons. And now I reach out, and I can't touch her. We have email, video messaging, all these new-age forms of communication, 'and what about longhand?' she asked me in her car outside Maidenhead station, the view through the windscreen dominated by a ghastly orange mobile phone advert. Sad, sad songs cried through the radio, just for the sake of the mood.

'Longhand we can do,' I tell her, 'although it'll be long-read as well, my writing is atrocious. Mail your address as soon as you arrive in Mumbai, please, but not by pigeon.'

It is too soon to say that I love her, but I know what love is and where it comes from and we have been feeding it for days. I pace my parents' house in Oxfordshire, lost and silent in brief but worthwhile grief. I have no idea how I'm going to deal with the next two months, all I know is that I think about this girl and my left arm goes numb, it still goes numb, a pulsing tickle through my tricep. *Why my tricep?* I wonder in the shower, why, of any part of my body, has this girl claimed my tricep? Such an arbitrary body part, until I remember she was number thirty three and that we kissed on our third date, and the revelation of threes comforts me somewhat as I reach around my chest and try to rub some life into the limp arm as water torrents over my face and down my chest, soaking me in sadness.

She flies tomorrow; I'm desperate for contact. She calls just after six and we talk for forty-five minutes. My mind is at rest, and even more so when I log into Facebook and see her Status:

Off tomorrow, I'll be missing someone a bit.

Strange how this Facebook thing has suddenly infiltrated our lives. I've not been convinced by some people's apparent need to share things that should remain personal; a public forum doesn't lend itself to taking cheap shots at exes or writing cryptic lines that everybody and nobody can understand. People use their Facebook status to send messages to people and frankly, assuming I'm the subject of Hannah's Status, I feel very warm indeed at seeing her quiet way of introducing me to her public. Now I feel better; I have been acknowledged.

She emails before bed, even making the faintest suggestion that she could come and join me on tour in Australia for a while. I respond with what I thought was a suitable preparatory travel checklist for her mid-morning flight:

> 1. *Put your passport under your pillow for safekeeping, and whatever you do don't remember to look under your pillow in the morning.*
> 2. *Go outside and let down your Mum's tyres.*
> 3. *Don't tell her what you've done.*
> 4. *Set your alarm for about 10am, that should do it.*
> *Gonna miss you gorgeous, keep safe x*

Thursday

A text comes through at twenty past ten:

> *Am afraid plan failed, am on plane, wearing a rather fetching pink t-shirt as it happens... Speak soon x*

She takes off at 10:35 and I spend the rest of the day wandering aimlessly, checking News 24 each hour in utter morbidity, taking comfort as each bulletin passes without a mention of a British Airways India-bound plane crashing somewhere. It's horrific, but I can't ignore the fact that with each extra minute she is further from me.

TEN

The New Year

Friday

Home is where the heart is and now, back in London, I just don't feel like I belong here. Every other thought involves Hannah and I have no idea how to just…well, be normal.

Saturday

I wake up with an epiphany; I think I'm going to go to India. I'd only do it if she gave the idea a nod, but by nature I know this is something I have to do. Hannah and I had such a fabulous beginning but there was no security in our kisses, only in our eyes. With thousands of miles between us and potentially months as well, there is a danger that our feelings will shrink into the ether. Distance sometimes makes the heart grow stronger, but it can also encourage weakness, and however good it was between us I'm not convinced that two weeks is enough of a foundation. If I have any power to give our relationship the strength it needs to survive (and I suspect this may mean more time to kindle the flames) then I'll do it.

It's time to pop the question:

> *Hypothetically, if I decided to write my book in Mumbai would I be able to have the pleasure of your company occasionally? X.*

Minutes later she writes back:

> *I'd make sure of it…and my weekends seem to be my*
> *own if I want them. My driver Dubey does love*
> *doing that airport run…! X*

I try to compose myself but I just can't function, everything I do is permeated by her. I'm still intrigued by the strength of this feeling and I slowly come to the crazy realisation that I am just designed to follow my heart. I can't do anything else. I'm going to fly to India.

Sunday

It's the last day of the year and I spend much of the morning queuing outside the Indian High Commission. Seriously, there are seven thousand people waiting by 8am, it's quite ridiculous. Eventually, just after noon, I leave with a new tourist visa stamped loudly in my passport. I shuffle across town and buy a return ticket to Mumbai, giving me nineteen more days with Hannah than I would have had otherwise. For the rest of the day I pack, preparing to vacate my room in the morning. And I can taste fear on my tongue, because of all the silly things I've ever done I'm not sure if anything rivals this, and I realise that even now I am terrified of what is going to happen with Hannah. Terrified of losing her, the fear consumes me and only subsides when she texts:

> *Been to Ghandi museum and met man with monkey*
> *on string – it's Christmas all over again! Would love*
> *to share this place with you x*

I reply but don't expect to hear from her, it's about half past six and I know for her and everyone else in Mumbai it is now a brand new year. I've been invited to a New Years party so pick up my feet and make my way to Wimbledon. They're a good crowd but my mind is elsewhere, and at some point it appears to be time to leave. I catch the last tube and stumble home, and when I walk through the front door I take one look around at tables overturned and papers everywhere and I realise we've been burgled by some little opportunist bastards.

Both of my laptops are gone, and my hard drives full of photos and video memories. Gone is everything I've ever created, bar a few random files and (mercy!) my dating diaries, which in a moment of instinct I emailed to myself before leaving the flat. Camera: gone. Money on my bedside table: gone. Phone: gone. Watch: gone. The place is a mess and then my heart stops. My passport, my fucking passport with the Indian visa in! Please, if there's any justice in this world, don't let them have taken my passport. I dash around the flat, clearing things up, calculating the cost of my loss, looking for the little maroon book which is the only thing standing between me and the girl I want to be with, need to be with.

And then after ten mind-boggling minutes during which I said more prayers than I had in my entire life leading up to then, I remember, it's in a little pocket at the top of my rucksack, and the thieving buggers left my rucksack right by the door. With nervous fingers I pry open the zip and there it is, my passport, untouched and unstolen, ready to take me to Asia. Thank flip for that. The immense sadness at losing so much is instantly replaced with relief. Just as I felt in 1999 looking down a verge at the overturned truck that I should have died on, the only important thing in my mind is love, and in my right hand it feels like I'm holding a passport to love, literally. I call my housemate and landlady, who spends much of her time abroad.

'They didn't take the cushions,' I tell her, 'can't have liked them. They didn't take any CDs either, I don't think.'

'Thank God I have rubbish taste,' she says.

Monday

Yet again my mind is playing tricks on me. My stomach is in knots, waiting for Hannah to get in touch. This distance, together with the relatively short time we've known each other, is making whatever we had seem almost unreal. The lines of her face and body slowly fade; the closeness we shared feels like it took place a century ago, resigned to the past. I imagine her so many thousands of miles away, forgetting me, pushing thoughts of me aside. I fret, all I want is contact from her, but at the same time I imagine that the next message will tell me she slept with someone else, that she's changed her mind, that she doesn't want me to fly anymore. I know I'm a fool, but I actually begin to play each scenario over in my mind, wondering how I'd react, rehearsing my lines, my actions. I could be forgiven for all of this madness if I was on drugs, but I'm not, I'm existing purely on natural adrenaline and other such sweet chemicals. All I know is I'm about to fly to a country to see a girl that I adore, but barely know. And it is this, this lack of understanding about how she acts and carries herself and what she wants that is creating a palaver in my head. I'm being unreasonable, unfair even, but in reality all I am is scared.

Not a great start to the year. Dad arrives and we drive out of London after I run through a report with the police, who have taken over 7000 calls through the night. My stomach is hollow at the information I lost on my laptops and hard drives and eventually I slump, head against the window, watching the pavements where Hannah and I walked along the Thames on our fourth date, then later we are running the roads of High Wycombe, the same roads along which we drove on Christmas Eve. Why is all of this replaying for me? I just want to be with her now.

Tuesday to Thursday

Impulsive, yes. Romantic, maybe? But oh God, what if three weeks is too long? I have my heart in my mouth, and it doesn't taste very nice. 19 days was, it turns out, a period that Hannah couldn't quite get her head around. He response was, 'Nineteen Days?!' I told her tongue-in-cheek that if she was sick of me after 19 days then it probably wasn't going to work out anyway. With hindsight, she probably didn't get the joke.

Friday

I am being shaken, quite violently.

'Sir, Omelette or Masala?' asks a firm female voice. I open my eyes and remember I'm on an aeroplane. 'Omelette or Masala, Sir?' comes the voice again, but this time it's like she's asking me whether I'd like to be shot or hung. Neither, frankly, and the prospect of curry for breakfast utterly terrifies me, so I pause for a while and stare into space. She doesn't seem to like that, and actually whistles at me, so I say the first thing that comes into my head,

'Er, coffee please'

'No, Omelette or Masala Sir?' she perseveres, so I give in.

'Omelette please.' I tuck in, and it tastes strangely like Masala.

I've never understood why airlines insist on feeding you the cuisine of the country you're heading to or escaping from, as if it's a culinary drip designed to ease the shock of transition to another country. I can safely say that was the most horrendous meal I've ever been dealt.

All the men in India seem to have moustaches; it's like a permanent Movember. Yesterday, just before I flew, Hannah sent me a text confirming that her driver was going to pick me up:

Dubey wears a white suit, has a moustache and should be holding a sign with your name on it. If he's

> *not there it's because he's been banned so get a cab to*
> *the office, Times of India by VT [Victoria Terminal]*
> *and call me x*

As I wander through the airport I wonder whether Dubey will be there or not. My heart is beating like a drum as I round the final corner and there is my name on a piece of paper, held up by a dapper short man with a round belly and a neat moustache. He looks like an Asian version of Charlie Chaplin after three Christmases in a row.

'Have you been waiting long?' I ask him as we shake hands.

'Yes.'

We walked to the car in silence. Blimey, is this the sweet man Hannah was talking about? In fact, he was. As we drove Dubey lightened up as I opened the flow of conversation. We chatted in broken pidgin, and when I wasn't asking Dubey questions about his favourite sport (cricket – we went through a list of players we mutually knew) and various districts of Mumbai, I sat there with a vast grin on my face, looking through the windscreen at my first views of India. It brought back my time in East Africa, huge billboards towering on stilts along the roadside, slums intermingled with clean, sterile car showrooms, roadside stalls and hawkers, inspired third world advertising – a ten foot strip along the side of a public bus read *this is India's favourite pen,* alongside a picture of an unremarkable blue biro - just brilliant.

Intermittent flashing LED signs hopelessly remind road users of safety – *Drive to care, not to Dare* – they proclaimed, as down below there was more daring than you've ever seen in your life. Cows stood on the pavement, ready for automobile sacrifice. At traffic lights beggars of all ages knock on the window to display their wares, anything from National Geographic to My Little Pony sets. Two small boys give up trying to sell me plastic flowers and start yelling 'Chowinum! Chowinum!'

'Dubey what are they saying?' I asked him, laughing at the wide smiles outside.

'Chewing gum Sir,' he chuckled, 'they want chewing gum, he he he.'

And then there's the transport. As soon as we left the airport it was carnage, no right of way, motorised rickshaws bisecting crossroads, the pilots barefoot with one leg crossed over the other. Open-back trucks packed with workers, and then the taxis, thousands upon thousands of black Ambassadors bumper to bumper at the side of the road, drivers sprawled out in the back trying to sleep off the combined pain of heat and waiting. Those lucky few – and when I say few I mean three million – taxis who have found custom join the throngs on the road, belching fumes and weaving from lane to lane, as if they were such things. Lanes, occasionally demarcated on the road, mean nothing here. On a three-lane highway the traffic is five abreast, so tight that many of the taxis have no wing mirrors, the vehicular equivalent to a receding hairline. I turn to Dubey, who has rarely taken his hand off the horn since our journey began, and ask about the taxis. He shakes his head,

'Taxis are very very bad, always stop, always go.' He said, which seemed a bit of a harsh assessment. Not long afterwards apparently without reason and as if to prove a point, a taxi swerved violently in front of us and stopped at an angle, the driver immediately getting out to remonstrate with Dubey, who shouted back then looked at me sideways when the man returned to his car. 'They're all crazy,' he said with a deep three tone chuckle. I nodded as his moustache twitched, staring bemused at the taxi ahead, amazed that this guy, carrying passengers and speeding along a busy three-lane road, had just stopped in the middle of the circus to have a little argument with Dubey.

'Does this happen all the time?' I ask him.

'Yes,' he said, with another laugh, 'very crazy taxi.'

After an almost timeless drive, which must have been an hour but felt like so much longer, we hung a left opposite the incredible Victoria Terminal train station and pulled up outside the Times of India Building. This is it; she's in here. No answer on her mobile so I had a message relayed from reception, 'she is in a meeting and will be some time,' one of three red sari'd ladies told me after replacing her handset, she ushered me to the waiting area and I sunk into a tight leather sofa, wondering just how long *some time* might be.

Half an hour later, there she was, a flash of blonde hair through the crowd, 'I can't kiss you here,' she whispers and I nod. Public displays of affection are not looked kindly upon in these parts. She takes me next door, to a meagre entertainment store with an upstairs coffee shop, and finally takes my hand as we climb the stairs. 'I need to go back to work,' she tells me, 'have a look through the guidebooks, I hope you can find somewhere to stay.' She looks nervous, worried even. I just want to kiss her but it's not possible, crap! 'I finish work at half seven,' she tells me, then looks at me sideways, shrugging, 'I hope you'll be ok, I just don't know what to do.' She gives me Dubey's number and full-well knowing that she hates me shortening names, I say, 'cool, I'll give Dubes a ring if I'm in strife.' She gives me that face I feel so used to, the one where I can't tell if she's pissed or pretending to be. Frankly, I've never been able to tell when a woman is faking. And then she's gone, down the stairs, out the door, along the street. Blimey, five minutes with the girl, then back to business.

I meet a Dutch man named Dave in the Welcome Hotel several hundred metres down a big pothole-shaped road from the Times. Dave must be in his forties and we chat for ten minutes in reception. He seems like he needs to talk. Poor bloke is missing a girl he's been travelling with, despite the girl running off with $8000 of his.

'She said she needed the security,' he told me, 'and she's proposed coming over and going half on everything once she arrives, which I suppose in the long run works out better for me because before I was paying for everything.' I conclude that love can rob you blind, and then go to my room to read a book.

A few hours later Hannah finishes work and joy of joys, I've found a room and she's staying over. I meet her outside work and we take a convoluted stroll to the hotel via a small café.

'Oh my God, there are white people!' Hannah exclaims, 'and that one has my book!' We sit and we're talking, finally, catching up, me telling my long and totally unnecessary stories, her politely ordering some food and filling me in on her first week out here. There's something in the air, the lack of allowed intimacy bracing the sheer oddness of the situation.

'Remember when I was sat opposite you on the train from Maidenhead to Cookham, and you said it was weird? Well,' I said, spreading my arms wide, 'not a pinch on this!'

After dinner we made the streets our own and eventually, completely raw from lack of lip contact, I leaned in to kiss her. She stopped me, 'Nooo, really mustn't do that.'

'Oh God, really? It's that bad?'

'Bad enough that they might stone me,' she said, which was a slightly depressing thought. But then she added, 'but holding hands is ok,' and as if to prove it she slipped a soft paw into mine.

We are sat on my bed, in silence.

'Can you turn the TV on, I'm a bit nervous,' she tells me in the room.

'Don't be.'

'I can't help it.'

We're in the middle of something that neither of us can fully comprehend. Exactly three weeks ago we were on our fourth date and now we're in Mumbai, together. I've chased this girl to India, and now I'm here there is no turning back, no second chance. As we sit here, in this bare hotel room with two thin single beds and curtains that have been made from a big doily I am reproached by dread, I'm not entirely sure that I've made the right decision. I never wanted to make her feel uncomfortable but it appears that almost without thinking I've done just that. I wanted to be here, she wanted that too, but somehow we're sitting on a bed staring at the walls. Fuck! Is it me? Did I blunder with my words when I told her how long I was coming for? A silly joke that gave birth to strain and doubt, and that's what we're dealing with now. Our contented walks and public kisses and rolling-in-the-bed nights in London are an entire developed world away, and ironically having met online a cyber space misunderstanding now threatens us. We watch TV and then eventually get closer. We settle, we whisper and then, slowly, we undress and slip beneath the sheets. And there, where it was supposed to be all encompassing and wonderful and the absolute summation of a ridiculously romantic idea to jet across the world in hot pursuit of a girl I would quite like to bear my children at some point, I simply feel as though I'm making love to her but that she's not to me.

I think she's still wary of me, can't bring herself to trust me, but what do I have to do? I adore this girl and I sleep little throughout the night, working myself up as she rests silently across the twin bed divide, convincing myself that our stilted reunion doesn't bode well, realising that for the first time since we started gaining pace that perhaps we don't have a future. And it's my fault. I created this make or break situation and perhaps rather than making us, I have done the wrong thing, and created fissures that didn't need to be here. A hollow stomach, I lie there in darkness, in silence, fearful. I'm just plain scared, and I finally drift off into a shattered sleep, peppered with dreams of Hannah and I walking in opposite directions, inconsolable, irretrievable.

Saturday

In the shower I tell myself I need to relax. I am here to be with this girl, but I am also here to write a book. I must start to concentrate on the book, because for too long now I've had Hannah on my mind and now it's becoming counterproductive to every bloody thing. Much like my fears of her not texting me back, I believe that I'm being irrational, that I simply need to be able to understand her more. In typical communication traits, I am the woman now and she is the man; she doesn't call, doesn't show constant affection, and I reach out to compensate. Cat and string theory, I need to back off a little. But it's so difficult because I just want to touch her, to kiss her, to hold her. And from the moment we wake up she's dying to get outside and walk along the beach, exactly the place where I'm not allowed to touch her.

Thankfully it's a weekend so I have her to myself. As the day progresses we travel all over the city. We just needed time. It feels like we've begun to find each other again after last night's nerves and unspoken doubts.

'You have no idea how hard it was to spend a whole day with you without a kiss,' I tell her finally, and seal it with a kiss.

'Character building,' she says.

'I'm not sure I want to build my character anymore,' I whisper, kissing her again. She's still making me chase, but now I realise it's not a game, it's her. I have some barriers to break down if I'm going to totally win her over, but this time as I peruse the cold hard facts instead of the mental creations of my irrational fears, it's obvious. We've just had a wonderful day together, in India, and it's not as though we're moving backwards. I almost feel happy, so I translate it into cheek.

'What does Dubes do on a day off?' I ask.

'His name is Dubey, and I'm not at all sure.'

'How do you feel about the fact that he chuckled when I called him Dubes after knowing him for ten minutes?'

'I think he misheard you.'

'Have you ever given anyone a nickname in your life?'

'No,' she says after a small thought. And then she does something that she hasn't done since we were walking hand in hand across Clapham Common what feels like several decades ago. She has this wonderful habit of taking a slightly awkward situation and narrating it as though she's a posh, well-constructed voice from the clouds on a very politically correct television programme.

'Dave persists in shortening the names of people he doesn't know, Hannah is embarrassed for him.'

I join in.

'Hannah is secretly angry that Dave is able to form quick bonds with strangers by calling them 'mate' or giving them wonderful nicknames.'

'Dave seems to have no idea that he's taking a man's given name, and desecrating it without thinking.'

'In Dave's mind, he calls Hannah 'H''

Eventually we both return to Earth, and as I look around it's quite obvious that I've just done what is almost certainly the most romantic thing I'll ever do yet have ended up in a place that is about as unromantic as it gets, apart from maybe Tikrit, or Gaza. No kissing or flirtation in public! Are you serious?! You can ride a motorbike without a helmet here, yet you can't kiss someone. Hannah decides to go back to her flat for the night and in an instant I feel like we're almost back to step one, the unknowing, the learning. Maybe it's jetlag but I lay awake alone in my room with a now familiar hollow stomach, feeling like this is just not going to work. I'm a rollercoaster carriage climbing and plummeting; life is so tiring when you have no idea what direction you're heading, especially if you can't get any sleep because of it. Although it's been a good day she's still a bit nervous and shy with me, the leftovers lingering from NineteenDayGate. I feel sick. I need water. I just want to hold her. Fuck it. I want *her* to hold *me*.

Sunday

I've made a right royal cock-up. At what point did I lose hold of myself enough to think that three weeks in India was a good idea? Crows glide above Juhu Beach, swooping onto hotel windowsills above, ca-cawing heartily as if laughing at the state below. Hannah sits opposite me, writing in her notebook, our legs and ankles occasionally brushing, they feel like dying touches. Yet there's still life in them. It's complicated.

We made love this morning, but I'm always wary of calling it *making love* until the *I love you*'s have been said. It was a rapid affair; I lost control in a flurry of delighted pumping.

'You turn me on,' I tell her, but she doesn't reciprocate. 'I'd like us to walk in a country where we can kiss,' I said to her yesterday as we held hands and played at the water's edge amongst dead fishes and pieces of glass. And it's not that she didn't concur, it's just that there was no confirmation of interest. Back to this morning, to our bed, I find her body enthralling but she pays mine no attention. Should I start to read the signs, or continue to ignore them? This girl arouses insecurities in me like no one else I've ever met. It has been a long time since I've slept with a woman who pays absolutely no interest to me, but I could accept that if there was a sign that it may change. But there is none, and I desperately need to start feeling wanted by her. We get on so well and I'd love for that to translate into the bedroom. Unfortunately for the time being, it isn't and it's starting to make me doubt whatever it is that we have, doubts that blossom throughout the night when she sleeps away from me. It's unlike the adult me to crave security from a woman, but I feel like a school kid again, virginal, unable to think about anything but the naughty stuff.

And an hour later I had no choice but to see the signs with my very eyes, as her eyes welled and reddened with anger and upset, pictures of her ex on Facebook partying with her friends at New Years. I knew it was soon for her, but the memories are raw and although he was mentioned only once during our courtship in London I'm forced to realise in a stinking Internet café in middle Mumbai that she's not quite as over him as she thought she was. It's a total, complete shock to me, yet at the same time I still manage to feel some guilt, the scars remain and I fear that I've contributed to reopening them. I have misread our situation, and my heart begins to sink, leaving a trail of scar tissue that eats into my belly. I am hollow yet again, but the ache feels irretrievable now, this reality is awful. When I flew here I did so because I felt that Hannah was someone, maybe The One. I came out here because I wanted to give our relationship a chance to grow, but in an instant of emerging tears I realise that it's impossible for this to happen here, because although we're both in Mumbai, we're not in the same place. My tears for my ex are long gone, Hannah's are not. There is no level emotional ground ahead of us; we are all of a sudden facing a different situation. Had the Me from before the dating challenge begun been sitting here now I would have handled things very differently. Then, I was more stable, less demanding, totally balanced. But now, two and a half months of intensive dating and even more inscrutable over-analysis later, I am pent up, emotional and needy. And that is really not what Hannah needs right now.

'I don't regret coming here,' I tell her, 'I just don't want you to regret it.' She stares away into the distance, and hits me with it.

'I guess I just feel like this is *my* Indian adventure,' she says, with extra emphasis on the *my*. She already regrets me being here. I feel like running away, leaving her to it and getting the next plane home, but I just can't distance myself from this. How I feel about her isn't fake, but my worries of the past week are now confirmed and compounded and it eats me up inside. I now know why I've been scared; it's because I had reason to be. She doesn't feel the same way as me.

Dubey has invited us to lunch and picks us up from the Welcome Hotel. He is full of good cheer and we chat away, asking him questions about the landmarks we pass. At a Hindi Temple near Malaba Hill he tells us Monday is for the monkey. I ask him what other animals are celebrated on other days, he says the elephant Ganesha is for Tuesdays, that there is a lot of God in India.

'Wow,' I say, 'Monkeys on Mondays, Elephants on Tuesdays, what happens on a Saturday?'

'On Saturday, it is Monkey,' says Dubey, slightly exasperated. Hannah and I grin at each other; neither of us are ever sure when we've been understood, or when we're understanding.

Later, after ten minutes of silence, Dubey pipes up with no warning, 'My wife is black.'

If I'd had food in my mouth, it would quickly have been stuck to the far wall. At lunch we fail to eat half of the offerings. Dubey's wife is indeed quite dark, but Indian. She is fasting for a week and the poor woman has to watch our meals go to waste. Hannah attempts to draw attention away from the mounds of food and asks if we can see the hospital next door but a man in there, perhaps a plain-clothed doctor, turns us away. Poor Dubey, his moustache drooped as he led us away, so embarrassing. Luckily the discomfort was short lived, for us, just as we'd started to ponder exactly how we were going to excuse ourselves Dubey said:

'Time to go.' We rose immediately leaving behind a large bowl of pudding, which was a concrete example of potential food poisoning. Hannah prodded me as I gazed out of the window on the drive north, and while I appreciated the touches I couldn't escape the very real truth that this was indeed a tricky patch of goliath proportions. She took about ten minutes out from niceness to tell me that effectively I was a fairly immodest chap, which hurt like buggery because it's not the type of thing someone says to you if they like you. It crossed my mind that she was being purposefully harsh to put me off her, somehow.

Once at Juhu we settled down for an oversize beer and both wrote for a while, and then, when the tension became just too unbearable, she spoke.

'Are you ok?'

Just be cool Dave, just play it cool.

'Not really girl. I'm quite uncomfortable.'

Nice one, very cool.

'Me too,' she says, 'do you want to talk about it?'

I leaned forward and took off my sunglasses; I could feel myself well up so stared at the beach for probably a bit too long, feeling her eyeing up my glistening sockets. I'm actually in the early stages of bloody crying, what is wrong with me?

'I do, yes...' I said, then added with a second of thought, 'but then again, I don't.' But I carry on talking, anyway. I tell her how I feel about everything, except the bit about her not wanting to touch me in bed. I tell her that I'd only just realised that she wasn't in the same place as me and I was trying to work out what to do with that. I tell her that I'd considered whether I was feeling this strongly because of the book, or because I actually did, and that I'd drawn the conclusion that actually yes, the book had nothing to do with how I was feeling, that you just can't control this shit.

You're rambling a bit now Dave, I told myself, you need to start being a bit cooler, you're like a cat with string again, just stand off for a bit. And then I ignored myself again. Silly inner voice.

'The thing is, I've totally and utterly fallen for you, and I can't do anything about it.'

Did I really just say that? I said be cool, man, now you're just sounding desperate. Say something else, take her mind off it...

'I have, I've totally fallen for you.'

Oh, come on.

Just stop to think, Dave. The big picture, do you think anything can ever happen with you two now you've made it very clear you're a total loser?

'I know it's ridiculous, I know it is, but it's there, that's it.'

'Yeah,' she said, 'you see, it's things like that which you should really keep inside.'

I went to the toilet and hit myself around the face. I move closer to the mirror and look at myself, trying to work out exactly where this part of me has come from. The spot by my nose is fading but a new one is lumping out from my left eyebrow, and I shake my head at myself. 'Good work mate, lose the plot and look fucking great whilst doing so. Get a haircut, get a plane ticket, go home and masturbate in a corner for the rest of your life, whatever you thought you knew about dealing with women, you don't. You Dave, are a loser.'

After that little talking to I felt strangely better, even though the manager of the hotel had walked in and caught me at it, which would have been ok but I was literally two inches from the mirror and must have appeared to be a serial killer. Outside, although she took my hand and we walked down the beach chatting like the old days (three weeks ago) I can just picture the messages she'll be writing home to her friends. *He totally freaked out, he told me he loved me, this is a nightmare...*

'Look,' she said to me, 'we're both young and in an amazing place. We fancy each other, so let's make the most of it.'

We fancy each other. Jesus. Do we, really? One hell of a fancy. Our wires were crossed over how long I should come out for and I started this mess. I should have held out for longer, but I couldn't. Ultimately, as we wander back to her apartment and a slightly grumpy Dubey, I can't see how I'm going to dig myself out of this one. I'm a bloody long way from home, I'm acting like a woman, and I'm quite sure I've just totally busted whatever chance I had with this girl. Dave, you're a freakin' idiot.

In the car Dubey asks to look at my phone.

'Ahh, it's a very nice phone.' He handed it back to me and once we'd stopped in traffic again turned, 'here's my piece,' he said, handing me his phone.

'Your piece!' I said, chuckling.

'Nokia 6236,' he told me, proudly. It just looked like a phone to me, as did mine. A few minutes later I was slumped in my seat, gazing into the middle distance.

'Are you ok Sir?' asked Dubey. Intuitive chap, this one.

'I'm ok Dubey, just tired.'

'You go to hotel and relax,' he says.

'I will my friend, I will.'

'Do you like drink?'

'You mean alcohol?'

'He he he, yes, alcohol.'

'I don't mind alcohol Dubey, now and then, all in moderation.'

'What is your brand, Sir?' I rack my brain for local beers,

'I like a bit of Kingfisher.'

'Ah very good Sir. Next Sunday, we will have some of that stuff.'

'Sounds good to me Dubey, sounds good to me.'

'Very good Sir.'

Back in my hotel, a long nap-ridden ride into the city from the north, I take stock. Yesterday was superb, so what happened today? Hannah's upset at photos of her ex tipped me over the edge. For days, maybe weeks, I've had a fear within me that what we shared wasn't quite bedded in reality, and her tears made that fear more real. I realised that I'd been scared for a reason, because I was vulnerable. From there I was never going to be able to hold myself together.

As soon as I realised that she wasn't in a position to be feeling the same about me I mentally began to switch off and back away from her, but physically and even geographically I'm still experiencing that same vulnerability. Somehow, in what seems like a rash finale to this bizarre relationship game I began in October, I've gone from being a distant date to tens of women to finding myself in a very foreign country with a woman who doesn't really want me to be here, a woman who I'm totally smitten with but who doesn't feel the same about me. It's a horrible three-pronged monster that I really didn't see coming when I boarded the 21:45 Virgin Atlantic Flight from Heathrow to Mumbai last Thursday evening. It's Sunday night in India, and I'm considering flying home. I feel like maybe I shouldn't be here, but I'm going to sleep on it and make a more valid decision in the morning. Chances are I could be in Mumbai for the whole week and still not see her, so is there any point in me staying? Is there any chance left with Hannah now? Even if I can find my senses and just be my normal self again has today been too damaging, for both of us?

Monday

Since I began dating my mind has slowly begun to work in a different way. I analyse things differently; I have become over-sensitive, I question everything and now, it seems, I'm possessive. In small doses these traits are not bad at all (except maybe possessive), but I have been living in a different world since October, totally consumed in an unrealistic intensity. My outlet has been my writing. If the world of relationships was my addiction, writing has been my medicine, my therapy. Here, in a hotel room in central Mumbai, I am writing properly for the first time since I started dating Hannah, and I feel so much better about myself, about why I'm here, perhaps even about what I have to do to avoid this trip being an absolute disaster. And the first step is to concentrate on the writing. Hannah continues to cloud my thoughts, yes, but not as much as she did during the first week she was away, not as much as she did over the weekend just passed. I am here to write a book, and I'm going to bloody do it. I can't force Hannah to see me and I've decided to remain quiet until she gets in touch.

My lowest ebbs yesterday came because I've done nothing for weeks but think about Hannah and maybe I'm wrong, but I think the only way for me to prove to her that I'm not actually an over-emotional desperado is to ignore her. I can't chase anymore, I'd just be opening myself up to hurt and this girl just isn't ready to be chased. She needs to have fun, she needs to enjoy herself, and I told her last week during our 19-days kerfuffle that if anything I just wanted to help keep her in a good place. Yesterday, I failed in that. However long I stay here, whether it's for another two days or two weeks, I'm going to put my head down and write this book and stop thinking so bloody deeply about everything. So far, it has proven to be nothing but a big pain in the neck.

I wrote all morning and went past 6000 words. I'm maybe a day or two away from starting to polish the diaries, and then the word count will really start to rise. The numbers give me something else to concentrate on, as did a good walk to Colaba this morning.

'Get some exercise and work whatever it is inside of you out,' Hannah told me yesterday, and she had a point. Doesn't mess around, that girl. So I walked. Not since 2001 when I wandered comfortably through tight-knit Kampala streets, dodging matatu minibuses and greeting Ugandans in their own language have I felt like I did today. I enjoyed myself, bantering with shopkeepers, skipping through crowds, covering my pockets. Alongside the City Mint a smart man with a badly cut moustache and a gammy eye sidled up and asked where in England I was from. Immediately I smelled a rat, con men sweat colourful stories and this lad gave me too much too soon. Game time.

'I'm from London,' I tell him, keeping my pace. He moves alongside but without a pavement there's only room for one at the roadside and he keeps falling behind me or skipping around blocks of concrete or parked taxis.

'How long have you been here?'

'In Mumbai?'

'Yes, Bombay.'

'A few weeks,' I say, knowing my lack of tan gives me away but not wanting him to think I'm fresh meat, ripe for the carving.

'You have been in Bombay for some weeks?' he says with an eyebrow raised.

'Yep,' I reply, 'I like it here.'

He disappears momentarily as a taxi beeps him off the road, and then breathlessly his little legs bring him back in line.

'I am heading for London,' he says.

'Really? When?'

'At the end of the month, I am setting up shop in Notting Hill.'

'Ah, that's a good place, what kind of shop?'

'Indian shop, trinkets, souvenirs. The Indian Boutique, it will be called.'

'Well good luck Sir, sounds like quite a venture.'

'Yes, but you know, with things like this it is always hard.'

Here we go, the sob story. Tried and tested method centuries old. He'll ask me to help him launder some money next. I smile and keep walking, a little faster so he's almost running now. He's only small, bless him.

'It's not easy setting up a business,' he's panting now.

I glance over at him and shrug my shoulders.

'Can we stop and talk please Sir?' he asks me, before adding, 'I don't want anything from you.'

Ah, I suppose he wants my address so he can send postcards of his new shop. I stop and look him in the eye, but don't say anything.

'Thank you Sir,' he says very quickly. 'Now Sir, for me, it is very difficult to get money in this country.' He pauses for effect, and I take a swig of water, not keeping an eye off him. His right eye, the gammy one, is almost shut tight now, the other one squints in the afternoon sunlight. He won't look straight at me, but he continues nonetheless, 'I have many Euros, Dollars and Great British Pounds in my shop near here, but I am not allowed to get traveller cheque. Can you help me get traveller cheque?'

'Exactly how can I get you travellers' cheques?' I ask him.

'The bank is just over there, Sir,' he points down the road, 'you get my traveller cheque and I give you 20%, it is a good deal.'

'I have some Euro coins that I can give you for rupees, if that helps? I say.

'No no Sir, not Euros, I don't want anything from you, just you help me with traveller cheque. We go back to my shop and I give you lots of cash.'

'My friend,' I say smiling, 'I'm not really interested in breaking the law.'

'No no' he says, shaking his head violently, 'this is all very legal.'

'Tell me again why you can't get travellers' cheques yourself...'

'It is just not possible.'

He didn't call me Sir, that time. Call it a hunch, but I don't really fancy going back to his shop. It's time to bring out two lines; the first gives me a time constraint, which means I can't help him right now. The second will suggest that I could help him sometime in the future but that in order to do so I'll need his address. If he gives me it, then I may well be wrong about his intentions. If he doesn't, it's because he can't risk me going to the authorities and dobbing him in.

'I have to meet a friend for lunch very soon,' I say, 'she is waiting for me.'

'But you can maybe quickly help me before this,' he suggests.

'I really must be on my way, but if you give me your business card maybe I can help at some point?'

'You really can't help now?' he says, sadness in his gammy eye.

'Sorry Sir,' I say, 'but you can give me your address and I may come to your shop, but I can't promise.' He rifles through his wallet, takes some time, thumbs a few old cards he has in there. Eventually he pulls one out, and hands it to me. I look at it, 'this is your name?' I point, 'you are Suresh?'

'I am Suresh, yes.'

'Well Suresh, it's been nice to meet you and good luck in London.' I turn to walk away.

'Is your friend Indian?' he asks,

'No, she's British. I really have to go, good luck Sir,' I say, and as I do he reaches out and plucks the card from my hand. I swear one side of his moustache had started to droop since we met. 'Goodbye Suresh,' I shook his hand, 'and good luck.' He doesn't say anything as I walk away. He may have even been a policeman; entrapment probably isn't illegal here, not like the good old black market.

Colaba has its own delights, especially the wonderfully named Hotel Prossers, which looked remarkably like a brothel. At least four times in the first hour I rounded a corner to have a thin man lean in and whisper 'Dope? Hashish?' into my ear, spitting as he did so. Two cats nestled together at the foot of a tree, one resting its head on the other's head. A young man selling world maps shouts at me across the road, 'Hey you, where are you from?'

'London!' I shout back.

'Not Shrewsbury?' he replies, disappointed. I shake my head, slightly baffled, and move on.

Later I find the Port Asia cyber café back in Fort. I email Will, Kate, Jo and Amanda, telling them all is not well in the world of Dave and Hannah:

Who knows what may happen, I tell them, *maybe with a bit of work it'll all be ok. If not, maybe you'll be seeing me sooner than expected!*

God knows what they're going to make of all this, they must think I'm loony.

Tuesday

A better day. I certainly feel more balanced, and with the word count growing I'm feeling much better about myself. Yes, Hannah is on my mind, but my wake-up analysis of our romantic plight was much shorter than yesterday's and I'm settled knowing I'm going to see her tonight. She hasn't been well since Sunday and I just want to put her at ease, mentally and physically, she needs some TLC, and having taken several steps backwards I want to ensure no more damage limitation is needed.

I may appear to be being too hard on myself, but no one is to blame here. We are both vulnerable in our own ways, and while I'm uneasy at the lack of commitment in the relationship I'm manoeuvring myself away from hope and I suppose, more towards an open friendship where anything could happen.

I take another walk in the afternoon, via Port Asia cybercafé where messages of *stick in there...* and *what doesn't kill you...* litter my inbox from friends. My favourite message is from Amanda, who threatens to fly out for a day to help me with some gin and wine therapy. What a star.

Wednesday

'Don't worry, I want you for more than just your oats.'

I'm rummaging through my flight bag in search of one last bag of porridge. Hannah hasn't been well and the poor thing now has another twelve-hour day ahead of her, but perhaps a new type of breakfast will settle her stomach. She stayed over last night but we kept our distance. She was low and needed looking after. We sat and watched a film on my computer, and although we were both fairly detached physically I took heart from the occasional stroking of the inside of my arm, a returned squeeze of a hand. I had no intention of trying to initiate sex and feel much better for not doing so; internally I am backing off to what I hope is a safe distance for both of us and although I'm still disturbed by Sunday's events and our now seemingly backwards momentum, I've begun to accept that us not working out is a fairly likely scenario.

When she says things like 'I want you for more than your oats,' though, it does make me consider that actually she might want me for something more than my oats.

'What're the chances of you coming over tonight?' I ask, knowing that an answer either way will stop me wondering about it during the day.

'Fairly minimal, I'm afraid,' she says, screwing her face up and looking at the floor to lessen the impact.

'No worries,' I say. I'm not surprised, I just want to look after her when she's unwell, and I want her to want me to look after her too.

We kiss passionately before she leaves, my laptop whirring in the corner in preparation for another day of writing. She looks at it:

'I'm jealous of you, being able to sit all day...' she says, tapering off as she heads for the door. *You should try sitting all day with what's bubbling inside my head*, I think as the door closes and another black space looms ahead.

Before I embarked for India I briefly discussed the situation with my mum, and we both agreed without question that it was a big move, one likely to make or break the relationship. So blindly fixated on seeing this girl, I didn't for one moment honestly consider that *break* was a likely outcome. Insufferably naïve, I was even thinking along the lines that we might share our first 'I love you's' before my return to the UK. A few days on, mortified and sheepish, I am still reeling in my stupidity.

4000 words takes me to 2pm, and then the first port of call is a haircut. I found a salon on Dr DN Road, wandered in, and became the subject of grins and chuckles for half an hour. Nobody there could speak English and I get the impression the boss was a bit sadistic, because he gave me to the youngest, most nervous kid in the room. Ten minutes of gesticulation kind of got my preferred style (short back and sides) across to him, and then he ventured forward with blunt scissors, cutting millimetres away at a time, stopping every ten snips to brush the hair away from the cape he'd ever so gently placed around my neck. In the mirror I could see an elderly man behind me take out a personal comb and meticulously style his own hair, before ushering his barber to continue cutting here, and here, and here. To my right a man was having his moustache trimmed, and all the while my hair was shrinking at a disappointing rate of knots. My young barber tried to get away with forgetting about the back of my back and sides - I'm quite sure he didn't understand the word mullet – but eventually we ended up with something half respectable. And then, just as I thought it was over, he started to ruffle my hair, very, very hard. It was like a massage, only much more painful. My right then left ears squished against their respective shoulders, chin struck clavicle, eyes rolled back in head, neck soaked up G-Force. Christ! Wasn't expecting that! I got up as quickly as I could, and paid him fifty rupees, about 60p. Amazing.

Hannah and I had talked about going to the Taj Mahal this weekend, so I went to Thomas Cook to enquire about prices. Despite advertisements all over the building and signs over several desks reading Holidays and Leisure Travel, I was told that they couldn't offer information about holidays or travel to Agra and the Taj Mahal, and instead I would have to go to the other office in Nariman Point.

'And exactly where is that office?' I asked.

'We're not sure.'

Excellent.

I found another travel agent in Colaba after a long and unsuccessful search first for the other Thomas Cook and then for alternative accommodation. The lady dealing with flights was very patient, if not a bit illiterate, and then I was moved along to the man who does the hotels. In short, this meant that he asked where I wanted to go, then went on the internet and read, word for word in horribly broken English, exactly what the hotel offered. Once I'd heard the spiel about 24hr conference rooms for the fifth time, I decided it was time to go.

I'm in India having an uncomfortable fling with a girl I'd quite like to have something more meaningful with, I've achieved nothing apart from an improved knowledge of southern Mumbai's geography and the only – and admittedly acceptable – saving grace is that I've gone over 12,000 words with the book. I spent this morning writing and chuckling at memories of past girlfriends, and frankly, it's good to laugh. I don't know what the hell I'm doing here, sat at half-past nine at night in the same dingy hotel room that I've been in every night since I arrived. Alone, not depressed but slightly uneasy, tired, considering a breakaway to Goa, and wondering just where things are going to go with Hannah. It's got the stage now that when she texts and emails, I'm not sure if she's doing it because she wants to, because she misses me, or because she feels that she needs to. The kiss this morning felt real enough, but I put myself in her shoes. If someone I really liked was in the same city as me, a city in which I knew nobody else, I probably wouldn't chose to spend the night alone. It's not easy looking at the cold, hard facts with this girl, because there are a mass of contradictions and very few direct pointers as to how she really feels. If only I'd decided to pop in to Mumbai en route to Sydney at the end of the month, perhaps the lack of pressure might have made things very different indeed.

There really is no telling what might have happened had I chosen a different path of action, so all I can do is accept what I've done, realise that were I not here I'd be at home kicking myself for not flying out, and maybe, just maybe, I can learn from my mistakes.

At least, in the absence of Hannah, I do occasionally have company at my hotel. There are some very small chaps in the corridor dressed head to toe in blue. They are very odd creatures, responsible for changing sheets and bringing food. They communicate with strange, guttural wails; so even from the safety of my room it's like several pre-pubescent

Chewbaccas are lingering outside. When Hannah stays over they hang outside the door, gently purring, hoping for even the briefest glimpse of the female. I know how they feel.

Thursday

I remember the last time she came over, a light knock on the door. Behind the door she stood, waiflike and pale like pouring milk bathed in a tight purple dress. 'Hi,' she smiled, 'everyone out here stares so much.'

I'm not at all surprised.

It's mid-afternoon and I've been writing all morning. Soon it will be time for my walk, stretch the legs, check Internet, clear my head. Over 14,000 words now and still haven't started dating, but the introduction is nearly complete. Strange, writing a book without having a clue how the thing is going to end.

Today is a funny one. Not *ha ha*. No plans have been made, and I am suspecting that tonight will be another one without Hannah. Strange, to have come so far with such high expectations and hopes, yet within a week they've all been but dashed. Just as I have convinced myself (although 'trained' may be a more accurate word) that Hannah won't be round tonight, I find myself doubting that she'll be around at all once I fly home. From a wonderful twelve days in England to a cataclysmic set in India, I am at a loss.

It sends weird shocks of pre-calculation through my body. If, as I am telling myself, this has no future, then what I am doing here? If I don't fly home I could get a train to Goa, get out of the pollution. *But there has to be something remaining,* comes the response, and in case of this you must sit, relax, and let her come to you. If you're in Goa you *know* that you won't be seeing her, and won't that be just as hard? Almost certainly, and yes I'm holding onto the scraps of potential that my being in Mumbai gives. I want to be level, understand where she's coming from and keep her in that good place, whatever that is. But without any indication from her I have no idea what she wants from me. So I continue to back off, protecting myself from further pain, because I've been hurting for days now and I can't keep doing this to myself.

In resignation, I'm forcing myself to feel much less for her than I did four days ago. Perhaps I can't stand being in such a helpless position, but however my psyche leads me through these things my conscience now tells me to walk away, cut my losses, and let Hannah find herself in a way that she so obviously wants to, alone. I think about our messages before I flew out. She told me that she was excited about seeing me, she said she wanted to share this place with me, but now I'm here she feels I am disrupting *her* Indian adventure. I wanted to give it a chance, but my flying over here, it appears, has created a weak footing, and with us both vulnerable and at least one of us unwilling to communicate I'm not sure either of us have the tools to fix the problem. What a total mess.

Even though we both have phones she's decided this week to only message me through email, so all I have left is to wander to Port Asia Cybernet Café to find out when I'll next be seeing her. I suspect, as we've been talking about a weekend excursion to either Goa or Agra, that I will have to wait until then.

Will writes:

> *Hey man, how's it hanging? To the left I would assume.*
> *How is India? And how's the book coming along? And of course, your burgeoning romance!?*
> *I went on a date with a girl on Monday evening, turns out she has a PhD in psychology and works with sex offenders! So, ummm, I kind of felt paranoid in case she saw through me. Anyway, very nice girl - smart but quite an awful kisser. Got to touch her boob though, woohoo!*

Can always make me smile, that boy.

Another bit of rubbish news, saw a bloke get hit by a bus today. It was like in the movies; one minute he was there, the next the side of a bus is speeding past. Five seconds of hysteria, his body is pulled off the street, and life commences for everybody but him.

Friday

This morning I'm leaning towards flying home sometime next week. A good rest would do me good before what will be a long and tiring tour of Australia, and the vibes are still not right from the camp of Hannah and I don't want to make things worse than they are, if that's possible. We're not leaving Mumbai this weekend after all, which is fine by me, but I'm meeting her outside work at 7pm tonight. Not sure whether that means I have her for an evening or a night, but time will tell. All I want is for everything to be ok again. In this dull, faded light it's easy to forget how good those two weeks in London were, and I'm almost horrified at how quickly the air has changed. After all, Christmas Eve was only two and a half weeks ago. It feels like years.

I am faintly aware that even as I write this Hannah is at the end of a hard week's work. She's been putting in 60 hours whilst running on less than a full tank, and as usual I've been navel-gazing and have had far too much time to dwell on the issues at hand. I cross my fingers that we can spend some time together this weekend and iron out the creases. If not, the end of my time in India is nigh. Goodness knows what repercussions this whole thing will have on my future relationships; it's like in a month I've been in and out of a serious thing. I suppose the fact that I'm even considering future relationships says it all, doesn't it. I'm a very foolish boy, sat at a small desk in the corner of a twin room in Fort, Mumbai, beneath a noisy, wobbly fan that clicks now and then as though it's speaking in Xhosa. Creeping towards 16,000 words, but I'm nervous, utterly consumed by anxiety.

It was, in fact, just an evening. But you know what, it was a good one. I met her outside the Times of India and she slipped her hand into mine. Almost immediately she told me that her drugs were at home and that she'd need to go back to Juhu tonight, and I glazed over for a minute or so, like us Cornthwaite men do sometimes. But she kept her hand in mine and over dinner she explained some more - that she has had no time to herself and that she wants the morning to write and because her work colleague is now staying at her guesthouse she gets even less time to herself.

'Please understand,' she pleads, 'I'm not giving you the brush-off. All week I've seen your word count rise and I haven't done anything. The rest of the weekend is ours.' And after that, I was just fine. All I've ever wanted is the full picture and as long as I'm involved somewhere then I'm happy. She's still not 100% but it's just so nice to see her and I'm glad we have some of the weekend to play with. It's a lovely evening, a cool breeze making the heat far from oppressive, and for the first time since I arrived we're just Dave and Hannah, chatting away about anything and everything, no tension, hand in hand, enjoying ourselves. In fact, it was just like London, bar the lack of kissing and the Indians everywhere. Even the street urchins swinging off my shirt and arms and the Krypton Factor road crossings were part of the fun. She needs to pee so we disappear into the hotel and then kiss frantically in the lift on the way back down, 'quick, quick!' she says as we descend, lips locked. I walk out and greet Dubey, who I haven't seen for days. We shake hands and then he comes in for a kind of half hug, which is slightly awkward but very endearing. 'See you tomorrow Dubey,' I say, and he shrugs with his whole body, which I think is quite a skill.

Tonight, alone in my room again, I am settled for the first time in a long while. I may well still fly home early, but now I'm a little more confident that perhaps I'll do so leaving things with Hannah on a good note. The time I've had to myself isn't good for me, all or most of the fears I've hoed up this week have been banished in just one good evening. There's a lot to be said for communication.

Saturday

An elderly couple who have spent decades together will one day be separated by death. The one which remains will be far from whole, because the time for them is certain to be nearing too and this may well be hastened by the fact that with their partner, much of their soul has already passed on. Although have had little time with Hannah, had I not come we would have had little to bond us for the ten weeks of separation Twelve days together in London, however wonderful was not enough to make either of us feel part-dead when we said goodbye. Although I must admit, I'm not entirely sure I was fully alive from when she walked down those stair with a small orange in her pocket after a goodbye at Maidenhead station.

I take my time en route to Juhu Beach, and along the way I knock off three new forms of public transport, each one an adventure in itself. First, the taxi; a fairground ride of a journey, bouncing off other cars, people, lampposts. The driver a picture of stoic calm, quite content for his vehicle to gain character as it makes its way to the train station. Then the train. Oh what joy, to sit by an open sliding door in a strangely empty carriage, my legs dangling just feet from the cranking wheels and the uneven, rubbish-covered verges. Shanty towns blur past, rented accommodation squashed into small holes in the ground right beside the railway track. At each stop my carriage becomes less my own and eventually I'm forced to stand, clutching my pockets. Near Juhu I leap to the platform and outside jump again into a new steed, this time a motorised rickshaw. What joy! To be speeding along at 3mph in a vehicle that is barely more than a horn with three wheels. I feel alive, today.

Sunday

Before deciding to fly to India, I sent Hannah an email entitled A Guide to Mumbai. It read something like this:

> *Hello you,*
>
> *I thought I'd familiarise myself with your soon-to-be temporary home and share some of the more interesting facts with you. I read somewhere (can't seem to find the url) that when you go to bed in Mumbai the last person you're supposed to think about is a bloke called Dave, but the writer seemed to be a bit pushy so I wouldn't take it too literally. Unless you want to, of course.*
>
> *Did you have any good pressies? I got a toothbrush and some dental floss from my Dad, a wheely bag from my Mum and a holdall from my bro(ther). So at least I'll be able to look after my teeth and carry stuff from now on.*
>
> *I was wondering if you know of any kind of Hannah antidote? Just can't seem to stop thinking about you and I'm struggling to do anything with my left arm hanging limp by my side. Really very annoying... x*
>
> *PS. Here's a guide to Mumbai that I...er...found:*
> *...apart from being possibly the most irritating place in the world for people named Dave, Mumbai is a melting pot of culture and westernisation, mixing Bollywood cinema with India's best nightlife, which incidentally, is not to be found at all enjoyable by blonde ladies going by the name of Hannah. Local snacks include idli, which is a type of steamed rice*

cake, and after filling their bellies the primate-lovers amongst Mumbai's 16.4 million population might find some cheeky buggers on the steps of Elephanta Island in Mumbai Bay...

Little did I know at the time that two weeks later I'd be wandering around Elephanta Island with Hannah, taking more pictures of monkeys than is decent. One of them launched itself at me from several feet away, climbing up my leg and swinging around on my backpack. I reacted like I was a twelve year-old girl, and Hannah developed side-ache from laughing too much.

It's been another good day, very loving, despite periods of extreme heat that could have caused bother. In such a strange place it is easy for moods and emotions to rise and fall, and now, sat in a Barista café in Fort drinking a sunset sparkle and more than halfway through an enormous chocolate sauce-covered piece of cake called, accurately, Excess, the anxieties of the last week have passed completely. Finally, after another submersion project, I feel like myself again. Whereas last week I couldn't have been in a worse place, the conclusion of three turbulent months of dating is here, in Mumbai, with a large piece of cake.

We talked all day. In bits and pieces, not seriously but frankly and openly and peppered with laughs, in cars and on boats and naked together in bed. Communication, so desperately lacking last week, has indeed ironed out the creases. And the creases, I have to admit, were widened by solo time and over-thinking. It isn't natural, the way Hannah and I have started out. Barely any time getting to know each other before she flew, and then more of the same on neutral but uncomfortable, unyielding territory. If it had been all easy maybe there would have been something wrong but as it is, I know for sure now that when I leave we might have enough of a base to build on if time allows, and this was my only hope by coming here.

I honestly can't say whether on my return from Australia in March Hannah will be waiting for me, or even if I'm going to want her to be, but as tricky as the first few days in Mumbai were I'm glad I did it, I'm glad I came. Because it gave us a chance. If we had parallel lives I suspect my early January was always destined to be difficult for me to get my head around. Either I'd have been at home stressing, or here stressing, both would have been about the same woman. It's strange, but I still can't categorise Hannah and I. I'm not sure that she's a girlfriend, I'm not sure she'd consider me a boyfriend, but now, in stark contrast to the nervous panicky me of low self-esteem last Sunday, I don't mind. We have something and have had something, and that seems enough right now, whatever happens.

I wrote to my friends at the end of last week that I'd see how the weekend went and make a decision about flying home after that. The weekend went better than I could have imagined but I've decided, flight availability allowing, to fly home early anyway. Some rest before Australia would be nice, I want Hannah to enjoy whatever time to herself she can, and also in utter selfishness I just can't face another week in Mumbai or Goa or anywhere in India because if I'm here I want to share it with her. But she's working hard and won't be able to spare much time, and I don't want any remnants of last week coming back. On all fronts, it's best that I leave. But I couldn't be gladder that I'm going to say goodbye with a smile.

Hannah returns to her flat in the mid-afternoon and I turn my attentions to Mumbai. I usually keep my ears clear in a strange city; to listen for traffic, dangers, get my positioning. Today, though, I listened to music. How liberating to block out everything, in streets full of hawkers I could walk in a straight line without interruption, and rather than lose my senses Bombay grew quickly in different colours, for without my ears I had to use my eyes doubly hard.

The cinema, at £1.70 a ticket, was a pleasure. A happy crowd all laughing and cheering, ever so strange for a Nicolas Cage film. Wonderful reclining seats (I suspect I was given an executive ticket for some reason) and a tradition sadly long dead in England, the half time break with ice cream and chocolates available on trays. Silly film, National Treasure, but sometimes one goes to the films for escape, not high art.

Monday

Following AA Gill's advice I always make an effort to write without a view. The spare desk in this hotel room is pushed up against a wall, but unfortunately there's a mirror attached, so now and then I find myself looking hard at myself, distressing at the swift growth of my facial hair, the top-heavy nature of this Indian haircut of mine, the lowness of my shoulders against my neck, the pale bags beneath my eyes. Hannah says I'm self-conscious, but she means I like looking at my own image. She's a fraction right; one out of ten times I see myself I have admiration, the other nine I have mild contempt, usually because the light is on. I suppose I could move the desk, but it would mean moving the other furniture, so draw conclusions from that - laziness succeeds over vanity.

Tuesday

I board in fifteen minutes. A wet, cold England awaits in ten hours or so, and by the time I arrive there Mumbai will seem like a far away dream. We parted well, last night's 'You're nice, well done,' and this morning's 'see you in March' mean more than the words give away. Had I been offered this ending en route to India in the first place, I would have taken it, mainly because it doesn't seem like a definite ending.

The week in England fizzes by. My lack of a home is softened by the kindness of Kara, Date No. 57, and her housemate Rach, who lend me one of the finest sofas in the land. They're wonderful, both sympathetic to my Indian misadventures yet welcoming and distracting in equal measure. While I was away Kate No. 27 decided that the best thing for her future career would be to quit her job and join me on tour in Australia, helping to organise talks and book sales. Of course, amidst the frantic build-up to a visit Down Under that was barely tangible when I began the Dating Challenge, I still dwelled on Hannah. Not for one moment did I regret flying to India, but for all intents and purposes my visit had compounded the very doubt in my mind that had precipitated it: what does the future hold for us?

Of course, I'd hoped that on return to the UK I'd be breathless, missing her, but left in no doubt that now we had enough time between us to get through the remaining time apart. Sadly, I was still as much in the dark as I ever had been, but still I felt like there was something to fight for, even if I hadn't heard from her since I flew home.

Eventually I found myself back at Heathrow, ready for a book tour, squeezed into an aircraft seat with just a whole lot of sky between my present and my future. Seconds before the engines start up, Hannah sends me a text:

> *If you can, drop some pins on the runway to stop take-off. Hold them up for 2 days if you can, then we can have snogs on the runway. See you when you get back, can't wait x*

ELEVEN

Back Home

For six weeks Kate No. 27 and I drove around Australia, talking about dating, and Hannah, and occasionally selling books. What a feeling, to see a book you have written up there on a shelf alongside Bill Bryson! The one downside to touring in Australia is that it's a big place, long roads, so much time to think (even if you're in a vehicle this time, and not on a skateboard). Straight after I took off from Heathrow, the communication from Hannah dried up. Perhaps she was mad at me for not dropping pins on the runway, or maybe she was even worse than I was at dealing with the distance between us.

As the tour draws towards a conclusion I receive a message from her, then another, but they're little nothings, barely more than 'Hi, hope you're doing well,' or 'How are the kangaroos?' She ignores any suggestions that we meet up when I get home and I'm dying to get this whole episode behind us, it's like trying to get a second date again. Thoroughly bored with this now. Jeez she's hard work. What gets me the most is that it bothers me so much.

I'm tired of it, of this unique and now dramatically unhealthy relationship. I still keenly refuse to read the signs for what they are, but I've distanced myself from the almost obvious truth, protecting myself from what feels like the inevitable. Since flying to India I hadn't for one moment thought about the Challenge, the fact that in hot pursuit of One Hundred Dates I'd found myself content to finish at Sixty Three, the importance of that girl putting the whole thing into perspective. Getting to One Hundred wasn't important to me, finding The One was, and I was willing to do anything for that.

In Sydney, a couple of days before returning home, I'm very aware that I haven't heard from Hannah for a few days. A gut instinct forces me onto MySingleFriend, where I run a search for the women who fall within my chosen variables. And there, at the very top, the place where the most recent logins are boosted to, is Hannah. My Hannah. Still looking for someone.

I'm worth a little bit more than this, I think. Were her lines on trust and time and unknowing and the other excuses just that, excuses? At the most cynical moments I wonder whether I simply provided her access to a convenient bed in London for a fortnight, or even that I was an even more convenient plaything for her in India, when she fancied? If she's still looking, if she's still dating, then I'm not the one for her, so why hadn't she told me after all we've been through? I've lost a little bit of respect for her now it's clear that she's not capable of being straight with me. After everything, the least she owes me is that. Yet another twist, I can't wait to be done with it, but these things should only ever be concluded in person, even if you did meet online.

On the plane home little fingers caress my feet. It's quite bizarre, knowing that there's a small and curious child in the seat ahead, wondering just what he or she is feeling behind their own feet. I waggle my toes, and the fingers disappear with a shriek.

*   *   *

Two days after landing I finally had a response from her, by text. All of my calls had gone unanswered, it was just a matter of time:

DATE

Do you want to meet for coffee?

No, was my reply.

I'm still, stupidly, prepared for anything. Six weeks of brittle communication has dampened the flame, and although it still flickers I truly have no idea what I want from her anymore. I was sure of just one thing, that not even the temptation of walking the London streets with No. 33 was justifiable if she wasn't prepared to be upfront with me. My emotional madness, my insecurities, my desperation for communication from her: all these were things I'd already packed into a bag and couriered halfway around the world. If she was ready for a relationship, so was I. If she wasn't, then I couldn't lose anymore of myself into a bottomless pit of doubt.

I reach the café, nerves creeping the length of my body. I haven't seen her since that morning in Mumbai when I flew away. She sits there in the corner, legs crossed beneath a small table. She doesn't stand when I reach her, so I lean down with an awkward half-hug half-kiss. I have no idea what I want from her.

'Would you like a drink?' I ask.

'Water would be good,' she smiles. We do the small talk, anything but the matter at hand. How all of that warmth and attraction can float away is beyond me, the chemistry has run its course, lost its momentum, fizzled away into a silence dotted with one-liners and two glasses of tap water.

I take in the lines of her face, note the eyes always averted. Her hair is still gorgeous, still flowing beyond her shoulders. She is being polite with her interest in the tour, but polite should stop once a relationship begins, polite becomes care, care becomes love. Polite evolves into effortless understanding. And what I can't understand here is how two months ago my heart was actively slamming against my chest, and I just stood there and let it happen without any sign of padding from the

293

culprit. The signs were always hovering like cupids on a day off and yes, now, the excitement has transformed through various stages of happiness, to confusion, then frustration, and now I am sat here just two feet before this girl who I believed I could have loved, and still could, but the reciprocation has completely gone. How should I feel about this? I'm not the guy to chase a girl that doesn't want to be chased; I have no idea what I should be wanting from her. I need answers, I'd be happy with that. Just stop the game, tell me we're not playing anymore, give me that at least, please, I beg of you.

'I can't give you what you want from me,' she says. 'I still fancy you, and stuff, but we want different things.'

I stare at her, and then at my water. For all of my preparations I can't dam the tears that fight their way out of my eyes; how is it that when you do want it to function, that gravity takes a holiday and allows water to flow upwards? My heart is not broken, but it's bruised badly. I do wish she'd just been honest with me long before this, respect is a lot more to leave someone with than silence.

'I have to go now,' she says.

'I'll walk you to the tube,' I say, being polite.

We don't say anything as we walk, hiding our brief history, watching it slide away casually without fight. That first hot chocolate smeared across my forehead. The second date with evolving smiles. The third, the revelation of her phone number, and the kiss! The fourth, with that missed train, the swift kick to the shin, and then much, much more. Christmas Eve, with her friends. India. It comes down to this, two people staring at each other outside Victoria Underground station, wanting the ground to swallow us up, to erase the final, fatal goodbye from memory. We hug and her hair sticks to my stubble like Velcro. She literally stands back and pulls it from my face. I can't help but laugh. She says goodbye and heads for the Underground, disappearing into a train station for the final time.

TWELVE

Conspiracy of Silence

Love can be brutal. I watched her go, knowing this was the last time I'd see her blonde hair, her back, the top of her head. Then she was out of sight. Gone. A bus caught my eye and I watched it pass. So many faces in there, so many other women out there to meet. But not right now, I'm not ready for that all over again. Back in Clapham I decide to go and buy a new sweater, to replace the old one I wore on Date No. 1, Date No. 37, Date No. 62, and so many in between. But I couldn't find one that was nice. Nothing fitted.

Serious daters, those looking for a long-term partner and just not a short-term shag, should put themselves first but their dates not too far behind. Self-respect is of the utmost importance, because the nuances of attraction can blur the lines between reality and uncertainty. I've learned that we should always be honest with ourselves, honest with those who appear to want something from us, and honest with the signs if we find ourselves chasing someone who may find us pleasant, but little more. Like it or not the signs are always there, it just depends whether we want to read them. Always remember, especially if you find yourself in the ascendency when it comes to dating that communication is the only remedy to complication.

Hannah's behaviour towards me, now I look at it with total hindsight, always kept me at arm's length. Occasionally I had the inkling that perhaps she thought she was better than me, or at least that she thought she could find someone better than me. Which begs the question, why the hell did I fall so heavily when the signs were so bad? I couldn't help myself, I suppose, and I totally paid the price. When you find yourself within an unwilling power game there's always the hope that you can gain some ground, even if a small angel on your shoulder is telling you for all its might that you have to step back and give yourself some space. Nobody else can help us in this situation, it's always down to us and it's very rare that we are completely in the dark about how someone else feels about us.

The problem comes when we begin to feel strongly about a stranger, because we don't know them. We want to, we'd give anything to, even our own pride, sometimes. I kick myself for my instincts failing, but perhaps my very first instinct with Hannah was correct, the one that struck me in the groin as she strutted off in front of me down the corridor in Leon, wiggling that fantastic bum, leaving me grounded, thinking that I didn't have a chance in hell with this woman. In reality, I never did have a chance, but as time went on I chose to ignore that because she allowed me closer than perhaps I should have been allowed to get. I simply didn't embark on this challenge to be one half of a fling but maybe I deserved it, just a little bit, for playing games with something so precious as love.

I do feel battered, but not surprised. I suppose I could see this coming, which explains the aching feeling in my heart from Day 31 onwards, but the lack of decency in the closure of this affair still leaves me feeling a bit used. If we don't protect ourselves we're susceptible to pain, but if we close off too much we run the risk of not giving love a chance. It wasn't just that I wanted more from our relationship than Hannah did. She became more important to me by the date, despite the fact that in so many ways we were different, lacking compatibility. I'm all-out, open, straight to the point. She didn't communicate enough for me. I'm endlessly flirtatious but she rarely gave anything away. She waited three dates before sharing her mobile number, yet she was willing to sleep with me before giving me her email address. Maybe she was an enigma, a mysterious, magnetic presence that left so much to be answered, maybe that was why I was drawn in so quickly, so deeply? That she was beautiful was of course a factor in play, but I would hate for this to undermine everything else. Her turn of phrase, her humour, her creativity and mannerisms all drew me in, as time allowed. I was prepared to love her and I would have liked the chance to do so, but there were so many signs that I chose to ignore. It's blind, love. We've all suffered it.

But what about the other women? Were there not others on this challenge that would have been worth finishing early for? Not that I knew of, even Nicola, who captured me for a while there, far more so than Hannah after one just one outing. My friends did nothing but laugh at me when in the pits of my deepest frustration I muttered, 'it's her loss.' Because you can't lose something you never had.

I've weighed it all up, and even with hindsight the dates I had with Hannah were exceptional. We clicked immediately and although you only get my side of the story, the fact that geography threatened to get in the way was devastating to me. Ultimately I'm a big believer in instinct. I'm happy I finished the challenge early, because I believe it was for the right reasons. But the key thing is how I felt when I was doing it; I had absolutely no doubt, I felt like I'd been honest to myself and not once have I looked back and wished I'd gone all the way to One Hundred.

Honestly, I think I learned far more by ending it where I did then I ever would have done by going all the way. If anything, completing the challenge would have applied more pressure to my relationship with Hannah (although perhaps the fact she wanted me to continue the challenge was the first pointer she gave me that in reality she wasn't interested in a long-term relationship), but at the time I wanted to give us absolutely every chance I could. Sure, it was nice to stop dating, by the time Date No. 63 came around I was absolutely sick of it all, but I wasn't looking for an easy way out. I was only ever going to finish for a very good reason, and I think I did. Hannah wasn't just a legitimate cause to end it all, she was an absolute in my eyes, and it proved that I wasn't doing the challenge for a book or a jolly, but that, actually, after everything, I *was* truly ready to meet someone.

There's a danger, especially with online dating, that we become mercenary, committed only to doing the very best for ourselves. Yes, we may like the person we meet, but if there's any hint of doubt then it's okay, we just shift right on to the next one. Ruthless, heartless dating. But, hold on! When the time comes, when that person walks around the corner and you meet and talk for the first time and cannot get them out of your head, that's when you know you've found something good. It is okay to be picky, because why should we be with anyone who doesn't make our head feel funny and stomach all tickly? But in the event that there's some chemistry with your date and all actions suggest that it's going somewhere exciting, follow the cardinal rule: if there's any doubt at all it means that there's something wrong, and only communication will solve this. We all deserve a partner who fits us perfectly, mentally, habitually and physically. And we all deserve to give it the very best chance we can.

When two people meet under the pretence of a potential beginning, there will always be the possibility of rejection. Where hope exists, hope can be dashed. If you feel strongly about someone you'll hold onto anything they do just to convince yourself that they feel the same, that you've got a chance. But when there's an imbalance in feeling, however slight, you must be wary, because two people in love should fall at similar rates. Why didn't I just face up to Hannah and ask her where it was going? I was scared to hear the truth, because deep down perhaps I knew what she'd say. I didn't want to face it, so kept schtum. If you're afraid to ask what's wrong, there's something wrong. The conspiracy of silence, the very same thing that haunts long-term couples whose love has become stale. We'd rather lie to ourselves than open up to being hurt.

Here's a lie: When you're in love, you feel that butterflies-in-your-stomach, excited, happy, romantic, lovey-dovey feeling all the time. If that feeling ever goes away, something is wrong.

If you accept this lie, no relationship will ever stand a chance because a partnership between two human beings, each with their own flaws and insecurities, is bound to have problems to work through and challenges to overcome. In a relationship that lasts, each partner wakes up every day and actively chooses to love their mate whether they feel warm and fuzzy, or not. Of course there should be romance, passion and excitement but not every moment is going to feel like a honeymoon in paradise. That's not the way life goes. The *Floating-on Cloud-Nine* feeling that many of us associate with love is actually a result of a chemical released in our brains during the first few months (or years, depending on the scientific study you refer to) with a new partner; it's not a definitive guide to how well a relationship is going. When we find ourselves in an established, long-term relationship with someone, a different chemical kicks in. One that makes you feel calmer, trusted and trusting, more secure and connected. This is a good thing - it means that you can actually come down from your whirlwind of can't-sleep-can't-eat-all-I-can-think-about-is-them and begin to build a solid relationship based on who you really are as individuals, a relationship rooted in reality, not excitement. The downside is that those initial butterflies that once felt so remarkable might subside a bit once you've hit this phase. It's completely normal and, frankly, unavoidable.

There's a pattern to successful relationships featuring three key elements. In the early stages two people are drawn together by chemistry, an essential mutual attraction based around personality and physical compatibility – the butterfly stage, the catalyst. It's brilliant! Once this begins to develop into something more tangible than flirtation then slowly the next stage becomes unity, when you're both right there together on the same level, existing together, sharing, and experiencing the harmony we dearly craved as singletons. This is love, true love. Yes, it comes in many shapes and sizes, but the couple that lasts through time and trouble manage to strengthen their bond with complete and utter mutual respect, and openness to each other's individuality. Losing your own personality and characteristics is the beginning of the end; your partner should understand you and let you be the person he or she fell in love with, and vice-versa. Once the butterflies have flown away (and they may return to remind you who is special now and then) a relationship formed on a solid foundation will survive, provided the respect and individuality continue.

We live in a time when humans are required to evolve and adapt at a quicker pace than they have ever had to before. The advance of technology has given us more tools of communication, which of course we can choose to use for good. But all too often humans fall at the offer of temptation, and in the same era that makes it easy to text a friend saying that we can't make the pub for a drink, marriages are also failing because we now have access to more potential alternatives than ever before. Why work at our current relationship if it's struggling, when the promise of new emotional and carnal excitement is so accessible?

I'll tell you why, because *new* doesn't last forever. I embarked on this dating challenge, on this book, because I found myself stuck in a perpetual circle of relationship failure. I know I'm capable of being a worthy, decent boyfriend, but I'm also just one in a million twenty-somethings who has found it commonplace to say, 'you know, I get bored after two or three years, it's like a switch got flicked.' What utter bollocks, I hit a hard patch and couldn't deal with it, using my youth as an excuse. I don't want to be that guy anymore, the one capable of destroying a relationship because I simply can't be arsed to work at it. In the process of losing a partner and being a major player in yet another heartache, I'm also dealing myself the same severe blows. Yes, I'm capable of being a scoundrel. Yes, I've made some almighty cock-ups in my time and yes, I've learned about my failures the hard way. I've not always been at the centre as my relationships have unravelled, but I know my faults and they'll stick with me forever. I've been desperately lucky to love the women I've loved and been loved by; my greatest teachers, my best friends. I miss them all, every one. History is like a dumping ground, isn't it?

What's the difference between relationships going stale in your twenties and later in life? Experience and maturity hopefully stand us in good stead to work harder at relationship problems. Breaking up is painful enough when you're young and aren't even sure that you want to stay with the partner you're saying goodbye to, but I'm quite sure that spending a life with someone you care deeply about beats the hell out of breaking up just because you went through a rough patch.

We're all capable of the *oooh look! I'm falling! Can't do anything about it!* feeling, but the situation and mindset is important. I've always been like that, open to it, not just with love but everything new and lovely in life. Yes, sometimes I haven't been ready for love, because my heart has been in another place; because of a lost girl, my work, a geographical situation. In Hannah's case I'd just been dating for two months, I was looking for a partner harder than most people ever will so I was primed to fall head over heels if the right girl came along. Right time, right person is so important. I'd put myself in the place, just needed the person. Then, BAM! My friends warned me that I was falling fast; they tried to reign me in – perhaps because they wanted me to finish the challenge! – but even though I knew they were talking sense I didn't listen. I chose not to.

It feels wonderful to bond with someone like that, but love is one thing where you're completely out of control, and it's scary as hell. Suddenly you're on a drug and can't bear the thought of it being taken away - it's the most addictive thing in the world. It's also important to remember that love doesn't always happen that fast. It can be brewed steadily, sometimes over months, sometimes years! It completely depends on the two people involved.

When I began The Dating I was full of optimism for the future and didn't for one moment think I'd end the challenge with some deep bruising to my heart. I didn't then and still don't believe that there's just *One* person out there for us, I think there are thousands, maybe more. We're whizzing about like molecules just waiting to collide and form a reaction.

Sometimes we meet someone on a Monday and it doesn't work out, whereas if that meeting had been delayed by a month, maybe even a week, then it would have had a chance. Hell, if I finished this chapter then went back on a date with everyone I met on this challenge then maybe it would be a different story. There is no way for us to know when the right time, place and person will come along, but we can only put ourselves in a position to be ready for them - in that sense it is a little bit of luck that you can only half make yourself.

You're living every bloke's fantasy, a friend wrote to me sometime around Date No. 40, but she couldn't have been further from the truth. It was a challenge, and finding someone shouldn't be such hard work! I stepped out into the dating scene in search of butterflies, and both gladly and sadly, I found them. It was magic while they lasted. It can happen so quickly, so suddenly, there's just no control, and I truly believe that this is how the early stages of love should present themselves: in a state of pure, blissful free-fall. Of course, sometimes the landing is hard and when it is a lesson is underlined, that love isn't to be rushed, or played with, and it certainly isn't a game. If you love someone you have to put your all into it, and with that in mind, with the glorious knowledge of experience slapping me round the face, I wouldn't recommend anyone serious about finding a partner to do so under the guise of an Endurance Dating Exercise - it's all far too confusing!

Hannah didn't give me, or us, a chance, and I'm ever so sad about that. But I accept it and I did all I could, I think. If things had been different, if feelings were mutual, perhaps I'd have had less doubt about the impending time apart and wouldn't have flown to India. Going there may have been the worst possible thing I could have done, but had I sat back at home and not done anything only to see Hannah and I fail, I would have regretted not buying that ticket. I'm glad I gave it a go, and I'd do it again in a heartbeat;.

One's recovery from lost love is often like an iceberg. The more that rests under the surface, the longer it takes to melt away. In truth, we didn't have much time together and I've suffered worse than my days post-Hannah. I caught myself just in time, the clouds of uncertainty finally sweeping away during my Australian tour, revealing with distance and hindsight what I'd suspected but refused to consider during the whirlwind that carried her, and us, towards Bombay – that I'd found a girl who totally knocked my socks off while hers remained firmly on her feet, because whatever tricks she was unconsciously playing with my head, I wasn't doing the same for her. I liked a girl and she didn't like me quite as much. So it ended.

Afterwards I went through waves of hurt, then bitterness, then guilt, then wondering whether there was any more I could have done, and then the final, cleansing stage of reality. Yes, my instincts had failed me in a fairly large way, but hey, once again I was single, free, and very unsure about where I stood in regards to finding a girlfriend. My balance had been over-weighted and I needed to find my feet again, because without your feet firmly on the ground it's quite hard to be sure where your head is.

Throughout your adult life you can look back at your relationship past and handpick those few who have made a stamp on your life. Some lovers are just that, lovers. Some are more and they become friends too, yet whoever you are and however much time has passed, beyond the hurt and sadness and regret that accompanies the end of the most wonderful partnerships, you can't ignore the impact that certain people have on you. Those early days when your head swims and you miss that person who you only met three days earlier. The loose, inexplicable ache of spending days apart, even if you don't truly know that person. Some relationships grow from friendship, others appear out of the blue, but the rarity of bumping into someone at the right time and in the right place is staggering. Here, when you search for something wrong purely because it all feels so right and still can find no fault, two people indelibly bond themselves to each other and whatever the future holds neither of you will forget what you meant to each other, whether it was for days, weeks, months or years.

I'm very glad to say that I've finally realised what question I should have been asking all along, rather than *how do you meet someone?* it should have been, *how do you know when you've met the right person?* And the answer is so ridiculously simple I can't help but wonder what all the fuss is about, because the answer is that you just know. You just know.

In little less than three months I experienced a wider range of emotions and experiences than most sensible people would in a lifetime. The intensity of the challenge left me distinctly unbalanced at times. I'd swing from self-conscious to cheekily confident, obsessive and desperate to nonplussed and casual, never really on the straight and narrow and then, as a consequence, probably never quite in the right frame of mind to be truly me with the right girl. That I was writing a book and heading for a goal undoubtedly corrupted what I always hoped would be a search for true love, and I think I made some mistakes along the way. For instance, I should have dated No. 1 again, I liked the way she picked spiders off her sweater. And I definitely should have made more of an effort with No. 3; I think if I'd met her one-month later things could have been very different. I didn't reply to No. 4's disappointed text message when, two weeks after our first and only date, I forgot her birthday. Admittedly though, it would have helped if she had told me about it in the first place. I had no idea what the next day was going to have in store, but my confusion with Rosie (Date No. 32) highlights a very important point: if you're not sure about someone, however well you're getting on, don't give them a foot rub. I would like to blame the wine but it's only partially responsible, so on that occasion I have to put my hands up and say 'Yes, Dave, you were an idiot.'

Sometimes I had good dates but I didn't get in touch afterwards. But only once, with No. 21, did I fail to get in touch after she had reached out. I was in the wrong. I think the onus is no longer just on the man to call; if you're interested in someone, you have no right to bemoan them not getting in touch if you fail to do so yourself.

It's been a while since I 'researched' this book and although I suspect most of my dates only needed a tube ride home to forget about me I wanted to be safe, so I gave it a couple of years before embarking on the long process of publishing. Which, by the way, is just as hard as finding a woman! At every opportunity, unless permission has been given otherwise, I've changed names, places and details to try and ensure that privacy had been maintained for all involved. In the back of my mind, I had fully intended to contact each of my dates to belatedly inform them about their unwitting involvement in my challenge and this book, but that pesky break-in on New Year's Eve meant access to my dating spreadsheet was lost forever. I hope, in the unlikely chance that you recognise yourself in these pages that you don't want to kill me.

At the time of writing, I'm glad to report that Kate No. 27 met a man online, and they've now been together for more than four and a half years. Oh, and they're marries, too.

Jo not only found herself a willing man through an online dating site but did so by eliminating the entire dating process and inviting him around to her house for a night of booze and Sing Star. They currently have a 2 year-old who is far less of a handful than mummy!

Amanda met her boyfriend when on a drunk night out on Clapham High Street. They've been together for four years.

David the Quizmaster is a regular on the telly these days, and is now married to a brilliant girl. He's still very funny and has just moved to LA to be a film star. I'm not joking.

It took barely two weeks for the MySingleFriend profile I wrote for Johnny (after Date No. 57) to bear fruit. He's now living with Lucy in Singapore.

Will still thoroughly dislikes the Northern Line, and he's just returned from Thailand with the marvellous soundbite, 'My God, ladyboys can be terrifyingly attractive!' He also accidentally had his nipple pierced, and can't stop touching it.

And me? Well, I may be able to interpret a female's body language at a hundred paces and I'd be lying if curly hair didn't still give me goosebumps, but I'm still working out the mechanics of relationships, and how to successfully conduct one at the same time as managing a career of haphazard journeys. For all of the highlights that come from a life of travel and adventure I have a sneaking suspicion that I'm missing something, or more specifically, someone.

The bits in between my adventures are the hardest, as I come home and grapple with the experiences that only I can fully understand. I'm looking for a woman to share my life with, to laugh with about the silly things we've both done and might do. I need her to offer up the consistency and stability that my career path simply can't provide, and I can't wait to make her a cup of tea every morning. Until I find that special someone I think a small part of me will always be searching for the one missing part of the puzzle. The promise of true love is eternally worth the risk of heartbreak, and until it comes along I'll always be a happy boy, but I won't be quite complete.

I tried my best in this challenge and despite a bout of aortic bruising I'm glad I logged onto MySingleFriend.com that fateful October morning. My serial dating days (especially to this degree!) were only ever going to be temporary, but although I now feel better placed to employ a certain degree of caution if again I'm faced with a woman fully capable of giving my heart a good squeeze, I'll still be the all-out, let the butterflies fly kind of guy.

Was it worth it, all of this? I think so. I now understand one true fact. There are rules and generalisations, experts and advice columns, more and more dating websites offering different ways to select your future partner, but at the heart of the matter finding the right person is the only true definition of fate dealing its card. We can't predict how or when it'll happen, men and women will continue through the ages to confuse the hell out of each other, and yes, relationships will continue to flourish, then crash and burn. True love exists, it's the most beautiful thing in the world and without it I'm not sure any of us can be truly whole. But here's the beauty of it all, I don't believe in The One anymore.

Walking on the surface of our lovely planet right now are countless people who, if the right things happen, could one day end up being your partner. There's no way of telling how many of them are out there, but to find them you've got to sort things out, open yourself up and look in that mirror knowing that you are more than worthy. You're a catch, I tell you! So, with that in mind, don't worry how many dates you might need to go on to find that special someone, you'll learn plenty as you search and you'll probably make some mistakes you don't need to be making later on. Just don't, whatever you do, give up. There's someone out there with your name on. There might even be One Hundred of them.

THE END

Thank You

Will Clive, for being a good mate and even more of a dating buffoon than me.

Kate Denham, for forcing this book out of me, saving the homeless, and generally being the best friend I could have hoped to find.

Nina Chang, for replying to the advert 30 seconds before the deadline. You've helped pull everything together my dearest Editor, thank you so much.

Amanda Shipp, for writing the profile and being there through the whole debacle. Sorry you never got to be a bridesmaid.

Kate Vere Hodge, for the company, the advice and the drive around Australia!

Jo Robinson, you still make me laugh, I'm glad I met you.

David Fynn, for hosting the best quiz night in…Clapham.

Emily Penn, for your patience and ears. Both kind of vital.

Mette Davis, for being there when it all kicked off.

Alice Harding, for introducing me to online dating and keeping a straight face during that bizarre birthday when everyone only had one degree of separation.

Joanna Hill, for being you.

Andy, my brother. Sorry you inherited the Thundercats Duvet!

Juliet Mushens, thank you for believing in this book, it gave me the confidence to take it further.

Sarah Beeney, for inventing mysinglefriend.com.

Kris Hallenga and Maren Hallenga, you're far more than a hippy and a runner to me, the most inspiring sisters I know.

Melika Harris, Jenny Hao and Nikki Baker, thank you for being able to feign both adoration and disgust in a single morning!

Sean Conway, because a picture usually tells a thousand words, and yours covers 100,000.

Lottie Brooksbank & Joanna Cable, I could have used your make-up assistance during the challenge, not just for the cover shoot!

Kara Dixon and Rachael Knowland for the sofa, Maltesers, and everything else.

My trusty proofreaders, Meghan Fitzpatrick, Charley Gould, Levison Wood, Lee Hughes, Annabelle Vernon,

Becky Osbourne, Charlie Masding and Christine Pettman.

And to all of my dates, thank you for meeting me, I hope you found someone special waiting just around the corner xx

If you enjoyed this book please do take a few moments to leave a review on www.amazon.com (or .co.uk). It'll help others decide to buy it (or not!).

To find about more about Dave's latest adventures and projects visit www.davecornthwaite.com.

He is also a regular contributor on Twitter (@DaveCorn), Instagram (@DaveCorn) and Facebook (/davecornthwaite)

Printed in Great Britain
by Amazon.co.uk, Ltd.,
Marston Gate.